Accelerating Trends in Law Firms

Consulting Editor **Peter Zeughauser**

Consulting editor
Peter Zeughauser

Managing director
Sian O'Neill

Accelerating Trends in Law Firms
is published by

Globe Law and Business Ltd
3 Mylor Close
Horsell
Woking
Surrey GU21 4DD
United Kingdom
Tel: +44 20 3745 4770
www.globelawandbusiness.com

Printed and bound by CPI Group (UK) Ltd, Croydon CR0 4YY, United Kingdom

Accelerating Trends in Law Firms

ISBN 9781787424227
EPUB ISBN 9781787424234
Adobe PDF ISBN 9781787424241

© 2021 Globe Law and Business Ltd except where otherwise indicated.

All rights reserved. No part of this publication may be reproduced in any material form (including photocopying, storing in any medium by electronic means or transmitting) without the written permission of the copyright owner, except in accordance with the provisions of the Copyright, Designs and Patents Act 1988 or under terms of a licence issued by the Copyright Licensing Agency Ltd, 5th Floor, Shackleton House, 4 Battle Bridge Lane, London SE1 2HX, United Kingdom (www.cla.co.uk, email: licence@cla.co.uk). Applications for the copyright owner's written permission to reproduce any part of this publication should be addressed to the publisher.

DISCLAIMER
This publication is intended as a general guide only. The information and opinions which it contains are not intended to be a comprehensive study, or to provide legal advice, and should not be treated as a substitute for legal advice concerning particular situations. Legal advice should always be sought before taking any action based on the information provided. The publisher bears no responsibility for any errors or omissions contained herein.

Table of contents

Preface _____ 5
   Peter Zeughauser
   Zeughauser Group

How to revisit your strategic plan in the wake of the pandemic _____ 7
   Peter Zeughauser
   Zeughauser Group

Talent management trends in post-pandemic law firms __ 27
   Jennifer Bluestein
   Perkins Coie LLP

How firms can successfully build culture remotely _____ 49
   Naomi Beard Nelson
   Naomi Beard & Associates

The accelerated pursuit of racial equity in law firms __ 99
   Tiffani G Lee
   Holland & Knight LLP

Building client relationships in a hybrid world _____ 113
   Michelle Holford
   Slaughter and May

The new normal: remote working, billing and law firm activism _____ 137
   Alex Dimitrief
   Zeughauser Group

***Pro bono* post-pandemic: our evolving commitment to serving others** _____ 151
   Sara Andrews
   Lisa Dewey
   Anne Geraghty Helms
   DLA Piper

How firms are leveraging technology and data to drive strategy, efficiency and client relationships __ 171
   David Cunningham
   Reed Smith

COVID-19's impact on lawyer innovation and decision making _____ 185
   Randall Kiser
   DecisionSet®

Law firm real estate: emerging considerations in a post-COVID-19 environment _____ 201
    Matt Brainard
    Savills
    Tiffany Winne
    Stream Realty Partners

Effective financial management post-pandemic _____ 215
    Thomas P Fitzgerald
    Winston & Strawn

Well-being of partners and the workforce _____ 227
    Eric Ho
    Health for Success

About the authors _____ 251

Preface

Peter Zeughauser
Zeughauser Group

When Globe Law and Business contacted me about publishing a book on law firm trends, much of the world was 'locked down' due to the COVID-19 pandemic. Law firms around the world were digging deep into their resilience to solve unprecedented COVID-19-related client challenges while working remotely. It would be fair to say that law firm leaders didn't know what to expect from week to week. Of course, my first instinct was to conceptualise a book that would address responses to the pandemic. But as I began to work with my editor and simultaneously experience the continuously unfolding impact of the pandemic, we became more and more convinced that the pandemic was accelerating change more than causing it.

As we developed an outline for the book and turned to inviting thought leaders to author chapters, we confronted the paradox that it would be impossible to write about accelerating change in the legal sector outside of the context of the pandemic. Indeed, law firms were responding to the time-tested Winston Churchill mandate not to let any good crisis be wasted. Thus, readers will find a pattern of pandemic-accelerated change woven throughout the book.

The pandemic wasn't the only powerful force accelerating change for law firms as we called on authors to contribute chapters. George Floyd's murder by a policeman in Minneapolis, Minnesota on 25 May 2020 imbued a greater sense of urgency for inculcating diversity, equity and inclusion in law firms than perhaps any other event in modern times. From *pro bono* commitments and undertakings to professional development and career opportunities it was as if a bolt of lightning had struck the legal sector, illuminating for many law firms centuries of systemic flaws and social injustice across all systems of government and society writ large, including western democracies, resulting in the sore inadequacy of diversity, equity and inclusion initiatives addressed in the book.

The scope of accelerating change, as readers will discover when reading this book, creates an imperative for the leaders of each and every law firm to revisit their firm's strategic plan, which is where this book starts. It moves on to cover how change is impacting the development and management of the law firm workforce, from partners to counsel, to associates to staff, addressing the vexing issues of integration, skills building and culture enhancement in the face of what appears to be an inexorable progression to remote work and all of its implications, good and bad.

Several of the authors address the expense savings brought about by accelerating change. An entire chapter addresses the reduced need for real estate. Another addresses the broad cuts firms made across vast numbers of budget line items. But the costs of change are also addressed in other chapters, from increased use of expensive new technology to the human toll of stress and anxiety many feel, the rising levels of substance and alcohol abuse and the ensuing increases in attrition rates, all experienced disproportionately more so by diverse people.

Indeed, reading the book raises the question of how firms will address the colliding forces of change in law firms. The pandemic accelerated greater use of technology, particularly with respect to remote work, which is depersonalising the experience of working in a law firm, on the one hand. And artificial intelligence, which is depersonalising society and decision making about people and the lives they lead, on the other hand. In revisiting their law firm's strategic plan, law firm leaders must ensure that the law remains a fortress for protecting the rights of all to experience the full humanity of life and that a career in law does not compromise any single individual's right and ability to do so.

Law firm leaders and other readers will find throughout this book fresh new ideas for addressing the inexorable force and accelerating pace of change in law firms across the globe. For their contributions, I am especially grateful to the authors of each chapter. Thought leadership is never easy, but each chapter author has contributed richly.

I also must thank the publisher, Globe Law and Business, for bringing the ideas contributed by each of the authors into the mainstream of discussion among law firm leaders through this book, and in particular my commissioning editor, Katerina Menhennet, for her remarkable guidance, patience and perseverance in bringing this book to print.

May we now carry on with change together.

How to revisit your strategic plan in the wake of the pandemic

Peter Zeughauser
Zeughauser Group

1. Introduction

Trends accelerate. John Naisbitt and Patricia Aburdeen nailed it in 1990 when they published *Megatrends 2000*,[1] describing what was beginning to shape the 21st century, including the rise of the Pacific Rim, the dawn of the age of biology, the triumph of the individual, the emergence of free market socialism, a religion revival, cultural nationalism and the booming global economy of the 1990s.

In 2015 McKinsey identified four global forces "breaking all the trends":[2]

1. Urbanisation will result in half of the world's $1 billion plus companies headquartered in emerging markets (down from 95% of the world's largest companies today) being headquartered in developed economies. The world added seven cities the size of Chicago each year between 1985 and 2015.
2. Technological change growing at an exponential rate beyond the power of human intuition to anticipate.
3. An aging world, with 60% of the global population in countries with shrinking populations.
4. Greater global connections, with over a billion people crossing borders annually, five times the number in 1980, and a complex, intricate, sprawling global trade system linked by technology.

Over the past 20 years, the percentage of China's population living in cities has doubled from 30% to 60%, a transition that took 90 years to happen in Europe and 60 years in the United

---

1 Patricia Aburdeen and John Naisbitt, *Megatrends 2000, New Directions for Tomorrow*, Avon, 1991.
2 Richard Dobbs, James Manyika, James and Jonathan Woetzel, "The Four Global Forces Breaking All the Trends", McKinsey & Company, 1 April 2015.

States.³ China's national urban development policy has shifted from building cities to building five economically and ecologically sustainable megalopolises connected to one another by a grid of 16 high-speed rail lines and housing half of China's urban population while generating half of China's GDP.⁴

The world has become more volatile, uncertain, ambiguous and complex. Big Law has boomed, arguably as a result. And changed. Among the rapidly accelerating trends over the last 30 years are:
- international expansion;
- consolidation;
- convergence;
- requests for proposal (RFPs);
- lateral cherry-picking;
- partner outplacement;
- market segmentation and specialisation;
- the rise of alternative legal service providers;
- the drive for diversity, equity and inclusion;
- brand rankings; and
- digitisation.

Then came the COVID-19 pandemic, emptying out the skyscrapers and hip, high-tech office parks that had been the comfortable preserves of lawyering, without answers for what to do next.

Some firms were blessed with client, sector and practice mixes that thrived. Others were badly wounded. The levelling question for all, though, is what their plan should be going forward, because as evidenced by each of the chapters in this book, basic assumptions about how lawyers do their work have changed overnight.

This chapter provides a coherent framework for revisiting strategy, whether the need is brought about by dramatic change or simply good business practice. The elements of developing strategy it contains can also be viewed as a menu. Each element standing alone can be used to shed light on the answer to the question that should be at the centre of developing every firm's strategy: what is it that the firm's partners aspire to build together for their firm's

---

3 Ling Xin, "What's Bigger than a Mega City? China's Planned City Clusters", *MIT Technology Review*, 28 April 2021, www.technologyreview.com/2021/04/28/1022557/china-city-cluster-urbanization-population-economy-environment/?utm_source=engagement_email&utm_medium=email&utm_campaign=site_visitor.unpaid.engagement&utm_content=05.12.subs&mc_cid=f5a695952a&mc_eid=083c0bcc9c.
4 *Ibid*.

practice? The framework brings to bear 25 years of developing best practices for teasing a consensus answer to that question out of a firm's partnership. The framework involves three pieces.
1. Assessing the competitive environment and the firm's position in it.
2. Articulating a differentiated vision of what the partners aspire to build together for the firm's practice.
3. Developing a set of goals, strategies and actions for achieving the vision.

2. **Why planning is rising in importance**

Common wisdom among Big Law leaders and pundits is that demand has been relatively flat for the better part of the century. If measured by hours sold, this is true. But how does one explain this proposition in an increasingly litigious, more heavily regulated global economy that has seen the rise over a quarter of a century of the European Union, China, an economic giant with a gross domestic product rivalling in size that of the United States, the largest economy ever and seven new Chicagos being added to the planet for at least 30 years running?[5]

The answer lies in technology and alternative legal service providers (ALSPs). Technology and ALSPs are devouring Big Law hours. Law firms are stabilising and growing revenue by persistently raising rates for the increasingly complex, highest stakes work. But when it takes less time to perform a given piece of work, it only makes sense that it takes more and more of that work to fuel revenue growth. It wouldn't be possible to raise rates if demand were flat or shrinking unless the number of lawyers was also shrinking, and it's not. The competition for the work intensifies if the speed with which the work can be accomplished outstrips the growth in the amount of work. This technology/demand paradox is the competitive environment treadmill on which Big Law finds itself.

In this environment, being top of mind for the work a firm wants to do means everything. For the highest rates driven by the technology/demand paradox, clients expect the best lawyers. Those who deliver the best service and the best results.

In an increasingly specialised profession, there are few worthy clients left who believe that any single law firm of whatever size is the best at everything, convergence to the wind. Where does this

---

5 Dobbs, *supra* note 2.

lead Big Law firms? It leads to making choices about the specialised practice and sector area expertise they want to be known for being among the best, or simply the best, at delivering for clients.

Planning is about making choices about what a firm wants to be known for being the best at in the minds of clients and talent. It provides a framework for making choices about how a firm wants to allocate its two most important resources: time and money. And, because firms have limited time and money, it is important that those resources be allocated for the common good of the firm, to wit: what it is that the partners desire to build together for the firm's practice.

At its best, planning is a journey to build a consensus about what the firm will look like if it is successful in the minds of its stakeholders: the lawyers who practise at the firm, the clients who hire the firm, and the clients and lawyers the firm would like to attract. A well-conceived plan sets forth who is going to do what, when and how to build the firm's image. Firms are turning to planning now more than ever because, as expressed throughout this book, the pandemic turned some key assumptions of how lawyers work and succeed on their head.

3. Articulating a shared vision

Building and articulating a shared vision of success is at the core of successful planning. There is no single way to do this. A strong leader or small cadre of leaders may articulate a vision that attracts followers. Latham & Watkin's Clint Stevenson told his partners, in what was then a modestly sized Los Angeles law firm known for its tax expertise, that if given the chance to lead the firm he would build it into the world's greatest law firm. Of course, before him, there was Paul Cravath. These innovative leaders attracted followers who found their visions attractive.

Eyeing the success of others, many firms simply follow observable patterns of the firms led by visionary leaders: open offices in the same places; build similar practice groups; and develop similar sector expertise. But what's missing is a vision shared by their partners. Laterals, groups and smaller firms are cobbled together without a shared vision. In a highly fragmented, undifferentiated, geographically disparate market this can work. But it begins to fall apart as market leaders differentiate themselves, grow in size and reap the financial rewards that follow. Building a consensus around a differentiated shared vision from a hodgepodge of practices, offices and industry sectors becomes a challenge for those who don't.

As Jeswald Salacuse points out in his book *Leading Leaders*,[6] a leader cannot lead a group of smart, talented, rich and powerful people someplace they do not want to go. If those lawyers don't like where their leader is going, they have other choices. So, the first task of the leader is to find out where her followers want to go. In a law firm, this is best accomplished by asking the partners a series of questions as the first step in the planning process.

4. **Interviewing partners**

There are two genres of questions that work well for teasing components of a differentiated shared vision from a partnership. The first is the 'What's your vision?' genre. For example:

- What's your vision for the firm's practice five to 10 years from now (or, what is it that you aspire to build together with your partners for the firm's practice?). What would the firm look like if you were successful?
- What clients would the firm have to have to achieve your vision?
- What would the mix of work have to be to achieve your vision?
- What practices would the firm have to build to achieve your vision?
- What offices would the firm have to have to achieve your vision?
- What size would the firm need to be to achieve your vision?

And so on. The second genre of question is the 'What's working well/what could be working better?' genre. This would cover topics like:

- What's working well about the firm's associate recruiting, development and retention programme? What could be working better?
- What's working well about the firm's compensation system? What could be working better?
- What's working well about partnership admissions? What could be working better?
- What's working well about how the firm addresses underperforming partners? What could be working better?

---

6 Jeswald Salacuse, *Leading Leaders: How to Manage Smart, Talented, Rich, and Powerful People*, AMACOM, 2006.

All told, there are likely about 30 topics that are relevant to creating a shared vision and a plan, about half of which may be relevant to a typical firm at any given point in its evolution.

In a large partnership, it's not a productive use of time to interview all the partners. What makes better sense is to interview the formal and informal leaders of the firm; opinion leaders whose views represent the views of others and whose involvement in the interviews can serve as a surrogate for similarly minded partners who would like their views heard in the planning process.

These conversations can be sensitive. Often, they are best undertaken on a not-for-attribution basis by an independent interviewer who synthesises the answers to highlight where there is consensus among the interviewees and where views are disparate.

5. **Collecting and assessing data about the firm's performance**

Building on a firm's strengths can contribute an important element to a successful vision statement, to wit: making a vision statement credible. Data about the firm's demographics and performance is the key to this endeavour. A comprehensive set of data should be collected and analysed by the planning team as part of its work.

The firm's performance data should be analysed to identify strengths, weaknesses, opportunities and threats. The first three can be identified from the firm's demographics. Of course, profit margins on work, attractiveness of the firm's client base and breadth and depth of the firm's practice areas and sector presence are important. But there are also opportunity costs. Underutilised lawyers, whether simply because they don't meet the firm's expectations for an 'all-in' commitment (billable and non-billable time) but also because of time spent unproductively, like working for less remunerative clients who don't pay the firm's full rates or ask for excessive discounts and write-downs. Underperforming offices that a firm might have once considered strategic but become increasingly less so for firms that have expanded into higher rate geographic markets can distract from management time and be a drag on a firm's performance, particularly if low-rate local work is the grist of an office's existence.

Reviewing and analysing data about the firm's size, growth and financial performance relative to its peers is also important. This data can be pulled together from various public and subscription services. Five-year trend lines on headcount, revenue, profits per partner and revenue per lawyer provide a big picture look at whether the firm is gaining or losing ground in the marketplace.

Takeaways from the data should be pulled together into a PowerPoint for use in the planning (described later in this chapter).

6. **Interview takeaways**
   When the interviews and data analysis is complete, the interviewer or someone working under the direction of the interviewer should pull together a set of takeaways, often best organised in the form of a PowerPoint with one slide for each question. The takeaways from the answers to each question should be organised into four categories: points on which there was a strong consensus, a consensus, what some people thought and what a few people thought. For instance:

   > Question: What practice groups will the firm have to have to achieve your vision for the firm? What will it take to get there?
   > - There was a strong consensus that the firm will have to build its private equity practice.
   > - Some people mentioned intellectual property.
   > - A few mentioned white collar.
   > - A few thought the firm would have to acquire or merge with a firm with strong private equity practice.

7. **Assessing the data and competitive environment**
   In addition to the interview takeaways, the data provided by the firm in response must be analysed for insights into how the firm is performing. Particular attention should be given to peer group studies and industry benchmarking. Benchmarking can be undertaken for areas of specific interest.

   Competitive intelligence that paints a picture of the firm's standing in the minds of clients and talent should be sought from the firm and from public and private databases. Often the firm's bankers and consultants are good sources of competitive intelligence. So are client service interviews, should the firm wish to undertake them as part of the planning process. If not, there are companies that provide competitive intelligence on client service, such as BTI Consulting Group.

8. **Forming a planning team**
   A planning team should be formed by the firm's chair, often in consultation with others, no later in the planning than after the interviews have been completed.

Planning teams should be designed keeping in mind the goal of getting broad buy-in for the plan from the partnership, but they also must be manageable in size. As is the case when deciding which partners should be interviewed, to achieve buy-in the planning team is best comprised of formal and informal leaders of the firm. A group of eight to 15 partners often complemented with the firm's chief operating officer (COO) is manageable in size. Too small a group and the team loses critical mass if a couple of members can't make the meeting. Too large a group diminishes the likelihood of adequate time for either robust, interactive discussion among all the members or efficient decision making.

Planning team members should be told that the planning will require a substantial commitment of time. Although it will likely be spread out over a period of several months, the total time commitment, not including travel time, could easily be in the neighbourhood of 80 hours or more.

9. Convening planning team meetings

Planning is an iterative process best accomplished with a series of planning team meetings. For a regional, national or international firm we have found it requires the planning team to meet over a period of several months. Although we have found it can be done if all of the participants are on Zoom, it is awkward to have some of the team members participate by Zoom and others in person and, in any event, it is far better if planning team meetings are in person.

We have also found that back-to-back half-day sessions are more productive than single full-day sessions. The half-day session format avoids meeting burnout and allows the team members to tend to client work, including calls and emails the morning before the first session and the afternoon following the second session. Member attendance at all of the meetings provides important continuity and sustains momentum. Social dinners during the evening between the meetings allows time for the team members to bond and share views about the team's work product. It also allows time for reflection on planning issues on which there are differences of opinion. Similarly so for allowing a couple of weeks' gap between planning meetings.

10. Agendas for planning team meetings

10.1 First meeting

The first meeting should start with the facilitator presenting an overview of the planning process, the reason to plan and the benefits of planning. Of course, planning is about making choices about what to grow and how best to grow it, but it is also about building consensus about those choices.

Once the overview and the reasons for planning have been presented, the agenda for the first meeting can be laid out, to wit:
- present and discuss the interview takeaways;
- present and discuss the takeaways from the firm data; and
- present and discuss the competitive environment.

These discussions should be interactive and robust, with the facilitator using Socratic questions. We often admonish planning team members not to hold anything back, saying that if they said to a partner after the meeting that "they couldn't believe nobody said 'X' or 'Y' then the meeting would have been a failure". After all, the planning journey is at least as important if not more important than the work product itself.

We have found that these three presentations and the discussion around them take at least a full half day and more often than not two full half days.

10.2 Second meeting

In the second meeting, the facilitator leads the planning team in a SWOT exercise (strengths, weaknesses, opportunities and threats). This is best accomplished in person.

The first portion of the exercise is brainstorming. The facilitator asks planning team members to free-associate the firm's strengths, weaknesses, opportunities and threats. The team should work spontaneously, with one suggestion triggering another. Brief commentary or questions are fine, but brainstorming is not the time for evaluation or analysis of the items that come up.

The facilitator is best off using two flip charts on easels. The top page on each flip chart is divided into a T chart, with a horizontal line across the top of the page and a vertical line down the middle. On one page, 'Strengths' on the left side of the T-bar, 'Opportunities' on the right. On the second chart 'Weaknesses' on the left side, 'Threats' on the right.

During the brainstorming, a team member may say that an attribute she is about to mention is both a strength and a weakness or a strength and an opportunity, or some other combination of two SWOT categories. The facilitator should ask the proponent to "break it down". What about it is a strength? What about it is a weakness?

While the members are free-associating, the facilitator is capturing their thoughts in the appropriate columns on the T-tables and prompting them for more thoughts. As each T-table fills up, the facilitator should hang it on the wall with tape in a place where the team members can see it and start a new chart.

When the brainstorming has been exhausted, it is time for a break. Team members should be encouraged to look at the work product on the T-tables during the break.

After the break, the team members should be asked if they have anything they want to add to the SWOT. The facilitator's job is to draw out the remaining strengths, weaknesses, opportunities and threats.

Once the brainstorming is finished, it's time to evaluate the SWOT. Team members should be encouraged to share their thoughts on the team's work product. What are the relative merits of each of the items? Is there overlap that should be eliminated? Should some of the items be reworded? Perfection shouldn't be allowed to get in the way of the good, but each item should get a once-over.

At the conclusion of the evaluative discussion, it is time to prioritise. To prioritise, we use a simple method called 'dotmocracy'. The requisite ingredient is 'sticky dots', the ~1/2" coloured adhesive dots often used to denote sale items in stores. At the outset of the exercise, the facilitator counts the number of items in each of the four columns – all the strengths, weaknesses, opportunities and threats. Divide that total by three and give each team member a commensurate number of dots. For example, if there are 21 items denoted as strengths, a team member would get seven dots. The same applies for each column. If each of the four columns has 21 items, each team member would be given 28 dots.

With dots in hand, the team members are asked to prioritise their top items in each column, in this example seven dots per column. This is accomplished by having the team members get out of their seats and place their dots on their priorities. Cumulative voting is allowed within columns. For example, a team member can place all seven of her dots for strengths on one strength. But team members cannot use dots allocated to one column in another column.

When the "dotting" is completed, the facilitator totals the dots for each item and notes it in the left or right margin of each of the categories. We now have a rough idea of where the team's consensus lies on the firm's greatest strengths, weaknesses, opportunities and threats. The SWOT is reviewed at the outset of the next session. All in, the SWOT exercise with prioritisation is likely to consume two to three hours. The work product will help inform the vison, goals, strategies and action items.

10.3 Third and following meetings

(a) *Articulating the draft vision statement*

Articulating a draft vision statement is a seminal point in the team's work. The vision statement is the font of the plan, from which the goals, strategies and action items flow. It states the partners' aspirations for what they want to build together for the firm's practice. It serves as a guidepost for leadership and management to use for making decisions about how to allocate firm resources and also for aligning the firm's structure and systems. A vison statement must differentiate the firm from its competition in a way that is favourable to the firm's clients and talent, and prospects for both. When they read or hear it the thought that "this firm is for me" should race through their minds. To accomplish these purposes, it must evidence the choices the firm has made about its future. These choices must serve as guideposts for allocating the firm's resources. Among the most important choices are those involving the markets (geographies, practice areas and sectors) in which the firm wishes to compete and the position the firm wants to occupy in those markets. Finally, a vision statement must have a horizon, or a date by which the vision will be achieved. This is typically expressed in a number of years. Too soon and meaningful accomplishments won't be achievable. Too far-off in the future and the plan may be out of date because of the changing environment. We have found that either three, five or seven years work well for a planning horizon.

For a vision statement to be optimally useful, all of the elements cited above should be captured in one to three sentences. How can this be done?

Drafting the vision statement begins after reviewing the takeaways from the interviews, the data, the competitive environment and the SWOT. To start, it is important to carefully lay out the elements of the vision statement set forth in the preceding paragraph. To build consensus, we have found it helps to start with brainstorming and word association, similar to what was done during the SWOT exercise, working with two flip charts again. The facilitator should ask the members of the planning team to volunteer words that they think should be in the vision statement. Two- and three-word phrases are fine. Each one should be written on the flip chart. All the while, the facilitator should be checking to see that words address each of the key elements of the vision statement in respect of:

- market position;
- practice areas;
- sectors;
- geographies; and
- talent.

As words start to mount up the facilitator should look for phrases to piece together, using the phrases to ask questions about and push back on their meaning. Words like "the best" and "firm of choice" speak to market position. These can be coupled together with geography, price areas and sectors. Ultimately, crafting one, two or three sentences together to form a draft 'straw-man' vision statement that can be critiqued, torn apart, revamped and tweaked by the group until a consensus is developed.

It's essential for the vision statement to be aspirational and credible. This need often presents a dilemma: should the vision statement describe what the firm is now or what it wants to be in the future? Balancing aspiration and credibility is often hard for lawyers. They yearn for clarity. Balancing aspirational and credible is often fuzzy. This dilemma comes up most often in deciding whether to use words like "Smith & Jones is the leading ... firm" or "Smith & Jones aspires to be the leading ..." Another stumbling block on clarity is whether to use "the leading" versus "among the leading".

In wrestling with these dilemmas, the planning team would do well to use poetic license. Fraud claims don't lie in the vision statement. There is no "truth in lending"-type required disclosure. Instead, apply the reasonable person standard. Don't get bogged down in precision for the first draft. Don't let the perfect get in the way of the good. Get a working draft of a statement on the paper up on a flip chart page for people to reflect on.

When the planning team has a workable statement on the table, check it against the requisite elements set forth in the first paragraph. The facilitator should push the planning team for ideas on how to address any missing elements.

A pitfall to avoid during the drafting of the vision statement as a group is for a member of the planning team who is not satisfied with the draft the planning team has derived to posit an alternative, or 'duelling' version of the vision statement. This is often divisive and counterproductive. Members of the planning team should stay focused on the facilitator's working draft. They should be encouraged to suggest modifications, but not wholesale alternative versions.

Other pitfalls to avoid are the 'website' pitfalls. There are at least two. The first is when members of the planning team ask whether the vision they articulate will be published on the firm's website. It might be, but it is more likely that the firm's marketing team will write website-ready copy from the version the group derives. The facilitator should steer the planning team clear of writing copy for the firm's website and instead leave that to the firm's marketing professionals.

Sometimes a member of the planning team will ask to see other vision statements. This gives rise to the second website pitfall, when members of the planning team visit other firms' websites to see what their websites say about the vision statements of their firms. If this occurs, it is important to keep in mind that those statements are likely the work of copywriters. Good for the marketing folks to research them as they copywrite, but not so useful for the planning team to use as a comparative for its exercise.

At the conclusion of producing the working draft of the vision statement, not infrequently as a result of compromises made in planning, a member of the planning team will read the planning team's work product and ask how it is different from other firms' vision statements. The dissenting member may read vision statements from other firms' websites. They may indeed sound similar. In response, it is best for the facilitator to ask the group how it can be differentiated. But it is also important to remind the group that every word in the vison statement is pregnant with the meaning attached to it when the group wrangled with each word. In writing the vision statement, it is truly the journey that counts. This surfaces most meaningfully when the group turns to drafting the goals, and again as the group turns to finalising the vision statement. At this stage, it is important to remember: the current version is a working draft of a proposed vision statement, not a final version for approval by the partners. It can and should be reviewed when the time comes for drafting goals, strategies and action items.

(b) ***Goals, strategies and action items***
All of the predicates for drafting the vision statement also serve as predicates for the goals, strategies and action items, and more. All of the data, the SWOT and the vision statement itself contain

ingredients. There are two exercises that are helpful in drafting the vision statement.

Milestones exercise: The first exercise for developing goals is the *Milestone Exercise*. This exercise calls on the firm's legacy. The group is asked to recall the defining events in the firm's history that made the firm what it is at the time the firm is planning. A timeline is made to mark the year each event occurred. These events would include, for instance: the founding of the firm; the year in which a key client or key clients first hired the firm; and the years in which the firm achieved certain financial metrics or opened important offices. Recalling these key milestones helps frame the planning team's mind for the order of magnitude accomplishments that ought to be considered for goals.

Stepping into the future: The second exercise is called *Stepping into the Future*. In the exercise, the facilitator asks the group to review the vision statement while considering all of the work that has led to this point in the planning, close their eyes and imagine themselves five years into the future. The firm has achieved its vision. With their eyes closed, they imagine that they have stepped five years into the future and are again gathering together as a reconstituted planning team to draft a new plan. Their first meeting is about to start. Before it starts, one of the planning team members turns to the person next to her and comments how remarkable it is that the firm achieved its vision. The colleague replies that it would never have happened except for a few main elements, and the two get into a discussion about the key accomplishments.

The team members are then asked to open their eyes and recount what it was the two members in the imagined conversation had said happened. The accomplishments mentioned must pass the 'but for' test. In other words, the vision would not have happened *but for* this event or accomplishment. This list of items serves as an additional starting point for goals. All goals must pass the 'but for' test. They must be outcome determinative of achieving the vision.

The reason for the 'outcome determinative' test for goals is simple: planning is about making choices in part because firms have limited resources, to wit, time and money. Planning is about marshalling those resources to achieve the shared aspirations of the partners. Firm leadership and the partnership writ large shouldn't waste its time and money on efforts that aren't outcome determinative of achieving their vision.

For the same reason, firms shouldn't waste time and money on goals that aren't reasonably achievable. It makes little sense to tilt at windmills. Big hairy goals, as Jim Collins calls them, are fine, as long as they are reasonably achievable and outcome determinative of achieving the vision.

(c) *Outperformers and drivers of success*
In 2007, using data Citibank had published, we identified a set of five drivers of success that distinguished a group of firms that had outperformed the market. We grouped their accomplishments into five drivers of success. We have often used these as a framework for considering goals. The five drivers are:
- a shared differentiated vision;
- disciplined growth in achieving the vision;
- talent management;
- client management; and
- marketing and communications.

When aligned and working well together, these five elements drive firm success. The elements of a shared differentiated vision that make it work have been covered earlier in this chapter. Using it as a divining rod to make decisions about how to allocate firm resources explains what disciplined growth is about.

We find that presenting these buckets after the Milestones and Stepping into the Future exercises help provide a framework for formulating goals, strategies and action items.

(d) *Talent management*
Talent management includes building a sustainable firm that holds out the promise of partnership in a stronger firm than the firm inherited by the generation of partners that came before. This includes strong professional development, well-managed work allocation affording all attorneys, including diverse attorneys, an opportunity to advance in their skill and knowledge levels and earn their way to partnership and maintaining strong alumni relationships with those who don't, 360 feedback and evaluation loops, high levels of utilisation, clear communication of expectations of staff and all attorneys, a merit-based compensation system that provides competitive rewards to the firm's high performers who meet and exceed expectations, and an 'up or out' system for attorneys who don't perform to purposefully set high levels of expectations.

In 2021, we looked at the performance of firms during the pandemic. Again, as we found when we looked at the Citi data about 15 years earlier, we found a group of firms outperforming the market with strategies and execution that fell into these five buckets. The single biggest change was in talent management. Firms have more tightly aligned their compensation systems with their strategy. Compensation systems continue to be less coupled to seniority and more coupled to performance, and also more elastic, with bonus components that enable firms to make material annual upward adjustments in compensation without affecting tier placement, or base compensation. This is particularly true for young partners and is reaching down even into the senior associate ranks.

Firm performance during the pandemic correlated with our long-held view that scale matters. Market research validates that known-for status correlates with gross revenue and size relative to market. Talent breadth and depth in core, high rate, preferably countercyclical markets drive the highest level of known-for status and financial performance. As noted earlier in this chapter, markets are geographic locales (cities and regions), practice areas and sectors. Firms that build breadth and depth where all three intersect. For example, Silicon Valley, Venture Capital and Technology practices, or Houston, Oil and gas, and M&A, out-perform those who don't hit the trifecta.

The benefits include better market knowledge and also yield the fastest and highest increases in financial performance because of compounding.

Finally, we learned from looking at the high-performing firms that they are strongly focused on building strong, diverse and inclusive talent pools with equity in opportunity and treatment for all. Not only has this been found to produce better results for clients,[7] but it also produces an environment more likely to result in attorney and staff well-being.[8]

(e) **Client management**

Client management can be broken down into two pieces. The first is curating your client list for high-performing clients in the firm's

---

7   Heidi K Gardner, *Smart Collaboration: How Professionals and Their Firms Succeed by Breaking Down Silos*, Harvard Business Review Press, 2017.
8   Justin Anker and Patrick R Krill, "Stress, Drink, Leave: An Examination of Gender-specific Risk Factors for Mental Health Problems and Attrition among Licensed Attorneys", *PLOS ONE*, https://doi.org/10.1371/journal.pone.0250563, 12 May 2021.

chosen markets and expanding your relationships with those clients. These are clients who pay your highest rates for the work your lawyers most want to do (in your core practice areas in which you have leading sector expertise) and who refer similar clients to you. Building large, curated client relationships enables firms to raise rates faster than randomly built, smaller client relationships.

The second piece is putting the best diverse collaborative team on the field for each matter each of these clients brings you and delivering a result that meets or exceeds expectations at a price that is aligned with the client's perception of value.

Client management includes seeking feedback on each engagement and significant milestone in the matter and relationship to ensure that this is happening and constantly improving.

(f) *Marketing and communications*
Marketing and communications should be consistently focused on burnishing the firm's brand, including by observing best practices in talent and client management, but also with fulsome profile-building initiatives that shape and enhance the market's awareness of how the firm is differentiated from its competitors in ways that make it the firm of choice for the most important client work in the firm's chosen core markets (again, geographies, practice areas and sectors).

10.4 Formulating goals, strategies and action items

The working draft of the vision statement, the work product from the SWOT, the Milestones and Stepping into the Future exercises, and the five drivers of success are the grist for formulating the goals, strategies and action items. Note that it isn't important to dwell on the semantics of what differentiates a goal from a strategy or action item. What the planning team should focus on is developing what needs to be done to achieve the vision statement and how the firm will be accomplish those things. In other words, the firm "is someplace now". "Where the firm is now" was discovered in part with the interview questions, in part with the assessment of the firm's data and the competitive environment, and in part with the SWOT. At the time of the planning it might be called "Point A". Where the firm wants to be at the time of the planning horizon is articulated in the vision statement. That might be called "Point B". The goals, strategies and action items articulate who is going to do what, when and how, to get from "Point A" to "Point B".

As long as the goals, strategies and action items encapsulate everything that needs to be done to get from "Point A" to "Point B" it doesn't matter what you call each of the components. What does matter is that those things clearly articulate what needs to be done and that there are measurable ways of determining whether what needs to be accomplished has indeed been accomplished.

Once all of this is explained to the planning team, the facilitator should lead the planning team in a brainstorming session, asking the group the question what needs to be done to achieve the vision. The group should be referencing all of the work it has done leading up to vision statement and, of course, the vision statement itself. Referencing all of the prior work and vision, the group should be asked and re-asked: "What else would need to be done?" And: "What will it take to do that?" Although it may not have been addressed specifically by the five drivers, the facilitator should tease out of the group what level of financial performance it would take to achieve the vision and what it would take to achieve that level of performance. When the group has exhausted its ideas, a fulsome discussion should be had to make sure each of the five drivers has been addressed and some attention should be given to refining the goals so that they are in "working draft" form.

11. Final drafting

We have found that once the goals are in working draft form it makes best sense to turn the final drafting of the goals over to a smaller group of two or three members of the team, with one specifically designated to take the lead. This smaller group refines the vision statement and the goals, and also fills out the strategies and the action items. Once this sub-group's work is brought back to the group for review, comment and revision, the final working draft of the plan is then presented to whichever body of the firm is going to approve it – the management team and/or the partnership. Their questions are answered and input sought for the planning team to consider as part of finalising the plan.

12. The gap exercise

Once a working final draft is completed, the facilitator should conduct a 'gap' exercise. In this exercise, the facilitator asks the planning team whether the vision would be achieved if all of the goals, strategies and action items were achieved. If the answer is "no" or uncertain, then the planning team should be asked what it is that remains to be done to achieve the vision and fill in the gaps. Brainstorming and evaluation can be appropriate at this stage, too.

13. Notes on buy-in and use of the plan

The framework set forth in this chapter is pregnant with opportunities for getting buy-in from the partners. Partnership, practice group, sector and office partner meetings can be taken advantage of to present and seek input on the then current state of the planning work. The SWOT and other exercises can be replicated in these sessions and the work product from them brought back to the planning team for use in its work.

The completed plan can be used to populate the agenda for the firm's executive committee and partner meetings. It can also be used as a starting point for each practice and sector group and office to develop its own plan, with the central question being what each will do to enable the firm to achieve its vision. Likewise for each partner having her own plan that answers the same question.

14. A few words about culture and values

Planning may invoke material changes in a firm, which may give rise to partner concern about changing a firm's culture. Culture can be amorphous and a firm's culture may indeed need to change in order to achieve its vision. For instance, we often cite the need for firms to embrace a high-performing culture or partnership.

To address partner concerns about changing a firm's culture, some firms choose to articulate a statement of their values. The values become a governor on change. In other words, a statement is included in the Values Statement that provides that the plan will be accomplished without compromising the firm's values, and then the values are listed. Some of the values often addressed include:
- diversity, equity and inclusion;
- collaboration;
- high performance;
- attorney and staff well-being;
- clients first ahead of partners and the firm; and
- firm first ahead of partners.

15. A closing note

In the end, the most successful firms have been driven by high-performing partners. A plan that clearly lays out what that means and the results it is intended to produce should be the goal for planning. The touchstones for partner performance should be:
- repeatedly demonstrating the ability to lead and manage diverse and collaborative teams in a core high-rate area of competency to produce innovative, customised results in

complex areas while achieving the highest levels of client satisfaction;
- doing that while aligning pricing, service and results in a way that meets or exceeds the client's expectations so that the client wants to return for another matter; and
- accomplishing the work profitably enough for the firm to attract, develop and retain more lawyers who unfailingly repeat that level of performance over and over again.

What will be measured in the way of partner performance?
- Client satisfaction, with results, service and cost (using tools like the Net Promoter Score).
- Client retention and growth.
- Matter and partner profitability.
- Attorney competency, recruiting, development and retention.

Talent management trends in post-pandemic law firms

Jennifer Bluestein
Perkins Coie LLP

For years, legal talent professionals have been hearing about the need for more inclusion, agility, reliable technology, focus on peer connections, cross-selling, diversity, etc. Some large law firms were able to make the shift and were rewarded with 'stickier' laterals, lower attrition and higher productivity. Other law firms didn't feel the pressure to change – they knew they would continue to get the best talent and charge their clients accordingly, without making any changes.

As profits per partner in the Am Law 50 kept rising and smaller firms started merging (or failing), some very successful law firms considered themselves almost immune from the need to change. However, in recent years, clients began taking a more demanding approach: suggesting partners move to particular firms, requiring electronic portals for case management, asking for measurable and regular reporting on diversity and requesting collaboration across law firms. Before this, some law firm leaders saw clients saying they wanted alternative fee arrangements or conducting reverse auctions to select firms, and then choosing the firm they'd been using the past decade anyway. As a result, large firms felt a pressure to innovate while others determined the pressure was false and that firms would not be held accountable.

The pressure and the earnest credibility of that pressure over the last several years began to increase significantly – just in time for the pandemic to send everyone home into a virtual world. The world paused in March 2020, only to pick up and start making up for lost time in the legal world in spring and summer 2020. During that time, legal talent professionals had to pivot for real – teaching new skill sets that included everything from recruiting remotely to understanding how to assign work and mentor attorneys effectively, supporting relationship-building without in-person experiences, and supporting well-being for a broad range of demographics in their talent pools.

This chapter focuses on recruiting remotely, building on the premise that attorney well-being is an important recruiting differentiator. It covers a variety of topics that are always relevant but which became especially challenging due to the pandemic, including:

- well-being during the pandemic – morale, connection, peer groups, benefits, staying connected, outreach and fighting burnout;
- flexible work, boundaries, parenting and work–life integration, working from home, meeting hygiene and use of videoconferencing;
- recruiting laterals in the Zoom/virtual era;
- integration and onboarding – best practices and how to do it during the pandemic;
- training and curricula for various development programmes by level (first-year training; new partner training; senior associate training; trial training), and how to deliver in the Zoom era – for instance, whether partners need to learn teaching/professional development remotely;
- transparency as a key to talent management: the new normal; and
- increasing reliance on professional staff.

1. Well-being

The cornerstone of recruiting is to convince prospective employees and partners that they will be happier and better off at our firm than at another. At Perkins Coie, our culture has always been a selling point, but we need to walk our talk both with our existing population and potential recruits. Every firm tries to sell its culture as a differentiator, but now more than ever a firm's culture must connect with well-being in order to demonstrate it has a desirable culture. First and foremost on everyone's minds during the early months of the pandemic was whether business and work would continue. Despite a lull in March and April, it certainly did. And by the end of summer 2020, talent professionals, law firm leaders and partners were hearing more about the newly termed "COVID-19 burnout" than pay cuts or lack of work coming through the door.

During the pandemic, my firm, Perkins Coie, participated in the annual survey by *Fortune* and Great Places to Work®,[1] which

---

1   *Fortune* 100 Best Companies to Work For ® 2021, www.greatplacetowork.com/best-workplaces/100-best/2021.

creates the ratings of Best Workplaces for *Fortune*. Perkins Coie has been participating in this programme every year for 19 years and has made the Best Workplaces list each of those years. When the pandemic hit, I asked myself whether it would even be a good idea to participate in the survey. People were "surveyed out" and working hard under very stressful conditions, often with small children and other unusual distractions in their homes. But in talking to various employees across departments, everyone was expressing such gratitude for the firm's approach and support during the pandemic that we decided to proceed with the annual survey. Fortunately, and somewhat to my surprise, the survey results were actually better than the previous year by three percentage points. With an increase in our already-high participation rate, 94% of our employees rated Perkins Coie a "great place to work" – an all-time high. From the survey results and the individual comments Great Place to Work® shared with us, I could see what was most effective in what we had done and were continuing to do. In April 2021, the Fortune Great Places to Work ranked our firm #1 for Consulting and Professional Service Firms and #23 in the country in its top 100 list. This was achieved despite the firm having temporary pay cuts in place. It was clear from the survey comments that people felt cared for by the firm during this difficult time, a key component for trust and well-being in a workplace. The public acknowledgement of that trust, whether in a Great Places to Work ranking or rankings in other media such as Vault or Chambers, is helpful in establishing a consistent brand in the talent marketplace. Just as firms want potential clients to think of us in a certain way, we all want potential attorneys and business professionals to think of us positively as well. Having a consistent brand helps on both sides of this spectrum.

1.1 Staying connected

The desire for in-person connection through going to the office or to events and retreats will not go away, and the pandemic has accelerated the many ways attorneys can connect and collaborate with clients. Whether firms are using OneDrive, Microsoft Teams, Zoom, Webex or other tools, there are benefits to being physically isolated, in that people have learned they can share documents, edit them together, and share conversations with good eye contact and the nuances of body language that make all the difference.

Most firms instituted a variety of check-ins and peer groups. One of the most effective efforts firms found they could undertake was actually the easiest – an old-fashioned phone tree, whether video or audio-only. Offices divided up their list of associates and staff and ensured that a partner from within the practice group or floor reached out to specific people they knew and had strong relationships with. The simple purpose of these calls was to check in to ask how the person was doing and what the individual needed. That simple exercise was valuable to the associates in particular, because they had indicated that they felt a bit forgotten and burned out.

1.2 Fighting burnout

According to a January 2021 article in the *Harvard Business Review*, "In 2019, burned-out employees were 2.6 times as likely to be looking for other employment. Researchers also estimate that workplace stress accounts for 8% of the national budget in healthcare."[2] Keep in mind, that information comes from pre-pandemic research. In a follow-up article from February 2021, "Beyond Burned Out", daily users of Zoom went from 10 million to 200 million during the pandemic.[3] According to Christina Maslach of the University of California, Berkeley, Susan E Jackson of Rutgers and Michael Leiter of Deakin University (who have studied COVID-19-related burnout and were cited in the "Beyond Burned Out" article), burnout has six main causes:
- unsustainable workload;
- perceived lack of control;
- insufficient rewards for effort;
- lack of a supportive community;
- lack of fairness; and
- mismatched values and skills.

Maslach *et al* advise that the tools employers have turned to and doubled down on during the pandemic (more of which is described below in the section on the ABA Well-Being Pledge) are effective for improving well-being, but not for preventing burnout. They conducted a survey of 1,500 employees, 67% of whom were supervisor-level or higher.[4] The results were astounding:

---

2 Margaret M Luciano and Joan F Brett, "Do You Know Burnout When You See It?", *Harvard Business Review*, 28 January 2021, https://hbr.org/2021/01/do-you-know-burnout-when-you-see-it.
3 Jennifer Moss, "Beyond Burned Out", *Harvard Business Review*, 10 February 2021, https://hbr.org/2021/02/beyond-burned-out.
4 *Ibid*.

- 89% of respondents said their work life was getting worse;
- 85% said their well-being had declined;
- 56% said their job demands had increased; and
- 62% of the people who were struggling to manage their workloads had experienced burnout "often" or "extremely often" in the previous three months.

In Big Law, we tend to think we have it worse: our stress levels are higher and surveys tend to show greater levels of career dissatisfaction. Well-being research conducted in 2016 by the American Bar Association suggests that some lawyers are really unhappy. Some 28% of lawyers experience mild or higher levels of depression, 19% experience anxiety, 23% experience chronic levels of stress and 20.6% of participants struggle with problematic drinking.[5]

And yet another ABA survey tells a different story: 87% of men and 72% of women were extremely or somewhat satisfied with their jobs. At the other end of the spectrum, 5% of men and 21% of women were somewhat or extremely dissatisfied.[6]

While the data aren't consistent across the board, one thing is clear: whatever was the case prior to the pandemic, burnout has increased and satisfaction has decreased and millennials (roughly those aged 30–41) are more negatively affected.

As law firms share the concerns of other industries that women (especially those with caregiving responsibilities) and diverse groups, especially Latinx and African-Americans, are losing ground or dropping out of the workforce during the pandemic, they've made fighting burnout and increasing flexibility a business necessity. Few talent professionals see this as a temporary need; instead, it is a catalyst for the future.

According to Gallup, the potential for burnout increases significantly once someone exceeds 50 hours per week and this is even more dramatic after 60 working hours. That might explain

---

5 PR Krill, R Johnson and L Albert, "The Prevalence of Substance Use and Other Mental Health Concerns Among American Attorneys", *10 Journal of Addiction Medicine*, 46–52 (2016), https://journals.lww.com/journaladdictionmedicine/Fulltext/2016/02000/The_Prevalence_of_Substance_Use_and_Other_Mental.8.aspx.

6 Debra Cassens Weiss, "Why Are Experienced Women Lawyers Leaving BigLaw? Survey Looks for Answers and Finds Big Disparities", *ABA Journal*, 14 November 2019, www.abajournal.com/news/article/why-are-women-lawyers-leaving-biglaw-survey-looks-for-an-answer-and-finds-big-disparities.

some of the increase in burnout during the pandemic – longer hours – but what else caused additional burn-out?[7]

In addition to not adjusting workloads down a bit in the pandemic, most employers, according to HBR, failed to give people enhanced control and flexibility, and they increased the number of meetings and video/screen time in particular.[8] The average employee spends 13% more time in meetings during the pandemic and on average works 48 minutes a day longer.[9]

Beating and preventing burnout is not an easy task, but if we use these methods as a tool for the future effective functioning of successful lawyers, it is worth the change management required. Law firms that help their staff and attorneys feel a sense of purpose, maintain a manageable workload and spend less time in meetings and video calls will find themselves further ahead on retention and engagement as the Harvard article predicts.[10] And just as importantly, employers that support management discussions with everyone on their mental health and frequent check-ins (in a meaningful way) are more likely to prevent significant burnout. Peer-to-peer groups that started during the pandemic, along with employee resource groups, will likely find a permanent place in the day-to-day running of our organisations. Another major aid is difficult to teach but easy enough to do with the right leaders and managers: empathetic managers. According to Helen Riess, the co-founder and chief scientist of Empathetics, this can increase job satisfaction and decrease burnout.[11] Law firms that support empathetic conversations and provide social forums like Teams or Pulse or Slack support a community of sharing without negative bias. Partners and managers who start meetings with "How is

---

7 *Gallup's Perspective on Employee Burnout: Causes and Cures*, Gallup (2020), https://spaces.pcc.edu/download/attachments/94211047/Gallup%E2%80%99s%20Perspective%20on%20Employee%20Burnout%20Causes%20and%20Cures.pdf?version=1&modificationDate=1595023177000&api=v2#:~:text=Gallup%20analytics%20show%20that%20the%20number%20of%20hours,their%20workload%20has%20a%20stronger%20influence%20on%20burnout.
8 Macaulay Campbell and Gretchen Gavett, "What COVID-19 Has Done to Our Well-Being, in 12 Charts", *Harvard Business Review*, 10 February 2021, https://hbr.org/2021/02/what-covid-19-has-done-to-our-well-being-in-12-charts.
9 Danielle Kost, "You're Right! You Are Working Longer and Attending More Meetings", *Harvard Business School Working Knowledge*, 14 September 2020, https://hbswk.hbs.edu/item/you-re-right-you-are-working-longer-and-attending-more-meetings.
10 Campbell, *supra* note 8.
11 Empathetics, http://empathetics.com.

everyone doing today? I can say for myself, it's been a rough few weeks" will be more likely to foster this kind of environment.

Law firms such as Mayer Brown, which has had an internal career coach, or Hogan Lovells, who has had well-being coaches on staff, are working hard to foster this kind of environment, while other firms are focusing on encouraging phone-trees and partner panels in associate programmes to remove stigma and encourage open discussion. Indeed, the focus on burnout will put much-needed focus on the well-being movement. It seems there is no end in sight to the significant stress staff and attorneys at all levels have been experiencing.

2. **Flexible schedules and time off**

The first thing Perkins Coie communicated to all personnel (referring to all professional staff and associates and partners) was stability: the firm was stable and everyone should just do their best. Before we sent everyone to work-from-home status, we introduced "Emergency Care Time" (ECT) to employees who had to track their paid time off (PTO). Knowing that employees could take extra days of PTO to care for themselves or others suffering from COVID-19 eased a great deal of stress. We heard over and over again, "thank you for the ECT – it has made a world of difference". Some employees who were older or at high risk simply wanted the freedom to go to the grocery store during off-hours; others took a few days to take care of elderly parents with COVID-19. We also offered staff the option of a leave of absence, a reduced schedule, or simply a flexible schedule. In addition, we let staff know that if they needed to change their work schedules to accommodate caregiving or e-learning demands, the firm would be understanding as long as individuals were transparent about their schedules with their supervisors. The firm asked for transparency from both a customer service standpoint as well as a legal compliance standpoint to meet the employer's responsibility to follow state and federal wage and hour laws. One critical point of this communication was that it was done in town hall meetings as well as in writing. All personnel received emails with information and a link to Frequently Asked Questions (FAQs).

By contrast to staff policies, associates have unlimited time off as they are judged on billable hours rather than hours worked. That was a more complicated issue because firms had no idea what was in store for the rest of the summer or year. There, many large law firms took a more flexible, if albeit vague, approach: do your best, and we will not hold low hours against you. As the pandemic continued, associates across the country at every large firm asked if they would get billable hours credit or reduced hours expectations in order to be bonus eligible. I have yet to hear of a firm that waived the hours requirement or reduced it, but most firms relayed the same message: focus on doing what you can and try not to worry. Perkins Coie explicitly communicated in a managing partner message, from me as the chief talent officer, and in associate town halls local and firmwide, this further message: associates with low hours for 2020 would not be judged or penalised in our performance review process for having low hours unless it was part of a larger pattern. Anyone who had low hours for 2020 alone would be judged on everything but hours. Moreover, we gave associates multiple choices: a no-questions-asked leave of absence until COVID-19 ended or until they otherwise felt ready to come back, reduced hours, or flexible hours. While we had a few associates reduce their hours, we didn't have many that took the full leave of absence, other than paid medical or mental health leaves.

In hearing how Perkins Coie leadership communicated with its attorneys, some attorneys at other firms asked how the firm communicated this level of empathy and ensured the messaging was reflected by individual partners. One critical component of getting consistency and buy-in was that partners were typically given the messages first and reminded that it was critical for the messaging to be consistent. Just as COVID-19 has been an opportunity for local leaders and politicians around the world to demonstrate leadership, it has been an opportunity for employers as well.

For Perkins Coie, the internal communication team was a vital force in ensuring that the firm followed a regular cascade for COVID-19-related communications: first, the management committee agreed on the messaging; then the managing partner, Bill Malley, shared it with the partners; then the town hall was held with the opportunity for individuals to submit questions to the moderator through a chat; finally, an email followed with a link to FAQs that were updated regularly. The answers in the FAQs were not always popular; some associates asked if the firm would be lowering its hours threshold for bonus eligibility. The answer to that question was "no"; however, associates were informed that individuals with low hours would not receive a negative performance review and it would not impact their partnership eligibility.

The critical point here is not what the individual decisions related to COVID-19 were, but how transparency helped build trust during a difficult time. And just as importantly, transparency goes along with thoughtful communication – having a plan to ensure all are told the same thing and in a variety of ways. At the same time, some associates indicated they felt that partners or clients sometimes forgot the extreme stress many of them were living with, particularly those with caregiving responsibilities. In turn, office managing partners and operational chiefs needed to remind partners regularly that the pandemic hadn't ended and kids weren't back in school. Instead, the new normal remained stressful, and even though months had gone by, numerous attorneys, partners and associates alike still had household distractions or responsibilities that competed with the focus and time their billable work typically required.

2.1 Supporting parents who rely on e-learning or who lack childcare

Starting about 20 years ago, many law firms started introducing Back-Up Childcare benefits for their employees and partners, typically through Bright Horizons. Law firms would typically give a set number of days to use the day care on an annual basis with a set co-pay that made it very affordable for staff and attorneys to use this backup day care when their own day cares might be closed or a nanny might be ill or out of town. The business case was fairly clear, especially for those billing their time: if it helped them bill an extra eight hours for each day they lacked childcare, the benefit paid for itself.

Bright Horizons likely never anticipated a global pandemic that would increase demand at all of its centres – or that would shut down any of its centres. But the agile company pivoted quickly to allow clients to add emergency care options to their contracts. Employees could use their own backup, including family members, to pay for their childcare and seek reimbursement from Bright Horizons. And by the time fall rolled around, Bright Horizons took it two steps further: they purchased Sittercity and provided free memberships as part of its benefit, accessing more sitters for their network. They also introduced learning centres where students age 8–13 could go for socially distanced e-learning (getting the kids out of the house and providing structure and supervision for parents who had to go to an office or needed some quiet in their households to work). Firms that used Bright Horizons were willing to invest more in this kind of benefit because they could see the positive impact on both productivity and well-being. And chances are these benefits will not go away; they will continue post-pandemic.

Perkins Coie saw the benefit of Bright Horizons and at first doubled the amount of days employees and partners could use the service, but eventually lifted all restrictions because it was clearly vitally important to a key demographic: attorneys with young children. Many large law firms either lowered co-pays for backup care or increased the usage available to employees – particularly attorneys – to encourage as much billable time as possible and to alleviate stress. While this is a necessary benefit in a pandemic world, there are other things to do to ensure the well-being of law firms' employees and partners that may enhance employee loyalty commitment and increase the well-being of our talent for years to come. It is benefits like these, which supported billable work and enhanced morale, that may have helped so many large law firms keep their talent loyal (and sane) and their billables high during such a challenging year for all.

2.2 Effective meetings – remote and otherwise in a remote world

As previously mentioned, there are some easy steps for meeting hygiene to increase efficiency, although this is admittedly hard for law firms that are more consensus-driven partnerships than others. As part of talent development, law firms took a step back (or rather forward) at the start of the pandemic and spent some time training their attorneys on how to operate successfully in a virtual environment, especially in light of an increase in formal meetings to keep people connected to one another.

Study after study notes that the percentage of worktime spent in meetings increased significantly during the pandemic, and the average workday increased by 48.5 minutes per day.[12] While meetings may be more essential for staying connected, the need for efficiency has therefore increased. The first step in increasing the efficacy of meetings, particularly in a virtual environment, is to empower people to decline the meeting in the first place. With the move to remote work, the number of meetings increased exponentially, perhaps to make up for the lack of unplanned interactions in an office environment. Empowering someone to decline a meeting might sound basic and easy, but for associates listening to partners or partners with demanding clients, it is more of an art than a science. Giving everyone a set of guidelines to ask before accepting a meeting is the first step. Those guidelines might

---

12 Kost, *supra* note 9.

include asking whether the individual has vital information to share or needs to collect or know some vital information before the meeting. The next factor for successful meetings is to ensure the host creates an efficient agenda, takes/shares notes with those who don't attend, and closes the meeting with clear and documented action items.

In the beginning of remote work, while everyone was focused on getting people to turn their cameras on, we quickly learned that the increase in meeting frequency coupled with the increased focus and attention required for video meetings created a higher risk of burnout. We assumed the associates would all join with cameras readily and that partners would have to be pushed to turn their cameras on, but the opposite was actually true: associates were much *less* likely to have their cameras on than partners. When we started asking people why, we heard a few different themes. First, associates were less likely to have a designated office in their homes. In addition, they were more likely to have young children or pets around and were more likely to work in their dining room or bedroom areas. As such, they felt less comfortable sharing their home life or living conditions with others, especially partners. Second, we heard exhaustion from associates sooner than we heard it from partners. Although it was unclear whether associates were more likely to have competing demands at home (including spouses also working at home), they expressed more concerns about stress and had a harder time focusing. Once we realised this, we stopped pushing people to put their cameras on and simply suggested that people do whatever worked best for them. That seemed to take some of the pressure off and we continue to see more partners with cameras on than associates.

3. How to attract laterals in a remote environment and across distances

3.1 Lateral associates

The lateral market is still extremely busy as firms continue to see a slight increase in client demand; firms with technology, privacy and health care practices are seeing sharper increases. While the sweet spot for recruiting lateral associates remains consistent at the third- to fifth-year levels, associates are often looking for things other than compensation. While lockstep compensation certainly makes it easier for associates to compare firms, associates are becoming more holistic and balanced in what they seek in law firms. Lateral candidates are more likely to move through personnel referrals or even LinkedIn than ever before, moving away from the traditional headhunter-driven approach. As a result, law firm recruiting pages with video interviews of associates discussing the firm's culture and nature of their practices are even more important. Firms that emphasise and demonstrate their dedication to community, through support of diversity and inclusion as well as *pro bono*, are pushing those issues in their recruiting process. In fact, in the last six months, numerous firms have announced 50–100 hours of billable credit for various diversity and inclusion activities. While the billable expectation remains in the 1,950–2,000-hour range for full-time associates for several years, the activities that count towards that minimum have expanded and will continue to do so.

Lateral associates are also often looking at potential in-house positions as options, and law firms have had to be creative in competing against corporate legal departments that continue to expand. Law firms that emphasise training, complexity of work and compensation are better able to compete with corporate positions, but there are still countless law firms losing talent to their own talents. The lure of stock options and the end of billable hours entice associates earlier in their careers than has been common in the past. At the same time, law firms need to be very careful in hiring associates during the pandemic. Many firms have had either public or quiet layoffs, so law firms need to be sceptical about those associates from firms that have experienced layoffs.

If anything, laterals coming from other legal markets have a greater chance of making the move because they are often moving closer to family support or away from crowded cities. Firms that do not object to long-term remote work after the pandemic are doing well in the lateral hiring market because associates are willing to switch firms simply to be closer to family or to have a lower cost of living. This has been especially true for firms wanting to recruit New York-based associates. Every year many young lawyers graduate from top law schools and go to work in large New York firms without necessarily thinking they will stay in Manhattan long term. When the pandemic began and restaurants closed and health concerns increased, the isolation young associates experienced took its toll and many moved back to their hometowns for the duration of COVID-19; now, many are looking to relocate there permanently if their law firms allow it. The larger their firm platform and the more flexible the law firm's management is, the more likely the associate is to stay. But for associates who work for firms that don't allow office transfers easily or that don't have offices in the cities where they want to live, looking for a new job became an easy decision in a very advantageous job market.

Finally, for associate recruiting, the current state of burnout makes new opportunities more enticing. Says one large law firm associate who wishes to remain anonymous:

We are having a hard time recruiting laterals. People are more burned out and there are fewer boundaries between life and work, so when candidates interview with me or my fellow associates, they hear the burnout. The narrative our partners give about it being a nice place to work no longer matches the narrative associate candidates hear from our current associates. Going in-house looks more appealing than ever.

The solution for the future is not easy, and perhaps there isn't one solution that will work for everyone. A certain amount of attrition is healthy, especially when most large law firms plan for that attrition and use it to weed out those associates that don't have some of the attributes firms now require for partnership. That said, if done collaboratively, going in-house can be a win-win because law firms realise that their clients hiring from the firm's associate pool simply cements the firm–client relationship. And for associates who are happy serving clients and managing their work in six-minute increments, some appreciation in the way of positive treatment and value and market-related compensation goes a long way. The simple effort of a practice group chair reminding associates to take time off during a pandemic, simply to turn off and relax, can help prevent burnout and the desire to find a greener pasture.

3.2 **Lateral partners**

Pre-pandemic lateral candidates wanted to know about the platform for partners, cross-selling and the culture of the firm. One things partners consider but rarely ask outright is whether their travel will be supported and whether they will be expected to be in the office every day. While some older partners do appreciate being in the office most days, a study of office security cards at two different firms showed a regular "show up" rate of about 25–30% – meaning only 25–30% of partners were actually coming to the office on a 4–5 day a week basis (pre-pandemic). This is a key takeaway for hoteling or day-officing space. How is the firm selling hoteling to partners who want their own office? Is that an option for all partners? While accounting and consulting firms started office hoteling 20 years ago, law firms wouldn't even consider it. Now that law firms have seen how they can work remotely, even though they often prefer to see one another in person, having a clear yet flexible plan for remote work is critical to attract laterals. And just as importantly, providing a comprehensive support model for lateral partners remains important. As many law firms are moving to 5:1 and 6:1 secretarial ratios and team support, laterals that are more accustomed to using centralised services may be drawn to a firm that still assigns one key secretarial contact to their desk, even if the actual work is executed by a team.

The mystery for law firms around hoteling, day-officing or shared offices is not about the real estate, it is about selling the idea to partners who are accustomed to large, book-lined offices that they consider their second homes. And, conversely, it is about selling the idea to associates, some of whom want to be back in the office to escape distractions and have more interaction, and some of whom are happy to never return to an office more than a few days a month.

Despite the inability to travel, lawyers, regardless of how many days they are in the office, still want to work for a firm that balances collegial culture with financial management. Attracting a lateral now and in the future will always involve the delicate balance of in-person connection, getting to know the firm and cross-selling. Firms that can show potential lateral partners that their integration and onboarding process won't skip a beat are more likely to get partners to change firms during the pandemic. As 2020 proved to be a busy year for lateral partner moves (although lateral partners in the 500 largest law firms dropped by 23% from the prior three-year average), there is reason to believe 2021 will pick up even more.[13] The pressure to provide larger guarantees for making a lateral move continues to increase, but also puts greater pressure on law firms to conduct accurate and thorough due diligence to minimise the risk of those significant guarantees.

Once the recruiting process is underway and the lateral partner questionnaire is completed, 2021 laterals indicate the pandemic actually made interviewing a more efficient process. By using video meeting tools instead of travelling, schedules were easier to arrange, and the process for most laterals is actually faster – finding an hour here and there is much easier than a day trip and coordinating the schedules of six or eight different people in one location.

---

13   *How COVID-19 Shaped Lateral Hiring – and What Happens Next*, Decipher, 2020, https://decipherglobal.com/how-covid-19-shaped-lateral-hiring-report/.

According to Decipher's Global Lateral Hire Risk Mitigation Survey, a recent survey of 30 Am Law 200 firms, 60% of firms prepare business plans for lateral partners before they join and an additional 20% do them in their first month, whereas 75% of firms have formal check-ins with laterals at least quarterly after they join the firm.[14] Surveys differ, but between 30–38% of lateral partners leave within five years.

The resulting change that is occurring will continue to be the focus on due diligence to truly understand client portability. For example, when a partner says he or she is doing $8 million for a large healthcare company each year and lists that on their lateral partner questionnaire, it is incumbent upon the recruiting firm to delve deeply into the nature of the client relationship – whether it was inherited, who runs the client relationship, and how many attorneys across the existing firm's platform currently work on those matters. Many failed laterals thought they could bring a large client with them, only to learn that either procurement or the general counsel's office wanted to limit the number of law firms, and the client entities value efficiency and e-billing more than the individual attorney relationships. Pandemic or not, these issues remain important for successful lateral growth.

3.3 Recruiting technology for law firm staff – but could it be used for recruiting attorneys?

One of the tools we looked at implementing prior to the pandemic was asynchronous video-based recruiting platforms. Once we saw the inefficiencies in recruiting, scheduling phone screens and first steps in the interview process, we turned to using web and video recruiting technology to save time and make things more convenient for those being recruited, especially those who didn't have time or privacy during the workday for a preliminary phone call with one of our recruiters. The technology is fairly straightforward: instead of scheduling a phone screen, a candidate is asked to upload their video answers to a few key questions. They get three to four chances to record each answer and upload it to their application. That way, the video upload replaces the need for HR to schedule and then conduct a phone screen altogether, instead relying on the uploaded videos. It is a bit odd for candidates, I realise, but it

---

14   Hugh A Simons and Michael Ellenhorn, "Recent Survey Shows Firms Aren't Doing Right Due Diligence on Laterals", *Decipher*, https://decipherglobal.com/recent-survey-shows-firms-arent-doing-right-due-diligence-on-laterals/.

is ideal for all because we no longer have to worry about syncing schedules, so it can all be done whenever each party wants. Our tool is called VidRecruit. And if a recruiting team isn't convinced of the potential time savings, talent teams can run time-scanner surveys for each member of their team to see where all of their time goes by department and level. These surveys then enable the team to reallocate time and automate whatever they can. It's a revelation in efficiency and flexibility, and perhaps we will see it being used on a broader basis for some attorney screening interviews in the future.

In terms of the actual recruiting process, lateral candidates at all levels report a more pleasant and efficient experience. The ability to meet for a half hour or an hour over video is more flexible than trying to bring someone in for back-to-back meetings with numerous people. It decreases the total time between seeing a resumé and having a few rounds of interviews when people can just fit in one meeting at a time instead of three- or four-hour blocks of availability. Moreover, candidates are less stressed about dressing up and "sneaking out" of their offices to meet with another firm; it is much easier to toss on a jacket and meet over Zoom. While the video meeting is rarely as rewarding as an in-person connection, new hires report that they were still able to get a feel for the people and the firm's culture, so the objectives were still met. Overall, recruiting has picked up again and the market is even hotter than pre-pandemic.

4. Integration and onboarding

Once law firms have sealed the deal with their laterals, the challenge starts all over again: onboarding and integrating people they've never gotten to sit down with and meet eye to eye or breaking bread. While the use of video is much more common and natural, most agree that it is still difficult to develop relationships and trust with that format. Nevertheless, firms that spend the time (and money) to have smooth, thorough virtual onboarding experiences seem to have navigated through the transition well. The first step in onboarding is to ensure that new hires receive a welcoming phone call that walks them through their technology and home office needs, especially for lateral partners. New laterals who were able to start on day one with worry-free technology, including the little things (for example, the ergonomic mouse or keyboard the partner is accustomed to), have an easier first few days.

Having a designated point person to help get files transferred and opened is another critical area for lateral partners too. Partners who can't get their files often spend more time dealing with that than getting their clients' needs met, which makes for a slower and tougher integration. Here, efficiency is clearly king, but having a designated, high-touch integration point-of-contact can make all the difference. As firms continue to focus on growth through lateral acquisition, the lateral acquisition manager role (or something similar) is becoming more and more common. Some firms have separate roles for this responsibility while others make it part of their lateral partner recruiting team, but one thing is clear: having a designated professional with responsibility for integrating the lateral partner (other than other partners in the practice group) is a trend that will probably continue to evolve.

While the old-fashioned "road show" with new laterals visiting various offices to get integrated and assess cross-selling opportunities used to be the preferred method of integration, COVID-19 forced firms to be more creative. The practice group virtual introductions at large virtual meetings are simply not as effective as those office visits. As a result, having an integration manager or business development manager create a plan for the lateral to meet various partners virtually, in a strategic way, is the best way to simulate the live experience. Virtual welcome cocktails with break-out groups may not be ideal from the standpoint of the wellness committees, but laterals report they are quite effective (and mocktails are usually quite creative as well) in starting new relationships.

5. **Development and training shifts to virtual**

As law firms continue to expand the training they provide for attorneys, especially associates, the training curricula provided by large law firms continue to expand and professionalise. While some of the largest law firms started emphasising distance and virtual training programmes years ago, the pressure to focus on their quality really took off in 2020. With hotel rooms and retreats cancelled for 2020, some firms held off on them altogether while others focused on the virtual experience. While some firms cancelled their summer programmes altogether, others opted to continue them with virtual training and social events. As a result, professional development is no longer viewed as something that can and should be done in person. Now firms know they can use technology effectively to promote both team building and skill building regardless of location. While some firms had eLearning technology and instructional designers many years prior to the pandemic, for many firms, they needed to bring in outsourced trainers to quickly adjust to virtual training methodology and platforms.

Similarly, virtual event management was rarely used by law firms prior to 2020, but now firms are starting to invest $50,000 and more in production values beyond the capabilities of Zoom or Webex. Invariably, law firms look forward to resuming in-person events, but they may be able to have long-term savings by having a mixed approach to training and retreats. For example, firms that might otherwise have a week-long orientation for first-year associates may find that an ongoing virtual orientation coupled with two days of in-person orientation is more successful. Now that firms have had to explore these options, they are more creative in how they use resources to develop the skills of their attorneys. Using high production values, services that are skilled at putting on remote events, a blend of recorded, live presentations and interactive sessions all yield more effective distance programmes. Ideally, a blend of live and remote learning can be the most efficient and effective method of providing training. For example, having a group watch or read some prework prior to a live, in-person programme can help participants, especially those who have to fly to a multiday programme, make the most of the time in the live programme together.

But the pandemic showed the legal industry that fully distant experience can be effective. For programmes that would normally be intensive multiday events, holding three- or four-hour programmes with breakouts and interactive sessions, over a period of a week or two, could be successful. However, scattering these programmes over various days to maximise attention and focus had one critical caveat: if associates have no backup and no support or understanding from partners to allow them to fully participate, holding sessions over a period of days or weeks will not work. For partner programmes even prior to COVID-19, a series of remote programmes on leadership or cross-selling could be very successful as long as nothing went over 90 minutes and they included interactive exercises within the cohort group. Critical to the success of these ongoing programmes that are done as part of a series is to record the programmes and send links to replay the programmes as quickly as possible. Allowing participants the flexibility to observe a programme right after it happens helps participants remain involved in a training series.

There are other advantages to remote training as well. Whereas a partner might have worked with associates across many offices to get a deal done, their interactions before COVID-19 may have been solely by telephone. But now with the increased use of video calling, those relationships are actually stronger by having a mix of video and phone calls. And we've been hearing the same thing from clients – clients trust the associates more now that they have gotten to know them and their pets, etc, in a different context. The trust and client development skills may be developing differently, but they are still developing in this virtual practice. In several cases, a few partners have commented on how they've gotten to know one another's children and it has made the working relationships stronger. Quite significantly, a number of partners indicate they will still travel to meet with clients, but they can do so less often and still maintain strong relationships. As such, desktop video is here to stay, even with some of the frustrating technical glitches everyone has endured during the pandemic.

There are, of course, a few caveats to help develop stronger professional relationships through video software. For one thing, attorneys need to remember they are still on a professional call, despite the kids and pets that may make for a confusing situation. Partners have indicated that they regularly see associates wearing casual T-shirts with graphics on them while on client video calls, and the casual nature of the attire as well as some of the graphics on the T-shirts gave the partners concern. Partners want to remind associates that they need to look more professional, but often partners avoid those direct conversations. As such, firms are better off reminding everyone in the organisation that business-casual attire is always a safe wardrobe decision and a minimum expectation for client video calls. For anyone who is uncomfortable with their actual background, whether it is a bedroom or something else, using a virtual background is a good solution. While some virtual backgrounds provide more distraction than anything (the palm trees on the beach), training everyone on how to use firm-specific backgrounds is an easy and worthwhile effort.

6. **Transparency is the new normal**
Evaluations and feedback are critical development tools for associates, but they used to take place under the code of silence and without associates knowing who said what. That has changed over the past 15–20 years with the implementation and awareness of state laws requiring that employers share their employee reviews and files with their respective employees. What was once shielded from view is now knowable by associates, and as a result, there has been a new emphasis on clear feedback, actionable advice and accountability.

If a firm is moving from an opaque system in which associates do not see reviewers' comments, there are many recommended steps to make that change successfully. The first step may be to ask both associates and partners to complete a survey on how they experience the current system and what recommendations each group has to make it better. Inevitably, associates who are not accustomed to seeing the original feedback will ask to view it. In many cases, partners will share that view, especially those who "grew up" in similar systems. Modern technology evaluation and feedback systems easily permit individual reviews and comments to be automatically combined into a summary report, with or without attribution. The critical issue in making this change is to give both fair notice and extensive evaluation training to those completing performance reviews, primarily partners and of counsel. Again, a remote environment requires online training, but it can still be interactive, whether done in a large broadcast or through small group sessions with interactive exercises. Using hypothetical situations, reviewers can learn how to take a fairly typical situation and document and properly provide feedback to the associate in both a conversation and formal written process. Once all have been trained on this process, including training associates on how to accept candid feedback, commencing an evaluation process in which associates are given their written feedback provides actionable results to truly help associates develop their skills.

7. **Changing staffing models: professional staff as trained business partners to attorneys**

   Another critically important change that has been occurring over the past few decades is accelerating both due to COVID-19 and due to client demands: professional staff are becoming trained business partners to attorneys. With clients looking to contain costs, increase ROI and enhance accountability, lawyers can no longer meet all of their clients' needs without the assistance of trained professionals. Gone are the days when a partner, some associates and paralegals, and legal secretary could fully support a client. Instead, law firms have started hiring knowledge management professionals, pricing experts, project managers, legal project managers and business managers to run individual practice groups as separate business lines. Firms also have client relationship managers partner with specific clients, and clients are looking to partner with firms on specific inclusion or *pro bono* initiatives which require a sophisticated level of staff. These individuals are often, but not always, former lawyers.

Moreover, they are often MBAs who have opted to specialise in law firm management. The pressure on law firms to provide these sophisticated (translation: costly) services means that law firms have had to find other efficiencies, such as moving administrative and secretarial work to shared service centres or pooled secretarial hubs within offices.

Under the guise of "never waste a crisis", numerous firms took the opportunity to streamline their administrative services support and laid off legal secretaries, client development staff and less productive attorneys. While work-from-home certainly made it more challenging for attorneys to work with their legal secretaries, some firms invested in ensuring attorneys had the same level of support while others took the initiative to double down on the shared service centres and reduce staff overhead in the administrative areas. While for some, this appears to be simply cost-cutting, other firms are shifting their spending to new technology and those more sophisticated staff needs. While some programmes have been deployed as early retirement programmes and others have been done as layoffs, again, clear and honest communication from management is critical in ensuring that staff and attorneys feel the decisions are both fair and reasonable. Decisions to lay off employees are never easy, but if management can avoid frequent layoffs and use them only with clear parameters and honest communication, the damage to employee morale can be minimised.

8. Conclusion

As law firms have had to hurry to be agile enough to weather the pandemic with grace and financial stability, they for the most part have succeeded in staying busy and meeting their clients' needs. The emphasis on client needs has been an important and, perhaps for some, humbling lesson in client service as it has forced law firms to refocus their business model and continue to invest in their attorneys and growth to ensure they can continue to compete. As the talent pool remains smaller and more competitive than large law firms would like, firms have had to think creatively and flexibly to find both compassion and operational efficiencies to be employers of choice for staff and attorneys (current and prospective laterals) alike.

How firms can successfully build culture remotely

Naomi Beard Nelson
Naomi Beard & Associates

1. **Introduction: navigating culture in unprecedented times**

    Speak with law firm leaders and they will tell you that the advent of the COVID-19 pandemic – and the changes it wrought on the business and operations of firms – necessitated rapid and profound shifts throughout their organisations. By late February and early March of 2020, perhaps the most immediate impact of the pandemic on law firms, their attorneys and professional staff was the immediate shift in the performance of their day-to-day work in a suddenly remote environment.

    For large- and mid-sized firms especially, remote work as the default arrangement has long been a rarity – the exception to the rule which places in-person, face-to-face work as the prevailing norm. The sudden shift to a fully remote workforce presented a wide variety of novel challenges. Beyond the mechanics and logistics of performing work remotely and the need to take stock of pressing financial forecasting and business, operational and technological issues, firms grappled with how they would remain connected with and supportive of their people. Law firms needed to ensure effective communication, maintain relationships and support productivity for hundreds, if not thousands, of individuals, most of whom were facing substantial personal challenges during a year of unprecedented hardship.

    Such sweeping changes to workplace norms inevitably evoked a change to the culture within law firms, and those cultural changes are still ongoing as firms continue to assess the scope of the pandemic's impact and its implications for the future of work. What is clear, however, is that firms which prioritised maintaining a strong sense of culture, while also addressing the existential issues raised by the pandemic, consistently saw better business outcomes overall – including higher productivity, lower turnover and better revenue.

The efficacy of outstanding culture can be seen in the recent performance achieved by McDermott Will & Emery, which posted record financial results in 2020. One important aspect of the firm's success, according to chairman Ira Coleman, is its culture: "We can only optimize our performance for clients and productivity internally by building a strong, happy culture."[1] He explained to *The American Lawyer*, "This [revenue growth] has been fueled by demand, lateral talent, client work and a great culture where people want to work hard."[2]

In addition, firms which recognised the importance of engaging *all* of their people – attorneys at all levels as well as all professional staff – in culture-reinforcing efforts reaped greater rewards in advancing collegiality, communication and productivity.

As a consultant and adviser to leaders in large law firms, I've observed a number of factors in effect among those organisations which have successfully navigated pandemic-related challenges. My consulting practice focuses primarily on large global law firms (often based in the United States, but with offices around the world), as well as some mid-sized firms – all of which found themselves making rapid adjustments to their business strategies and operations in response to the pandemic. Within firms of such size, maintaining culture has been both particularly challenging and especially important as changes rippled across multiple offices and large workforces.

In reviewing the literature and observing the activities of my clients, I've found that the law firms which approached the changing landscape with proactive determination and a commitment to resilience achieved continuity – and in some cases enhancement – of strong firm culture. In fact, many firms proved their ability to preserve and even deepen a strong sense of culture within their organisations – even accelerating aspects of their talent development offerings in the process.

While many law firms entered 2021 in the enviable position of having closed 2020 with strong financial results and ample work to support their continued growth, the focus on maintaining and

---

1	Interview with Ira Coleman, Partner and Chairman, McDermott Will & Emery, 8 February 2021.
2	Patrick Smith, "McDermott Posts Huge Gains in 2020, Even Though it 'Never Felt Safe'", *The American Lawyer*, 22 January 2021, www.law.com/americanlawyer/2021/01/22/mcdermott-posts-huge-gains-in-2020-even-though-it-never-felt-safe/.

cultivating the cultures of these organisations remains front and centre. Such efforts are critical to their continued success, requiring intentional, strategic effort as remote work arrangements continue for the foreseeable future.

1.1 The importance of culture in law firms

The concept of 'culture' can seem amorphous and thus easy to relegate to low-priority status. Yet culture is a core component of law firm success; in many ways, it is the glue which holds high-performing teams together and drives engagement. A strong firm culture provides attorneys and professional staff with clear values and purpose. When individuals feel that their work is part of a cohesive group effort centred on a shared mission, they are more productive, collaborative and committed to their firm's success.

Firm culture also drives retention by enabling colleagues to build strong relationships, which engenders loyalty and supports retention of top talent. Heidi Shepherd, chief talent officer and assistant general counsel for employment at Goodwin Procter, shared that the strategic importance of maintaining a strong sense of culture at the firm is situated among the very top priorities for the firm's leadership. As Shepherd put it, "the subject of firm culture is a critical piece of every discussion with the chair". Shepherd acknowledged that day-to-day expression of the firm's values of "collaboration and connectivity" had to quickly pivot once the pandemic forced the abrupt shift to remote work. Firm leadership is strategically focused on how to continue to reinforce the firm's culture as remote work continues, and to revisit ways in which firm culture can be further reinforced once a broad return to work is permitted. Shepherd envisions a return to the office in which heightened emphasis is placed on the quality of in-person interactions.[3]

Many firms also acknowledge the challenges of promoting retention in an era of remote work, when some firms find it much harder to fully distinguish and express their cultures in an all-remote environment. Richard Rosenbaum, executive chairman of Greenberg Traurig, observed:

> *If you have people with good practices and they don't feel culturally wed to the firm, it's much easier for them to say it's time to go. If ...*

---

3   Interview with Heidi Shepherd, Chief Talent Officer and Assistant General Counsel for Employment, Goodwin Procter (3 February 2021).

they don't feel this strong cultural bond, after a while they may start thinking, "I feel disconnected" and be much more available for that phone call from the next firm.[4]

1.2 Challenges to maintaining culture presented by remote work

Senior leadership sets the tone in shaping and maintaining culture within larger law firms. These leaders articulate the firm's vision, values and objectives, model firm culture and incentivise behaviours which sustain it. At the same time, a firm's culture is realised and reinforced in concrete ways at the team and individual level. Firm leadership may set the tone and articulate the norms which define a law firm's culture, but for that message to come to life, individuals at all levels must embody and espouse those principles. The extent to which each attorney and professional enacts the firm's values in their daily interactions with colleagues determines the strength, cohesion and consistency of the culture over time. Leaders at all levels must not only espouse values, they must also model them in their behaviour and create policies which enable and motivate others to follow suit.

The COVID-19 pandemic introduced a number of challenges for individuals in all aspects of their lives. If left unchecked, these struggles could undermine their ability to embody the firm's culture. The advent of the pandemic and the sudden, forced shift to remote work it demanded left many attorneys and professional staff feeling unsettled and uncertain due to factors such as:

- loss of long-standing routines which govern workflow and time management;
- disruption of fundamental assumptions about day-to-day functioning;
- increased anxiety and uncertainty regarding established norms and procedures; and
- lack of access to physical spaces which promote intra-firm relationships and standard work practices.

In many cases, the pandemic has also imposed a profound and deeply taxing personal toll on the day-to-day lives of people.

---

4   Ben Seal, "Disruption and Disconnection: Greenberg Traurig's Richard Rosenbaum Expects a Tumultuous 2021", *The American Lawyer*, 20 November 2020, www.law.com/americanlawyer/2020/11/20/disruption-and-disconnection-greenberg-traurigs-richard-rosenbaum-expects-a-tumultuous-2021/.

1.3 Factors promoting success in maintaining culture remotely

Firms which had strong cultures when the pandemic began were particularly well equipped to make a smooth transition to remote work. Michelle Egan, managing director for talent development at O'Melveny & Myers, observed:

> *O'Melveny knows who it is and has articulated and lived by its values for decades. Firm leadership viewed the advent of the pandemic as an opportunity to demonstrate those values in action and to further strengthen those norms. As a result, we were able to enter uncharted territory with a clear vision for our strategic approach, which was to continue to advance the growth of the firm while using our existing talent development framework to ensure that both our existing and new programs and offerings were responding to the individual needs of all of our people. The sense of connection, cohesion and shared mission advanced by our strong firm culture made achieving these goals not only possible, but very successful.*[5]

Erica Murphy, chief human resources officer at Ropes & Gray, expressed a similar view, noting that the firm went into the pandemic with a strong culture and reservoir of goodwill: "The firm had really strong relationships and a sense of community going into the pandemic, and we continually look for new ways to build upon that strength."[6] In a similar vein, Jami Wintz McKeon, chair of Morgan, Lewis & Bockius, said that "one of the great advantages we had was we started out with a culture that everybody chipped in and everybody participated and everybody looked out for each other".[7] Proactively maintaining existing culture through intentional virtual communication and facilitating cross-office collaboration enabled the firm to reinforce that culture during the challenges of 2020.

Other factors which helped to strengthen law firm culture during the pandemic included:

- decisive, effective and nimble leadership which – despite rapid and substantial pandemic-related challenges – placed

---

5   Email from Michelle Egan to the author (29 January 2021).
6   Interview with Erica Murphy, Chief Human Resources Officer, Ropes & Gray (8 February 2021).
7   Brenda Sapino Jeffreys, "When the Pandemic Ends, Will Law Firms Still Have a Culture to Return To?", *The American Lawyer*, 29 November 2020, www.law.com/americanlawyer/2020/11/29/when-the-pandemic-ends-will-law-firms-still-have-a-culture-to-return-to/.

communication with the people within their respective firms among the very top business priorities;
- a transparent, methodical, trust-inspiring approach to ongoing communication within firms;
- a willingness to embrace and leverage the powers of the latest technology facilitating real-time connection;
- recognition of the importance of culture by firm leaders and supervisors at all levels; and
- an ongoing commitment to enhancing and augmenting the firm's existing talent development resources and benefits programmes to respond to the needs of their people.

1.4 Strengthening the core elements of culture during COVID-19 and beyond

The consensus is that there will be no return to normal – in the sense of a reversion to pre-COVID-19 cultural norms – inside or outside the workplace. While the full impact of the pandemic on the world of work remains unclear and will only be fully understood with the passage of time, it is clear that changes forced by the pandemic will have a lasting impact on how work is performed across all industries, even when remote work is no longer mandated by the pandemic itself. Law firms are already translating the lessons learned in 2020 into improvements and refinements to their cultures for the long term. Importantly, they've identified aspects of how they've operated and reinforced culture during the pandemic which they seek to preserve, even in a post-pandemic environment.

In more than 25 years of working in and consulting with law firms and their leaders, I've increasingly observed that effective functioning in the following six areas is most crucial to successful culture-building:
- leadership and communication;
- talent development programmes and initiatives;
- recruiting and onboarding practices;
- relationships, engagement and collegiality;
- diversity and inclusion; and
- wellness and work–life balance.

Adrian Davis, chief attorney development and knowledge officer at Latham & Watkins, described the firm's successful pivot to remote training and development: "With tremendous agility and effort, we repurposed and expanded our training programs. We were pleased to see that this shift actually enabled greater engagement in training and development programs." Davis found this trend towards increased participation in remote group events and training to be consistent across multiple cohorts, from summer associates to first years to optional conversations for wider groups of people to join programmes on important issues of the day: "There was an appetite and hunger for these kinds of programs, and we really met that need." Multiple groups across the entire firm have followed suit, providing trainings on a range of practical issues and allowing for more interactive sessions: "Our intentionally organized meetings have enabled colleagues across the firm to feel more connected, helping strengthen existing relationships and forge new ones." The impact of these group meetings also paved the way for more one-on-one interaction, enabling teams to remain more directly aware of the particular challenges some of their fellow colleagues may have been facing at a given moment. As Davis put it, "leaders at all levels asked themselves 'who is my flock and how do I take care of them?'" and then reached out to their groups accordingly.[8] How the firm handled the challenges posed by the pandemic, in part by finding ways to strengthen and reaffirm the firm's strong sense of culture, was a source of pride for the firm's people.

Set forth below is a discussion of the principal ways in which law firms successfully rose to pandemic-imposed challenges to protecting and cultivating their cultures and how organisations can apply lessons learned during this time to make continued strides in these critical areas.

2. Leadership and effective communication

When law firm leaders adapted to the financial, technological, productivity and personnel challenges brought on by the COVID-19 pandemic, many also recognised the need to maintain a close connection with their people. After all, a law firm's greatest asset – its working capital – is its talent. As noted by McKinsey & Company: "Your people are your law firm … Support employee flexibility, collaboration, and connectivity through technology and frequent communications from firm leaders."[9]

Those law firms which experienced the greatest success in navigating the challenges to their culture in 2020 ensured that leaders at all levels – from firm to local offices, practice groups

---

[8] Interview with Adrian Davis, Chief Attorney Development and Knowledge Officer, Latham and Watkins (6 February 2021).

[9] McKinsey & Company, "COVID-19: Implications for Law Firms", 4 May 2020, www.mckinsey.com/industries/financial-services/our-insights/covid-19-implications-for-law-firms#.

and teams – developed and maintained a regular cadence of communication and sense of connectedness with their people. As Michelle Egan of O'Melveny noted: "One of the keys to our effectiveness in promoting a unified sense of culture is by empowering our leaders at all levels, including associates and counsel, to embody and advance our firm's norms and values."[10]

2.1 Communication

Law firm leaders have long recognised the need for ongoing, clear communication with their people, and the pandemic brought into sharp relief the importance of transparency, consistency, frequency, accessibility and responsiveness in top-down communication to maintain strong culture.

(a) Transparency and consistency

The pandemic sparked rampant uncertainty, anxiety and speculation – a recipe for undermining productivity, loyalty and a strong sense of culture. Firms which recognised this risk prioritised transparency in communications, inspiring hope and forward-focus, while acknowledging uncertainty and hardship. In doing so, many leaders not only maintained but improved the culture of their organisations. Key aspects of transparency in leadership communications of particular import during the pandemic included:

- stating clearly what leaders did and did not know;
- providing realistic messages of hope while remaining honest about ongoing challenges;
- sharing decisions as well as the rationales behind them;
- relaying updates about the financial health of the business, including any plans regarding layoffs or furloughs;
- disseminating clear and reliable information about COVID-19, including firm policies and procedures;
- maintaining the regular rhythm of operations-focused communications (eg, workflow, technology, hiring and recruiting);
- informing all employees about additions to compensation and benefits and ensuring all information about those topics was easily accessible; and
- distributing information about concierge services to address emerging needs such as childcare, flexible hours arrangements and technology support for working remotely.

---

10 Email from Michelle Egan to the author (29 January 2021).

Leaders who were candid in their communications consistently saw their workforce respond with a willingness to support their firms and their colleagues, even amidst the individual, personal challenges they faced. In addition, ensuring that messages from all firm leaders maintained consistency in both tone and content helped law firms produce and maintain a cohesive culture – and promote a sense of trust.

(b) Frequency

Frequent communication, coupled with transparency, was crucial in combating the uncertainty which can undermine culture. Many firms adopted a cadence of weekly or biweekly town hall-style conversations led by senior firm leadership, coupled with strategic outreach by practice group, office and team leaders more frequently.

These live conversations were coupled with other means of communication to reinforce messaging from senior leadership, including:
- emails highlighting important new developments and offerings;
- voicemails from local leaders touting recent successes; and
- one-on-one outreach by supervisors and managers to the members of their teams.

Communication from key parties at regular intervals became paramount at Kirkland & Ellis. Chiara Wrocinski, Kirkland's chief administrative officer, described how she developed a weekly communication, first centred on important COVID-related health and safety updates, that then morphed into a fulsome weekly piece highlighting pandemic updates, firm initiatives, important benefits and personal interest stories. Over the course of the past year, that communication has been instrumental in promoting Firm culture inside and outside of the office.[11]

(c) Accessibility

Successful firms also ensured that attorneys and professional staff at all levels were included in all communications and that information was shared fully across the entire organisation. By communicating in a wide variety of formats, leaders ensured that information was accessible to all. Effective communication formats included virtual

---

11   Interview with Chiara Wrocinski, Chief Administrative Officer, Kirkland & Ellis (23 February 2021).

town halls, webinars, emails and voicemails, with town hall-style video updates and webinars generally being the most useful formats for disseminating information widely. Individual outreach was also a crucial tactic for firms to include everyone in communications. One way in which firms maintained this crucial one-on-one interaction was to divide responsibility for connecting with individuals among multiple leaders.

Breaking down hierarchies also improved accessibility in communications. The old-school approach to maintaining a sense of hierarchy between attorneys and other law firm professionals, a practice which had been fading in recent years, receded rapidly during the pandemic. Firms have more widely embraced the fact that it is only when all people within their organisations are included that a cohesive and strong sense of culture can take hold and flourish. Town hall-style conversations were delivered across entire populations, sometimes diminishing the traditional barriers between attorneys and staff. A concerted effort was made to be sure that law firm leadership communicated not only with equity/capital partners and other attorneys, but also with law firm staff, who were increasingly recognised for the crucial role they play in the proper functioning of these organisations. Describing the monthly calls between the chair of McDermott and members of the staff, Lee Anne Petry, head of communications and strategic initiatives, office of the chair, noted: "Our calls between the chair and the staff were among the most fun and engaged conversations within the firm."[12]

Indeed, many 'support groups' established by firms during the pandemic invited membership by any interested party, an approach which further blurred the attorney–staff dividing line and forged new, close relationships between people in various roles but sharing common challenges. Janet Stone Herman, director of attorney development and women's initiatives at Morrison & Foerster, told *The New York Times* that firm-wide support programmes helped establish deeper relationships during the pandemic: "People are so much more sympathetic across the board and see each other as human beings first," she said. "I'm hoping that sticks."[13]

---

12 Interview with Lee Anne Petry, Head of Communications and Strategic Initiatives, Office of the Chair, McDermott Will & Emery (8 February 2021).
13 Shira Ovide, "Using Tech to Teach – Smartly", *The New York Times*, 15 May 2020, www.nytimes.com/2020/05/15/technology/coronavirus-distance-learning.html.

Chiara Wrocinski of Kirkland & Ellis identified the opportunity that Zoom, Remo, Microsoft Teams and other virtual networking tools had on bringing the global Firm together – across all offices and roles: "We are one population, one firm. This experience has provided us an opportunity to get to know each other better than ever on some level. Ironically, we are socially distanced, but closer than ever."[14]

(d) *Responsiveness*

The effectiveness of communications was vastly improved when leaders invited dialogue and responded to questions and concerns from employees. Effective methods included responding to questions during meetings (either in the moment or submitted beforehand), inviting questions and comments during video meetings using the chat functions of those technologies, taking polls regarding pressing issues and sharing the results, inviting feedback through regular surveys, providing mechanisms for the anonymous sharing of feedback and questions and holding regular virtual office hours during which people could drop in to ask questions. Pillsbury Winthrop Shaw Pittman saw this as a particularly effective approach; chief human resources officer Kathleen T Pearson said: "Communication is a two-way street. By giving our entire population several different avenues to share their concerns and fears, we build trust and stability within our culture."[15]

2.2 Empathy and action

The humanising effect of the pandemic – the sense of fellow-feeling created by shared concerns and suffering – pushed many leaders to place increased focus on empathy in both their words and actions.

(a) *Genuine empathy*

Frequent communication from law firm leaders set the tone at many firms. Particularly outstanding leaders used an authentic, caring tone in their communications, maintained a regular cadence of outreach and evinced genuine understanding of the needs of their people. This included messaging to acknowledge the special burdens carried by people assuming caregiving responsibilities – whether for

---

14   Interview with Chiara Wrocinski, Chief Administrative Officer, Kirkland & Ellis (23 February 2021).
15   Interview with Kathleen T Pearson, Chief Human Resources Officer, Pillsbury Winthrop Shaw Pittman (12 February 2021).

children or other family members – and an awareness of both the systemic and individual hardships brought by the pandemic. Some leaders coupled this messaging with a range of offerings meant to recognise the unique burdens shouldered by caregivers.

Firms developed an array of creative offerings to respond to the specific needs and circumstances of various individuals; for example, augmenting their telehealth offerings, promoting participation in virtual exercise classes to promote a sense of shared experience and launching an array of remote contests (ie, childhood photo contests).

Tim Henderson, chief recruitment and professional development officer at Finnegan, Henderson, Farabow, Garrett & Dunner, explained that leaders at the firm were instructed to "be respectful of people's time given the fact that they're not only at home working but also that they might have children who are learning virtually or providing ... caregiving services to children and people who are ill". The firm offered attorneys up to 50 hours of billable credit for COVID-19 caregiving – and instructed practice group leaders and partners to reach out to individuals who seemed to be struggling to offer support and resources for their specific circumstances.[16]

(b) *Meaningful, concrete action*

Many firms conveyed messages of "shared sacrifice" or "we are all in this together" to their people – and those firms which followed through with policies reflecting those principles advanced a strong sense of culture by building trust. In fact, messages of solidarity from leadership were only effective when followed by concrete actions which had meaningful impact on staff and attorneys.

Tim Henderson observed that leaders following through on their stated intentions was important to supporting culture at Finnegan. Early in the pandemic, the firm clearly communicated their plan to support people, then executed that plan: "Senior leadership took a team approach and handled communication really well. Leadership kept everyone apprised of the plan ... and acted on their word – this approach was very helpful to morale."[17]

---

16   Interview with Tim Henderson, "May the Record Reflect", 6 October 2020, National Institute for Trial Advocacy, www.buzzsprout.com/441178/5602066-12-career-development-in-the-time-of-covid-with-amy-hancock-and-tim-henderson.
17   Interview with Tim Henderson, Chief Recruitment and Professional Development Officer, Finnegan, Henderson, Farabow, Garrett & Dunner (4 February 2021).

2.3 Effective management practices

The importance of effective self-management and management of others also emerged as a priority in maintaining positive firm culture. Some law firms seized the opportunity to revisit their leadership structures and more fully define the roles played by leaders at all levels. This practice accelerated leadership development in some firms, while highlighting leadership development as a key priority for other firms.

(a) Leadership at multiple levels

While senior leaders set the tone for cultural values and work priorities, the most successful firms were intentional about developing and supporting leadership at all levels. By elevating the visibility of more leaders within law firms, senior leadership was bolstered by the contributions of local, practice group and team leaders. Adopting a flat, more widely distributed leadership structure broadened the effectiveness of management and empowered teams to move forward more quickly once decisions were made.

Leaders such as office managing partners, practice group leaders and team leaders played a fundamental role in supporting and enacting firm messages. Strong leaders employed a variety of successful management tactics, including:

- holding routine group meetings and individual well-being check-ins;
- mindfully balancing work expectations with awareness of and support for individuals' needs and circumstances;
- setting standards and modelling existing best practices for remote work, while adjusting those standards as effective approaches evolved;
- showing openness to new technologies and practices which aided efficiency and business development, such as process improvements, pricing creativity, financial reporting and data analytics; and
- supporting incentives (eg, games, contests, recognition) which aligned with firm culture to promote engagement.

(b) Leadership from partners

All partners in a law firm are leaders, and developing the talent of other attorneys and achieving high performance on their teams is a key aspect of their contribution to the firm. During the pandemic, one successful strategy for leveraging partner leadership was ensuring more junior attorneys had a specific partner who was responsible for their individual development. While the design of the partners' roles varied, key elements included the responsibility for giving feedback, supporting development opportunities through work allocation, providing formal training, promoting high utilisation levels and ensuring that career goals and progression were actively managed. Conducting annual reviews and formal follow-up sessions during the course of the year was another important role of partners. This approach enabled even the most junior partners to cultivate their own leadership skills while also reinforcing individual relationship-building efforts.

(c) **Management training**
A culture of excellent management requires training and resources to help those who supervise others – regardless of their seniority – manage more effectively. Firms which promoted excellence in their management culture undertook a number of actions.
- They helped managers provide meaningful and ongoing feedback by providing routine check-ins, updates and team meetings so that attorneys could develop their skills during remote work. Such activities required proactive effort on the part of senior attorneys, especially those working with associates they didn't know well at the time of the shift to remote work.
- These firms emphasised the need for compassion, not only with the stress caused by the pandemic, but also regarding the limitations imposed by an individual's personal circumstances (including respecting boundaries and work–life balance).
- They offered formal trainings and informal mentoring relationships to engage managers in cultivating effective habits and to help them provide resources to associates in need of support.
- These firms engaged with associate committees more frequently and, in turn, encouraged those committees to engage more frequently and directly with the associates they represent.
- They centred the need to develop future leaders, nurturing younger attorneys to champion the firm's values and culture and become the talent pool from which future leaders can be drawn.

3. **Talent development programmes and initiatives**
Professional development is one of the most powerful tools in creating a culture which drives engagement, loyalty and long-term success in a law firm. Firms which invest in the growth of their

people demonstrate a genuine commitment to the attorneys and professionals who work there. Talent development also contributes to a culture in which individuals achieve more success and, in turn, devote themselves to the firm's success.

Quite remarkably, most larger law firms maintained or increased the cadence and scope of their usual formal talent development offerings in 2020, while also responding to the demands of the COVID-19 era. Law firm talent development professionals adapted to the demands of remote work, rapidly learning how to provide valuable training online. That adaptability was an important part of maintaining and preserving culture by promoting attorney engagement, retention and development.

3.1 Formal talent development offerings

Maintaining formal training programmes was a vital aspect of supporting law firm culture during the COVID-19 pandemic, with some larger firms offering hundreds of training programmes in 2020. Successful firms also substantially augmented their existing programmes with training specific to the challenges of 2020, adding content ranging from using remote technology tools to building remote presentation skills, supervising remotely and developing clients from a distance.

In addition to adding remote work-specific topics, firms improved the outcomes of their talent development programmes by shifting standard approaches to better fit distance learning needs. Successful strategies included:

- augmenting internal training resources;
- developing rich libraries of content;
- rolling out a range of learning models tailored for different skill sets;
- reducing the length of trainings from several hours to more bite-sized durations; and
- making the programmes themselves highly interactive.

By identifying and responding to the changing needs of their organisations, professional development departments played a foundational role in strengthening culture in the face of 2020's challenges.

3.2 A strong feedback culture both up and down the chain

Firms with a strong feedback culture – one in which senior attorneys and staff provide ongoing feedback to their teams as part of regular work practices – produce better performance by individuals, more effective teams, greater retention and stronger relationships. Through a combination of formal reviews and ongoing feedback, senior attorneys and staff ensured that employees received the hands-on guidance they needed to develop while working remotely.

(a)   Performance reviews

In 2020, many firms sought to ensure that feedback provided through performance reviews was substantive and actionable, including developmentally appropriate advice. By maintaining their usual schedule of performance reviews – and, in many cases, further reinforcing the review processes – these firms provided a sense of continuity and ongoing career development even amidst uncertainty and disruptions in other areas of work. Firms which did not have robust performance review practices in place sought to bolster their existing programmes to engage attorneys and professionals in their continued development and a long-term view of their career trajectories. Overall, firms found that taking a fresh look at their review processes and adjusting them to reflect existing realities produced better outcomes.

Paul Hastings LLP had begun revamping their approach to annual reviews prior to the pandemic. Managing partner Greg Nitzkowski told *The American Lawyer* that the changes the firm had begun to implement were important in making reviews more effective in the face of 2020's challenges:

> *We had the same process that everyone has had for years: an annual review, at year end, that fed directly into bonuses. It fulfilled a process, but it didn't really relate to the development of skills, or talent or opportunities generated … We started giving midyear feedback that was development focused. We started doing more informal reviews every four months or so, and only committed them to writing if there was a performance issue.*[18]

According to Nitzkowski, this new approach allowed the review process to account for the various life circumstances among attorneys, the effects of which were heightened by the pandemic: "If you are a 15-year partner, your life is one thing. You probably have kids that

---

18   Patrick Smith, "How Year-End Attorney Reviews Might Look a Little Different This Year", *The American Lawyer*, 20 November 2020, www.law.com/americanlawyer/2020/11/20/how-year-end-attorney-reviews-might-look-a-little-different-this-year/.

are close to college aged. If you are a first-year associate, you probably don't have kids and probably aren't married. Those situations are so individualized." Ira Coleman, chairman of McDermott Will & Emery, echoed the need for performance reviews to provide individualised evaluations which help attorneys grow their skills: "[W]e need to focus on development and performance improvement. Personalize it. Someone could have great stats but if you don't have the qualitative elements, then there is something missing."[19]

(b) ***Informal feedback***

In addition to formal performance reviews, ongoing informal feedback is crucial to attorney growth and development. Attorneys continually assert their desire for input from their supervisors, and these calls were more profound in 2020. Managers who took time to provide such continual feedback created invaluable learning opportunities and contributed to a stronger feedback culture at their firms. Without in-person opportunities to offer substantial, real-time feedback, successful firms built practices to encourage and enable online interactions, such as standing virtual feedback sessions and checkpoints within workflows designed to elicit input from supervisors during the course of a project.

(c) ***Up-the-chain feedback***

A central aspect of a strong feedback culture is the welcoming of feedback which flows upwards as well as downwards. Formal programmes such as upward reviews – in which associates and staff provide anonymous feedback about their supervisors – improve the performance of managers and offer attorneys and staff a meaningful voice in firm culture. During 2020, many firms created channels for such up-the-chain feedback, such as:

- monthly surveys to ascertain levels of wellness and satisfaction;
- feedback questionnaires to evaluate the effectiveness of support programmes and resources;
- dedicated channels for employees to ask for resources they needed; and
- surveys to measure the strength of the firm's culture at all levels.

In addition, many firms implemented more thorough upward review programmes or embarked on such initiatives if they had

---

19   *Ibid.*

not done so in the past. Efforts such as these gave firms actionable information about the success of their culture-building efforts and boosted morale by demonstrating that feedback is a two-way street throughout the firm.

3.3 Mentoring relationships

One of the most powerful forms of professional development is mentoring. Whether through formal firm programmes or informal relationships, one-on-one connections between senior attorneys and those more junior are critically important to both individual attorney development and a sense of cohesive firm culture. Firms which prioritised mentoring during remote work found it to be a valuable measure in promoting professional development and relationship-building.

Formal mentoring programmes, which match associates with more senior attorneys (typically partners) whose practice areas align with their career goals, are a hallmark of law firms which promote a strong learning culture. These programmes are also crucial to ensuring that associates who do not develop an organic informal mentoring relationship are not left behind in their development. Associates (especially junior ones who were newest to their firms) who did not have mentoring relationships in place at the outset of the pandemic found themselves with far fewer opportunities to receive guidance from senior attorneys when working remotely. Some firms answered this challenge by increasing the scope of their formal mentoring programmes. In the shift to online collaboration, professional development departments succeeded in supporting mentoring programmes by:
- proactively reaching out to both attorneys and staff to solicit participation;
- following up with participants to ensure they had adequate resources to support their communications;
- providing tip sheets to both mentors and mentees to facilitate valuable online communication; and
- encouraging supervisors to take on mentoring roles for attorneys in particular need of support during the pandemic (such as those in dwindling practice areas).

Informal mentoring relationships also proved key to associate success, and firms with a strong feedback culture tended to foster opportunities for such relationships to develop organically. In 2020, the onus was often on associates to actively seek such relationships, both with their supervisors and other senior attorneys in the firm.

3.4 Career advising and alumni support

In the midst of the economic downturn wrought by COVID-19, many attorneys and law firm professionals felt a growing sense of unease about the future of their careers as several firms announced layoffs and furloughs. By prioritising career advising and alumni support programmes, firms demonstrated their commitment to supporting the entire arc of an individual's career – including, when applicable, through successful exit from the firm and maintenance of ongoing alumni connection.

An additional aspect of career support – one which successful firms were mindful to pursue in 2020 – is career transition support for attorneys leaving the firm. Law firms offered outplacement consulting programmes to help attorneys who had been laid off secure new positions. In addition to providing material support to attorneys, these offerings created a lasting bond with alumni and improved morale for attorneys, who recognised the firm's genuine investment in the careers of all attorneys.

In-house career coaching programmes helped attorneys navigate worries about and changes to their career trajectories. Professional development departments offered one-on-one coaching to address individual issues such as a reduction in work for certain practice areas, attorneys' desires to pivot to new practice areas and planning progress towards professional goals and milestones.

3.5 Skills development

The economic shifts which drove changes to firm business strategies in 2020 created an increased need for certain skills. Successful firms supported attorneys and staff with professional development in key areas, which benefited both firms and individuals. In fact, the remote work environment created many new opportunities for attorneys to develop skills – another way in which firms promoted ongoing engagement with their people. This was primarily due to:
- partners' increased focus on and acceptance of training needs for attorneys, especially for new associates;
- a levelling of the playing field, allowing smaller and mid-sized firms opportunities to expand their areas of expertise;
- an increase in collaboration across practice areas to meet changing client needs, opening the door to opportunities for attorneys to learn new skills; and

- opportunities for junior attorneys to shadow partners and attend events like client meetings, depositions and even court appearances without the cost of travel.

In addition to developing skills which were of immediate benefit to firms and attorneys managing changing business needs, skill-specific talent development offerings reinforced a culture of learning and career growth.

(a) **Pro bono work**
Firms which maintained – or increased – their support of *pro bono* work provided substantive opportunities for developing talent. The pandemic rapidly increased the need for *pro bono* work and legal services in a number of areas, including employment law, domestic violence cases, immigration and support for small businesses.

Such opportunities allowed attorneys to build skillsets, expand their networks, work collaboratively with colleagues and nurture their professional interests. *Pro bono* work also fostered much-needed connection among colleagues and reinforced a sense of culture with social bonds and a commitment to helping others.

(b) **Business development training**
Highly effective firms ensure that business development is part of the fabric of each attorney's work, in ways appropriate for their seniority. An increased focus on business development training was an important aspect of professional development during the pandemic, especially as the shifting market necessitated changes to firm strategies. In 2020, the visibility of business development teams within firms grew, and many such teams took the opportunity to partner with professional development departments to offer training programmes in areas such as:
- cultivating proactive efforts and consistent habits;
- mining and cultivating contacts;
- leveraging online presence and use of technology resources;
- developing an awareness of fee structures and sensitivity to billing issues;
- collaborating with colleagues to cross-sell services; and
- engaging in discovery discussions with clients to learn more about potential new ways to serve their needs.

Direct client service is perhaps the most effective way for attorneys to hone their business development skills. Rather than being a

hindrance, remote work offered a variety of novel opportunities for attorneys at firms which embraced a business development culture.
- Associates were able to attend more client meetings because travel costs were not a consideration.
- Attorneys forged more personal connections with clients over video; when both parties were working from their homes, a deeper level of intimacy and human understanding could be achieved.
- Attorneys who effectively leveraged online communities found more opportunities to grow their networks and develop business relationships in an environment where many potential clients were particularly open to forging connections.

With a heightened focus on the importance of cutting-edge technologies as a means to remain connected with one another and with clients came greater open-mindedness around the various data analytics and customer relationship management tools which can be used to assess markets, streamline aspects of legal practice and track marketing and sales efforts.

3.6   **Role-specific talent development**
By taking a proactive approach to promoting growth and talent development for specific cohorts, law firms adjusted to a radically changed work environment. Firms found that the remote environment produced particular challenges for certain types of attorneys, and they adjusted their programmes and approaches to increase opportunities for connection and cohesion of their talent development efforts.

(a)   ***Summer associates***
Many firms worried that the 2020 summer associate class as a whole would suffer from a lack of in-person training, but they showed determination and creativity in overcoming the challenges of a remote environment, coupling orientations and substantive training sessions with virtual events, such as:
- themed weekly meetings to address topics specific to new attorneys;
- scavenger hunts to help summer associates learn more about the firm;
- programmes to connect summer associates with a variety of other attorneys;

- invitations to join discussions related to the practice of law and history of the firm; and
- games and social events to reinforce a sense of connection and camaraderie.

(b) **Laterals**

As lateral hires join a firm, ensuring that their professional development does not stall is crucial in promulgating a strong culture of ongoing learning and growth. During the pandemic, firms focused on bringing laterals into professional growth opportunities from the start of their tenure through activities such as:
- mindfully and proactively developing lateral integration plans;
- working with laterals and supervisors to define shared expectations;
- setting development goals and benchmarks for measuring success;
- establishing lateral-specific mentoring relationships;
- leveraging the use of remote technologies to foster more connections with more peers, more quickly and deeply than pre-pandemic patterns had typically enabled; and
- engaging laterals in proactive business development initiatives.

(c) **Associates**

While formal talent development programmes are crucial for associate development, the need for associates to take a proactive approach to their own development and success emerged as an increasingly clear trend during the pandemic. This messaging is something that many firms sought to integrate in their ongoing communications with associates.

In practice, the need for associates to take responsibility for their own development often translates into securing meaningful work assignments. Meela Gill, director of professional development and attorney training at Weil, Gotshal & Manges, offered practical advice for associates, noting that: "While there are many ways to refine skills at large law firms, the most effective route to advancing your professional development is by learning and mastering legal and professional skills on substantive work assignments." Gill counselled associates to take a proactive approach by communicating their interest in and availability for assignments, reaching out to maintain professional relationships and remaining visible to colleagues and supervisors while working remotely.[20]

Amanda Rose, partner at Fenwick & West, echoed the importance of proactive networking for career advancement. She observed that the pandemic has, in some ways, presented new opportunities for building relationships which further professional development, saying:

> *Get out of email and pick up the phone and talk to people. COVID has created so many alternatives to easily connect with people through video calls and virtual events. Take advantage of these. It makes it so much easier to attend events, especially for working parents.*[21]

Law firms have varied approaches to assigning work, from formal processes to more flexible free-market systems. Regardless of a firm's approach to work allocation, associates whose firms ensured they had ample opportunities to volunteer for valuable assignments and secure strong relationships with partners strengthened their culture of excellence and teamwork.

3.7 Salary and bonus consideration

Alongside professional growth and career advancement, attention to compensation is necessary for a culture which incentivises and rewards success. The economic downturn in 2020 presented challenges for firms in terms of revenue streams and projections, which required a thoughtful approach to compensation programmes. Successful firms found a balance between making necessary budget cuts and maintaining, even increasing, compensation packages which were competitive and supported loyalty.

Firms which chose to temporarily reduce salaries in the spring faced the likelihood of diminishing morale and undermining retention of their top talent. Strategies they employed to combat this potential backlash included:

- following a "shared sacrifice" philosophy in which salaries were reduced for those at the highest echelons of leadership

---

20 Meela Gill, "Ask A Mentor: How Can Associates Seek More Assignments?", *Law360*, 11 January 2021, www.law360.com/pulse/articles/1342535.
21 Tasha Norman, "How I Made Partner: 'Connect With People. Take Small Steps and Be Positive', Says Amanda Rose of Fenwick & West", *Law.com*, 22 January 2021, www.law.com/2021/01/22/how-i-made-partner-connect-with-people-take-small-steps-and-be-positive-says-amanda-rose-of-fenwick-west/.

by the same or a greater percentage than salaries for more junior employees;
- communicating with transparency and compassion regarding the reasons for cuts and the timeline for restoring salaries;
- reverting pay cuts as quickly as possible in accordance with firm finances; and
- providing back pay, when feasible, upon restoring salaries to normal levels.

Bonuses are another fundamental aspect of attorney compensation and are usually tied to billable hours. As financial performance at large law firms began recovering – and in some cases skyrocketing – in the fall of 2020, firm 'bonus wars' to retain their top talent ignited. The need to retain talent caused some of America's wealthiest elite firms to increase their associate bonus programmes, competing with other firms to offer the most competitive options.

While increased bonuses were a boon to high performers at law firms which pursued aggressive bonus incentives, attorneys whose billable hours were diminished due to the pandemic's impact on their personal lives were at risk of seeing their compensation decline – a particular concern for working mothers who bore the brunt of childcare when schools were closed or converted to online learning. Some firms recognised the need to adjust their usual bonus structures to ensure that their culture didn't suffer the blows of demoralisation and gender-based pay disparity. Many firms reduced billable hour requirements for bonus eligibility and leveraged operational savings which stemmed from remote work to reallocate funds to bonuses and incentives for both attorneys and staff.

Kirkland & Ellis, for example, offered special bonuses for staff members in recognition of their dedication during the pandemic. Chairman Jon Ballis said in a firm memo posted to *Above the Law*: "While Kirkland & Ellis is an institution built on the foundation of legal and operational excellence, it is also a firm that embodies the long-standing qualities of perseverance, resilience and grit – never more evident in our staff than in this past year."[22]

---

22 Andrew Maloney, "Big Firms Roll Out Bonuses and Other Payouts for Stressed Staffers", *The American Lawyer*, 7 December 2020, www.law.com/americanlawyer/2020/12/07/big-firms-roll-out-bonuses-and-other-payouts-for-stressed-staffers/.

4. Recruiting and onboarding in a remote environment

The culture of a firm extends beyond its walls, and the way a firm conducts interviewing, hiring and onboarding establishes its culture from the first moment of contact with a potential hire. An attorney's journey from contact to onboarding has the potential to lay the foundations of a productive relationship and integrate new hires into the firm's culture.

The disruptions of the COVID-19 pandemic changed the usual cadence and timing of recruiting, hiring and onboarding programmes. While shifting daily work operations to a remote environment in 2020, firms faced the further challenge of moving their hiring processes online, as well as fundamental shifts in the volume and pace in recruiting to meet changing business needs. Among top law firms, even those which furloughed or laid off attorneys and staff continued recruiting and hiring, both to shore up expanding practice areas with lateral talent and to maintain the pipeline of emerging talent.

Successful firms quickly adjusted long-standing programmes to the demands of remote communication and seized new opportunities for building culture online through strategic lateral hiring and shifting recruiting and hiring timelines.

4.1 Strategic lateral hiring

The rapidly changing 2020 landscape saw many firms pivoting from existing business strategies to instead devote resources to practice areas which expanded suddenly in response to novel challenges wrought by COVID-19. While lateral hiring fell overall during 2020 – a decline of 30% compared to the previous year[23] – some high-performing firms strategically increased lateral acquisitions. For instance, *The American Lawyer* reported:

> *Several prominent firms have bucked the 2020 trend of slowing down intake of new blood. Citing the presence of previously unavailable lateral options and steady firm performance during the pandemic, these firms have been able to expand their lateral hiring strategies.*[24]

---

23 Andrew Maloney, "No Opportunity Wasted: Even as Lateral Hiring Cratered in 2020, Some Stayed Busy", *The American Lawyer*, 25 January 2020, www.law.com/americanlawyer/2021/01/25/no-opportunity-wasted-even-as-lateral-hiring-cratered-in-2020-some-stayed-busy/.

24 Patrick Smith, "Opportunity in Crisis: These Firms Seized on an Unusual Lateral Hiring Market in 2020", *The American Lawyer*, 12 October 2020, www.law.com/americanlawyer/2020/10/12/opportunity-in-crisis-these-firms-seized-on-an-unusual-lateral-hiring-market-in-2020/.

Acquiring high-quality lateral talent was crucial for such firms – and a key element of successful lateral hiring was firm culture. Legal recruiter Michelle Bigler, founder of MB Attorney Search, noted:

> COVID caused people to reevaluate what was important to them, their family, the future of the legal industry, and how they can remain competitive in their practice without sacrificing their personal life. This was all happening while partners were being squeezed financially to keep their firms afloat.[25]

Given that environment, a positive firm culture was an important component of attracting lateral talent.[26] Armstrong Teasdale, one firm which focused heavily on lateral recruiting in 2020, offers a pertinent example. According to managing partner David Braswell:

> People want to join a firm right now that is looking ahead instead of hunkering down and braving the storm. We are getting talent from firms that are not dealing with [the pandemic] as well. Some firms are dealing with it in a more dramatic way than us, and I do think that has caused some partners to consider Armstrong Teasdale. We are using the pandemic as an opportunity instead of taking things away from people, such as lowering head count or reducing salaries.[27]

Ensuring that laterals seamlessly integrate into the culture of a firm – and contribute to that culture – when joining remote teams required innovation and ingenuity. Approaches firms used successfully included:

- one-on-one virtual introductions with peers – both within and across offices;
- regular check-ins with supervisors, partners and HR representatives;
- personal outreach from practice group leaders, client relationship partners and office heads; and
- remote lateral integration circles and virtual coffee breaks and happy hours.

---

25   *Ibid.*
26   Justin Henry, "Finding a Cultural Fit When Lateral Hiring Goes Virtual", *The American Lawyer*, 22 January 2021, www.law.com/americanlawyer/2021/01/22/finding-a-cultural-fit-when-lateral-hiring-goes-virtual/.
27   Smith, *supra* note 24.

4.2 Shift in recruiting and hiring timelines

Changes born out of the new remote environment – in businesses as well as law schools – and the changing economic landscape had profound effects on firms' timelines for recruiting. Many firms took this as an opportunity to bring potential new hires into their culture more thoroughly and build stronger relationships in the process.

(a) Summer associate recruiting

When it comes to interviewing summer associates, large firms have highly structured programmes. As most law schools delayed their on-campus recruiting programmes in 2020, firms had to adjust their timelines. *Business Insider* reported that on-campus interviews "typically held before law students' second years, have been pushed back to after the fall semester … With the extra half-year's time, law firms are getting creative with how they reach out to prospective candidates".[28] With this elongated timeline, many firms have taken the opportunity to offer law students resources – such as interview prep sheets and virtual roundtables – which enhance their chances of success and nurture their development early on.

(b) Lateral recruiting

Whereas summer associate programmes saw extended timelines in 2020, firms increased the pace of recruiting and hiring lateral attorneys to meet business demands; these compressed timelines were made possible by the ease of scheduling interviews remotely. *The American Lawyer* noted that lateral hiring at the partner level generally takes at least six months due to the time required for attorneys to visit offices in person for multiple meetings and meet-and-greet sessions, but remote meetings shortened that process to as little as six weeks.[29]

Bob Bodian, managing partner at Mintz, Levin, Cohn, Ferris, Glovsky and Popeo, reflected: "The experience here is that it's much easier to get availability. You're not setting up in-person meetings, which require more of a time commitment."[30] Thus,

---

28 Yoonji Han, "5 Top Law Firms Run Through Their 2021 Summer Associate Recruitment Plans, from Using '3D Resumes' to Interviewing Students from Lower-ranked Schools", *Business Insider*, 9 November 2020, www.businessinsider.com/top-law-firms-summer-associate-recruiting-oci-virtual-interviews-students-2020-10.
29 Dan Packel, "From Six Months to Six Weeks: Lateral Hiring Is Speeding Up", *The American Lawyer*, 29 July 2020, www.law.com/americanlawyer/2020/07/29/from-six-months-to-six-weeks-lateral-hiring-is-speeding-up/.
30 *Ibid*.

the combination of the uptick in lateral hiring and the shortened hiring timeline facilitated by remote work has been a boon to firms pursuing seasoned talent to support changing business strategies.

4.3 Shift to video-based communication

Conducting interviews and onboarding sessions virtually presented similar challenges to holding meetings remotely – with the added difficulty of ensuring candidates and new hires became acquainted with the firm's culture without being present in person. Many firms successfully leveraged video technology to overcome these hurdles and even found silver linings in the unique opportunities presented by the video format.

(a) Personal connections enabled by video

In *The American Lawyer*, Armstrong Teasdale managing partner David Braswell noted that interviewing via videoconference allowed for more authentic interactions: "The tone on a virtual interview is different. People are more relaxed. When you're on the hot seat, in a room full of several suits asking questions, that can be stressful."[31]

San Francisco-based legal recruiter Avis Caravello added that meeting candidates virtually in their homes supported these personal connections: "You're meeting the dog, the kids, the spouse, the postman, who knows. It gives them a more human feel and allows for connections to be made more quickly."[32]

Building deeper personal relationships from the start can help a firm bring a lateral attorney into the culture more quickly and effectively, as well as ease the transition into onboarding once a hiring decision is made. "When you come out of the recruiting process as a lateral, you're completely exhausted," Caravello noted. "You've been on airplanes for months, you're meeting tons of people. Now, candidates go into the on-boarding process a lot more fresh than they did in the old days."[33]

(b) Creative use of video technology

Translating their existing processes into remote experiences during the pandemic allowed firms to leverage technology in creative ways which enhanced connections and culture. *Business Insider* reported

---

31   Ibid.
32   Ibid.
33   Ibid.

on some of the successful techniques used by five top law firms in recruiting new associates, such as:
- using video-interviewing platforms like LaunchPad;
- hosting meet-and-greet events via Zoom breakout rooms;
- providing TikTok challenges for 2020 summer associate candidates;
- offering mock interview sessions and presentations for law students; and
- hosting special events like presentations from notable public figures and video tours of interesting locations.[34]

Firms employing such techniques found that interactive video sessions provided ample opportunities for candidates to get to know their culture and forge connections with attorneys and leaders. One attorney recruitment manager observed that such virtual connection also benefits the firm by giving it a preview of potential star candidates by allowing more varied and personal interactions with potential new hires.

5. **Relationships, engagement and collegiality**
Ultimately, a firm's culture is enacted by the forming of relationships among colleagues and with clients. The restrictions on face-to-face interactions engendered by the COVID-19 pandemic presented obstacles to building relationships on all fronts – both personally and professionally. Firms which undertook ongoing efforts to support both existing and new relationships among attorneys and staff found that such initiatives played a vital role in maintaining culture.

Kirkland's successful approach to engagement offers a compelling example. The firm convened an 'employee engagement task force' that pulled together senior professionals from all administrative departments within the firm (IT, admin, HR, talent development, business development, etc) to form a cross-departmental group which, according to Chiara Wrocinski, "overnight created a plethora of engagement initiatives that have become foundational to how we interact with our people". Wrocinski described the array of activities launched by the task force such as (i) fun social events meant to bring people together, including pumpkin carving

---

34   Han, *supra* note 28.

contests, cooking contests, virtual cafes, staycation ideas, picture collages of 'life in quarantine', a firmwide book club, a talent competition and firmwide trivia games with 3,000 participants and (ii) substantive communications regarding practical issues of critical importance regarding the health and safety of the firm's people. The firm developed vast COVID-19 resources – from in-home COVID-19 testing to travel and quarantine restrictions, to vaccine support and updates, customised by each locale. As Wrocinski put it: "We haven't been able to give vaccines yet, but we are able to sort through the complex and overabundant information, and synthesise it in ways that are helpful to each person in their own locale." All of these initiatives – the social events and the informative resources – were highlighted in Wrocinski's weekly firmwide emails.[35]

5.1 Leveraging technology to advance engagement and collegiality

Active efforts to promote a sense of engagement and collegiality at law firms – something many worried was in jeopardy with the absence of organic, in-person interaction – was crucial to strengthening culture in 2020. For some firms, these activities even reduced geographic barriers to relationships and promoted connections among people who would not otherwise have had a chance to interact. Successful tactics undertaken by managers and firm-wide leaders included:

- creating frequent opportunities for online engagement, including virtual meetings, to maintain connections among employees at all levels;
- offering career counselling and development resources to underscore the firm's ongoing investment in individuals' success;
- scheduling regular check-ins with attorneys and staff to simply ask "how are you?" and evince support; and
- reallocating attorneys in slower practice areas towards *pro bono* matters, training and development or new firm practice area capabilities, rather than making quick decisions about potential exits.

At Pillsbury Winthrop Shaw Pittman, such virtual engagement yielded excellent results. Chief human resources officer Kathleen T Pearson explained:

---

35 Interview with Chiara Wrocinski, Chief Administrative Officer, Kirkland & Ellis, (23 February 2021).

> *Engaging remotely via video allowed Pillsbury to bring colleagues together from around the world for Shared Experience Forums. We have hosted over 20 internal forums which each has a specific topic for open discussion. To date, we have brought together over 1000 colleagues from around the world at all levels.*[36]

What successful firms learned from such activities is that managers must help establish norms of working which foster engagement and inclusion for the entire workforce. Firms based their decisions in these areas on analyses of which type of talent was most needed and which roles were most important to business needs. Many firms also leveraged analytics tools to understand and promote connectivity and engagement, such as social network analyses and listening tools such as mobile text platforms.

Erica Murphy, chief human resources officer at Ropes & Gray, noted that, once the pandemic necessitated a shift to remote work, the firm was focused on "(i) maintaining meaningful connections with and between the firm's professionals and clients in a virtual world; (ii) providing resources to help employees balance both their professional responsibilities and general well-being; and (iii) continuing to train and motivate their professionals in the absence of in-person mentoring". Leveraging technology became essential to accomplishing these goals. Using an array of means – email, video presentations, virtual events and initiatives – the firm sought to find ways to not only replicate its culture during remote work but adapt in ways that were responsive to the needs of their people (eg, online resource centres related to COVID-19, video communications both from firm leadership and fellow employees; a speaker series on topics ranging from history and the arts to social justice and entrepreneurship; employee resource groups and benefit programmes; practice group "pods" in which ongoing challenges could be discussed; and internal newsletters devoted to evolving efforts and initiatives).[37]

5.2 Embracing innovation

Advancements in technological resources have made remote work possible, and such advancements in recent years have enabled

---

[36] Interview with Kathleen T Pearson, Chief Human Resources Officer, Pillsbury Winthrop Shaw Pittman (12 February 2021).

[37] Interview with Erica Murphy, Chief Human Resources Officer, Ropes & Gray (8 February 2021).

companies across a wide range of industries to develop high-performing distributed teams. Since nearly all law firms were forced to adopt remote work to at least some degree in 2020, it followed that all individuals needed to become fluent with the technological resources which shifted, virtually overnight, from 'optional' to 'essential'.

A culture of innovation and future-focused thinking was bolstered within firms which readily adopted technologies to enable efficient workflows and relationship-building. In an industry often seen as averse to new technologies, tools such as videoconferencing software, asynchronous messaging platforms and cloud-based project management systems enabled attorneys and staff to remain connected and to collaborate meaningfully in firms that chose to embrace such technologies. In addition to facilitating business operations during quarantines and social-distancing mandates, these changes have laid the groundwork for more creative and flexible interactions into the future.

Some law firms seized on the unique benefits of online operations (eg, increased flexibility, opportunities for new ways of connecting) and overcame long-standing industry biases against remote work. Firms which continually iterated on technological approaches and provided robust training and resources to help attorneys and staff use technology effectively eased the transition to remote work. These firms also accelerated a culture of innovation which will serve them well even when work norms shift again in the future.

(a) **Video communication**
Perhaps the most notable technological shift has been in a near-universal acceptance of video-based forms of communication, including Webex, Zoom, Microsoft Teams and BlueJeans. This became a foundational means by which law firms maintained a sense of connection with their people during the pandemic. Attorneys, in turn, quickly identified video communication as critical to their ability to serve and cultivate clients. A whole body of training and programming focused on effective use of video technology has emerged during this time.

(b) **Adoption of new communication channels**
Coupled with widespread use of video technology has been a pronounced uptick in the use of new platforms for internal communication, such as Slack, Microsoft Teams and Google Hangouts. These messaging platforms combine characteristics of email and text messaging – providing the promptness of real-time

communication when all parties are available while maintaining the opportunity for asynchronous communication necessary to accommodate various schedules. These platforms enabled firms to replicate, in some ways, the varied types of communication inherent to in-office work. Further, firms explored new possibilities created by more online project management tools – such as Asana, Exterro and Clio – to enable efficient workflow for remote teams.

Chiara Wrocinski of Kirkland noted that the pandemic opened up new pathways for communication: "The pivot to all-remote work opened up a whole other world of communication among our people. We took the best of our people's knowledge skill-sets and collective wisdom to create new, deeper forms of outreach."[38]

5.3 Personal connection

Developing personal connections with colleagues and supervisors is foundational to a strong sense of culture. Without the opportunity for such interactions to occur spontaneously (eg, chatting with colleagues in the breakroom, elevator or hallway), firms had to create intentional spaces for casual connection and relationship-building.

Ultimately, these efforts are about genuine human connection, and a firm cannot replicate in-office interactions perfectly in a remote environment. Firms succeeded by seeking creative ways to replicate such interactions, as well as by seizing new opportunities provided by online collaboration tools. Some successful practices firms undertook included:

- scheduling time at the beginning of team meetings for informal chatting and ice-breakers;
- establishing open-invitation office hours in which leaders were available online and welcomed people to drop in;
- creating spaces within online collaboration tools like Slack dedicated to fun topics and casual chatting; and
- hosting multiple social activities, including virtual escape rooms, firm trivia nights, mixologist classes, cooking classes, virtual walks, photo contests, recipe sharing, holiday parties and book clubs.

Large law firms have long tended to have fairly formal cultures. Creating a more relaxed environment which allowed for personal connection has been an exercise in intentionally shifting the culture.

---

38   Interview with Chiara Wrocinski, Chief Administrative Officer, Kirkland & Ellis (23 February 2021).

Those firms which succeeded in this adjustment were able to maintain and advance their cultures not only for the current climate, but also into the future.

Firms have sought to cultivate a sense of personal connection in creative ways, even at a global level. Jennifer Fox Crisp, global director of talent management at Baker McKenzie, spoke to how the firm's "Baker Band" sought to build a sense of authentic connection among their approximately 13,000 people spread across 77 offices by conducting a remote performance of the uplifting song, "Lean on Me". Members of the band located across the United States, Singapore, Vietnam and the United Kingdom met virtually to rehearse. Ultimately, the remote collaboration was recorded and released across the firm. Said Crisp: "Baker has historically had a big meeting and travel culture – connecting in person is endemic to who we are, and the band is always a favourite at firm meetings. Because of the pandemic, we had to give that up, so we found a way to bring that back in a different way. It reminded us of who we are that's truly unique." The message of the song was one that was reinforced by the firm's chair in some of the many internal blog posts he wrote.[39]

6. Diversity and inclusion

Advancing diversity and inclusion (D&I) has long been central to maintaining a healthy firm culture, and diversity initiatives have made an impact in recent years. *Business Insider* reported that: "In 2018, minority associate representation increased to 24.2% in law firms, up from 19.5% in 2010, and women have made up about half of law-firm associates for at least a decade."[40] Yet deep disparities remain, especially at the leadership level. Partners and firm leaders are still overwhelmingly white and male.

The heightened focus on D&I during 2020, driven by an increased awareness of racial injustice and the disproportionate impact of COVID-19 on communities of colour, has further cemented the import of law firms making specific commitments to and progress in these areas. Many prominent firms made strides towards meaningfully improving D&I by elevating diversity experts within senior management and launching a variety of initiatives.

---

39 Interview with Jennifer Fox Crisp, Global Director of Talent Management, Baker McKenzie (2 February 2021).
40 Samantha Stokes, "Meet 7 Diversity Leaders Who Are Fighting for Equality and Inclusion in Big Law from Firms Like Baker McKenzie and White & Case", *Business Insider*, 5 February 2021, www.businessinsider.com/diversity-execs-white-and-case-baker-mckenzie-top-law-firms-2021-1.

When done authentically – with clear intentions and measurable goals – these efforts were well received and positively impactful on firm culture.

6.1 Firm-wide programmes

Diversity committees, affinity groups and specific initiatives have moved beyond event and sponsorship planning. At successful firms, these groups became instrumental in driving a more challenging and meaningful debate about structural change. In 2020, many firms strengthened their culture by creating specific D&I targets focused on advancing women, improving racial diversity and supporting LGBTQ+ attorneys and staff. Crucially, firms are focused on improving representation of these groups at the leadership level.

Maja Hazell, White & Case's global head of diversity and inclusion – who led the firm in achieving Mansfield Certification Plus in 2020 in recognition of their diversity achievements – placed emphasis on the need for increased D&I success among the echelons of leadership. *Business Insider* reported:

Hazell said one thing she was focusing on was teaching leadership and management skills to partners and empowering them to lean into uncomfortable conversations, like the history of slavery in the US and that people in the country are treated differently based on their skin color.[41]

In addition to ensuring representation at every level of seniority, leading firms focused on making meaningful contributions in their communities. Last year, Baker Botts entered a three-year partnership with Official Black Wall Street to provide legal services to Black-owned businesses. The firm's director of diversity and inclusion, Kathy Bowman-Williams, told *Business Insider*: "We could have taken the easy road by making a donation to a legal-defense fund, but we decided to take a stand to see how else we could help the African American community."[42]

6.2 Work allocation and professional development

During 2020, firms with a strong D&I culture were particularly attuned to developing initiatives to directly engage with and

---

41   *Ibid.*
42   *Ibid.*

monitor workloads of individual attorneys in order to evenly apportion hours and equalise access to interesting and challenging work. This approach supported efforts to ensure that attorneys of all races, genders and identities are able to grow as professionals and advance their careers.

Concordant with equalising access to valuable work opportunities was ensuring professional development opportunities were also equally available to all attorneys. A central question firms must grapple with, as posed by *The American Lawyer*, is "How can a law firm ensure that lawyers – particularly those from a group that was already marginalized in Big Law prior to the pandemic – aren't compromised by the transformed reality of a post COVID-19 world?"[43] Taking into account the various challenges faced by historically marginalised communities and creating programmes which overcome the inherent inequities those groups face was – and will continue to be – a foundational activity for firms advancing D&I in their cultures.

In addition to taking an inclusive approach to attorney growth, firms which led the way in D&I in 2020 ensured that all employees were part of their initiatives. At Perkins Coie – another firm which earned Mansfield Certification Plus in 2020 – chief diversity and inclusion officer Genhi Givings Bailey focused on expanding firm programmes to include professionals as well as attorneys. As she told *Business Insider*: "Law firm DEI initiatives have historically not included staff, which is a missed opportunity." In the coming year, Bailey said she was "focusing on including law-firm staff, like secretaries, business-side professionals, and paralegals, in diversity initiatives so everyone is represented".[44]

6.3 Countering bias in hiring practices

The way a firm conducts recruiting has a profound effect on the diversity of its workforce. The practice of recruiting new attorneys only from a select group of top-ranked law schools is seen as a key contributing factor to reduced D&I at large law firms. *The American Lawyer* explained: "It's not that law firms actively seek to

---

43 Patrick Smith, "In a Remote Environment, Talent Development Is Fraught With Risks", *The American Lawyer*, 25 August 2020, www.law.com/americanlawyer/2020/08/25/in-a-remote-environment-talent-development-is-fraught-with-risks/.
44 Stokes, *supra* note 40.

deliberately limit the diversity of their workforce. But going back to the same schools each year with the same criteria in mind leads to what most firms deal with now: a homogeneity of mostly white males."[45] Tomas Chamorro-Premuzic drove this point home in *Harvard Business Review*:

> *We still hear managers and organizations self-congratulate on their attempts to hire for "culture-fit," but this is often incompatible with the desire to harness and nurture a diverse and inclusive culture … On the surface, hiring people who "fit right in" seems like a great idea. But when you become really good at this you will inevitably overlook, if not reject, the people you may need the most: individuals who can bring a different perspective, set of values, and backgrounds therefore augmenting cognitive diversity and expanding rather than consolidating your culture.*[46]

Some forward-thinking firms began leveraging emerging technology to better address D&I in hiring, especially in their law school recruiting programmes. Willkie Farr & Gallagher, for example, partnered with Suited, a new artificial intelligence recruiting platform. Suited uses a standardised method to identify the law students most likely to thrive with a particular firm's culture. "We are hoping to get a broader range of schools than we had previously", explained Tony Yanez, partner at Willkie and a firm recruiting chair, in *The American Lawyer*. "The way to previously get access to a law student was to put people on campuses and then set up next steps after that. This allows us to remove some of those barriers and have a broader reach."[47]

Suited CEO Matt Spencer emphasised that the platform is built to root out bias: "We are [working] with data scientists to interpret that data, and [they] are trained to … look for bias in the underlying data."[48]

"The issue of bias and removing bias from the process are front and center to [Suited]", Yanez said. "Anything that gives law students great access to firms is a good thing. We can always do

---

45 Patrick Smith, "Big Law Firms to Test New Recruiting Tool, Using Tech to Combat Bias", *The American Lawyer*, 15 December 2020, www.law.com/americanlawyer/2020/12/15/big-law-firms-to-test-new-recruiting-tool-using-tech-to-combat-bias/, accessed 30 January 2021.
46 Tomas Chamorro-Premuzic, "Thriving in the Age of Hybrid Work", *Harvard Business Review*, 13 January 2021, hbr.org/2021/01/thriving-in-the-age-of-hybrid-work.
47 Smith, *supra* note 45.
48 *Ibid*.

better, and we are always looking for ways to improve, and with Suited in particular, we can expand our reach into law schools."[49]

The use of technologies like Suited can augment traditional interviewing processes to help recruiters overcome inherent bias in the hiring process, while fundamentally improving the culture of a law firm.

7. Wellness and work–life balance

Attorney wellness and mental health concerns have been hot topics for some time, but implementation of programmes to address these issues has always competed with the realities of the billable hours model. As firms faced the challenges of COVID-19, many realised for the first time the true significance of these issues in sustaining high performance – and the heightened importance of wellness as the strife of 2020 wore on.

Firms whose culture already included a commitment to wellness were well prepared to expand their efforts to meet their people's increasing need for support during the pandemic. Krista Larson, director of employee well-being at Morgan, Lewis & Bockius, explained how her firm built on their existing value of gratitude to strengthen their wellness culture:

> *Expressions of gratitude have a positive impact on both the giver and the receiver. Law firms can even facilitate easy ways for lawyers and staff members to express gratitude to each other. For example, my firm established a gratitude-card exchange program in our offices in 2019, and continued the program last year through an online application for sending virtual cards during the pandemic. We exchanged a remarkable 2,600 virtual thank-you cards in 2020.*[50]

One firm which proved especially successful in supporting a culture of wellness during the pandemic was O'Melveny. The firm won the top spot in *Vault*'s "Best Law Firms to Work For" in 2020 and took top billing in 12 sub-categories, including the wellness category. *Vault* ranks firms based on an annual associate survey – an excellent indicator that the attorneys at

---

49 *Ibid.*
50 Krista Larson, "A Lawyer's Guide To Setting Well-Being Goals In 2021", *Law360*, 14 January 2021, www.law360.com/articles/1344696/a-lawyer-s-guide-to-setting-well-being-goals-in-2021.

O'Melveny found the firm's wellness programmes to be highly effective throughout the year.[51]

According to Jennifer Fox Crisp, global director of talent management at Baker McKenzie, the firm created an opportunity for those who were interested to take what they called a "COVID sabbatical". In locations that offered the programme, people could choose to take sabbaticals ranging from six weeks to three months, while maintaining a level of pay as well as full health benefits. This offering itself marked a cultural shift, creating more opportunity for more people – including business professionals – to take sabbaticals in a culture that hasn't broadly offered them.[52]

Those firms which grasped the increased need to support attorneys and staff – and responded with appropriate urgency – enhanced a culture of wellness. Both heightened awareness and meaningful action were the key factors in driving this success.

7.1 Increased awareness at the leadership level

Many law firm leaders are people who have learned to thrive despite an environment which can make wellness difficult. Although the pandemic affected each individual in unique ways – and had a disproportionally large impact on people of colour and marginalised populations – it simultaneously presented new challenges to work–life balance and wellness which were felt at every level of seniority in law firms. As partners and firm leaders navigated the adjustment to remote work, effective leaders became acutely interested in supporting people working remotely.

This shift in awareness and mindset enabled some leaders to embrace new attitudes focused on increasing wellness for both themselves and their employees, such as:
- expanding the definition of professionalism and growing more flexible in the acceptance of people's personal needs;
- appreciating the sacrifices made by high performers who produce outstanding work while handling the demands of children, pets and other personal obligations;
- increasing awareness of the deleterious effects of unreasonable expectations of availability; and
- recognising the crucial role of effective work–life balance in avoiding burnout and encouraging sustainable success.

---

51   Vault, "2021 Best Law Firms for Wellness", www.vault.com/best-companies-to-work-for/law/best-law-firms-to-work-for/wellness.
52   Interview with Jennifer Fox Crisp, Global Director of Talent Management, Baker McKenzie (2 February 2021).

7.2 Embrace of changing norms

Radically new ways of living and working affected everyone in 2020, and both the news and personal conversations were littered with discussions of the 'new normal'. Indeed, cultural norms did shift rapidly in response to the pandemic, and law firms' cultures followed suit. Firms whose cultures were strengthened during this time were those which acknowledged and embraced the opportunity to evolve their cultures. Important actions undertaken by leaders at all levels included:

- connecting on a personal level with individuals and empathising with the hardships they faced;
- evincing sensitivity about mental health issues and offering resources;
- forming committees dedicated to providing resources and soliciting input from attorneys and staff; and
- elevating flexibility as a core value among managers and leaders.

In an industry whose culture is often considered cutthroat, this trend towards humanising and deepening empathy was an opportunity for firms willing to embrace changing norms to elevate their cultures and lay the groundwork for ongoing improvements.

7.3 Increased resources and support

The pandemic has heightened the focus on well-being and awareness of the need to provide emotional and social support, including support of mental well-being. Firms which translated their awareness into meaningful policies and material actions were most successful in cementing a culture of wellness. Some of the most successful actions firms took were:

- encouraging managers to hold regular one-on-one check-ins with those they supervise;
- hosting a range of virtual social activities which included firm leaders;
- expanding flex-time and vacation policies to support changing needs;
- offering stipends for public-interest fellowships and one-year sabbaticals;
- providing resources and benefits for working parents and those caring for dependents;
- extending benefits for healthcare, including mental health services and telehealth, and expansion of the range of benefits offered through Employee Assistance Programmes;

- offering programmes or subsidies to support physical and emotional health; and
- providing workload management support.

McDermott Will & Emery, for example, provided assistance to parents and people caring for elderly relatives, as well as offering a 25-hour billable credit to each associate to use for wellness and mindfulness activities.[53] Another leading firm, Morrison & Foerster, engaged a family therapist to provide online seminars – available to all of the firm's 3,000 attorneys and staff – to provide support for issues ranging from parenting in a remote-learning environment to managing feelings of isolation and loneliness.[54]

Firms also contributed to wellness by ensuring staff and attorneys had the resources they needed to find social support from peers and colleagues. Many firms encouraged the formation of peer affinity groups of all kinds, such as online book clubs, socially distanced walking groups and support groups for those with unique challenges (eg, working parents, single people), and provided online platforms and firm resources to enable individuals to engage in such peer support.

8. Conclusion: applying the lessons of 2020 to the future of law firm culture

The COVID-19 pandemic has upended deeply held workplace norms and practices within law firms. The full impact of the pandemic likely won't fully be appreciated for years to come, and will no doubt leave a lasting imprint on how law firms – especially large- and mid-sized ones – operate. The successful shifts we've seen this past year will contribute to an evolution in how firms work and build culture. Amidst ongoing challenges, one silver lining is the integration of new practices and beliefs into the ecosystem of firm culture for firms which choose to embrace this opportunity to continue building on successful efforts undertaken in 2020.

8.1 Proactive leadership

Changes to the economic landscape and workplace operations will persist as the progression of the COVID-19 pandemic and the varied responses to it by government officials continues to unfold. While

---

53 Smith, *supra* note 2.
54 Ovide, *supra* note 13.

the nature, scope and impact of those changes remains unknown, the ability of leaders to adapt quickly to changes has proven to be instrumental in maintaining a strong culture.

Lingering concerns remain about potential, long-term adverse impacts of the pandemic, both on culture and on developing talent.[55] Challenges presented by remote work may have lasting consequences which leaders must proactively combat, including:

- a reduction in work for some associates, especially those in practice areas which have contracted in new market conditions, potentially delaying the substantive development of their skills;
- fewer occasions for senior attorneys to observe junior attorneys in person as they perform their work and provide apprenticeship and mentoring;
- fewer opportunities for summer associates to receive training and develop relationships as they exit law school; and
- the diminishment of organic, face-to-face interactions which build relationships among colleagues and reinforce culture.

While proactive leadership has helped maintain and even reinforce culture with creative new approaches, leaders must remain vigilant in their commitment to the successful practices they developed (or observed in other firms) in the past year. Leaders must:

- combat the weight of 'pandemic fatigue' – the tendency to grow weary of change and to revert to old habits – both in themselves and with their workforce;
- maintain frequent and transparent communication, leveraging multiple communication channels which enable productive conversation;
- continually seek new avenues to provide hands-on training for attorneys and support the kind of on-the-job learning which is crucial to attorney development;
- extend formal talent development programmes and targeted support (such as coaching and skill-specific training); and
- continue to find ways to redress the most persistent, ongoing challenges faced by some of their professionals, for instance – and perhaps most notably – the challenges working parents

---

55   The Young Lawyer Editorial Board, "Circumstances Changed, but Expectations Didn't. Young Attorneys Are Frustrated", *The American Lawyer*, 27 January 2021, www.law.com/americanlawyer/2021/01/27/circumstances-changed-but-expectations-didnt-young-attorneys-are-frustrated/.

face in meeting the expectations of the firms in which they work while meeting the needs of their children.[56]

To capitalise on advances made during the pandemic, firm leaders will need to model adoption of new tools and methods; productive next steps and a future-forward outlook must come from above. As the potential for working together in offices becomes more and more accessible, complacency can easily undermine the strides firms have taken towards positive culture development. The challenges faced in 2020 can serve as a powerful reminder to all firms in recognising that culture must be proactively nurtured – regardless of external circumstances – in order to evolve and thrive.

8.2 Long-term planning for talent development

Given that remote work will continue in some form well into 2021, law firms are recognising the need to continue to find innovative and effective methods for mentoring and training young attorneys from a distance. Those who began their careers in the last few years – and especially those who entered the law firm landscape last fall – have in many ways missed out on the irreplaceable informal mentoring and training which has typically taken place in person. With young lawyers unable to connect with potential mentors in the hallway or at lunch, law firms must continue to seek ways to replicate those connections in a remote world.

In addition to building on existing programmes and expanding new programmes created in 2020, firms must empower their talent development departments to address potential skill gaps faced by their most junior attorneys. At the same time, managers need ongoing support in supervising effectively in remote and hybrid-work environments, building robust distributed teams and advancing their leadership skills. Both attorneys and professional staff at all levels worry about the ways in which they may be falling behind developmentally – and continued attention from leaderships is required to prevent talent from stagnating.[57]

---

56   Dylan Jackson, "Big Law's Working Parents Are Hurting. Money Is Not The Answer", *The American Lawyer*, 26 January 2021, www.law.com/americanlawyer/2021/01/26/big-laws-working-parents-are-hurting-money-is-not-the-answer/.
57   Zack Needles, "Law.com Trendspotter: The Pandemic Has Put Associate Development Back on the Back Burner", *Law.com*, 7 September 2020, www.law.com/2020/09/07/law-com-trendspotter-the-pandemic-has-put-associate-development-back-on-the-back-burner/.

8.3 Thoughtful approach to return-to-work questions

Changes to the attitudes regarding remote work in the legal industry have been rapid and profound – and have included some surprises. Many senior attorneys and leaders who have long viewed remote work and flexible schedules as impediments to productivity have been pleasantly surprised, both by the speed with which large workforces could pivot to remote work and by just how much good, productive work could actually be accomplished notwithstanding the suddenly all-remote working environment. For attorneys who, in an effort to attain a level of work–life balance, for many years have been requesting the ability to work remotely, the debate about whether remote work can be done effectively has been settled during the pandemic. The likelihood that it will continue, at least to some degree, is all but certain.

The potential of widely available COVID-19 vaccines has many firms anticipating a return to working in person. At the same time, the emergence of new, highly contagious strains of the virus (for which vaccines are not effective) threaten to derail plans to bring workforces fully back into the office. Successful leaders will continue to embrace online collaboration approaches, setting themselves up for success in remote, hybrid and in-office work environments. As Ira Coleman, chairman of McDermott Will & Emery, pointed out on *Law.com*'s "LegalSpeak" podcast, "COVID is just accelerating trends that were eventually going to happen" such as using videoconferencing in place of travel for meetings.[58] Many firms which strengthened their cultures in 2020 were already paying attention to these trends and adopting new models for collaboration – those which wish to build on that success will continue to invest in such innovations.

At the same time, an eventual return to a preference for in-person collaboration, coupled with a more tolerant and flexible approach to remote work arrangements, may be where most larger firms land. Said Cozen O'Connor CEO Michael Heller: "There's no doubt that in-office work is better at creating professional affinity among [colleagues]."[59] Tim Henderson of Finnegan offered a similar

---

58 Interview with Ira Coleman, "Zooming Through 2020: COVID-19, Surviving Remotely and a Few Silver Linings", *Legal Speak*, 18 December 2020, legalspeak.libsyn.com/zooming-through-2020-covid-19-surviving-remotely-and-a-few-silver-linings.

59 Justin Henry, "Finding a Cultural Fit When Lateral Hiring Goes Virtual", *The American Lawyer*, 22 January 2021, www.law.com/americanlawyer/2021/01/22/finding-a-cultural-fit-when-lateral-hiring-goes-virtual. See also, "After Gauging Firm's Pandemic Responses, Will Associates Be on the Move?", *The American Lawyer*, 2021, www.law.com/americanlawyer/2021/01/26/after-gauging-firms-pandemic-responses-will-associates-be-on-the-move.

observation, which reflects the views expressed by the majority of senior leaders with whom I've spoken on this issue: "We don't envision the firm opting for an all-remote environment. Even with all our successes in building connection among our people, you can't replicate the benefits of in-person culture or the attorney apprenticeship model remotely."[60] Or, as Lee Anne Petry of McDermott put it: "There's no substitute for the connective tissue that's built through in-person working relationships."[61]

The current consensus appears to be that a return to in-person work is anticipated, likely with greater acceptance of partially remote work arrangements, but with an awareness of the import of in-person work – both to build culture with intention and to optimally support the attorney apprenticeship model which, through side-by-side work, provides attorneys the extra degree of insight and skill that can make a true difference at this level of practice. Rather than mandating such returns, however, firms will likely focus on the benefits for those who return to work, in terms of advancing career growth and satisfaction – while also showing greater openness across the board to an array of remote-work arrangements.

(a) ***Implementing new technologies***

Firms must accelerate their adoption of new technologies which enable remote work to be just as effective as in-office work. The legal industry has traditionally been regarded as slower than other industries to embrace new technology. The past year has proven that they *can* do it – and the coming years will prove that the firms which lean into innovation will particularly thrive.

Effective remote work was already important for firms with a global workforce and teams working across multiple offices; even if everyone returns to working in the office, continued innovations are crucial for business success and open new avenues for effective workflows. Firms which continue to use these new approaches will be better poised to remain nimble and attract top talent.

As Level Legal CEO Joey Seeber noted: "One positive effect of 2020's enforced deep dive into remote working is a new openness to innovation … the emphasis on technology will drive new solutions

---

60   Interview with Tim Henderson, Chief Recruitment and Professional Development Officer, Finnegan, Henderson, Farabow, Garrett & Dunner (4 February 2021).
61   Interview with Lee Anne Petry, Head of Communications & Strategic Initiatives, Office of the Chair, McDermott Will & Emery (8 February 2021).

for practicing lawyers, for use both internally and externally for clients."[62]

(b) Focusing on equity in hybrid environments

Hybrid arrangements, in which some work remotely while others return to the office, may be on the horizon for many firms, but the possibility raises questions regarding whether issues of equity could arise in such circumstances, such as for those professionals who, for whatever reason (caregiving responsibilities or disability status, for example), cannot return to work on the same timeline.

Many argue that learning the practice of law is a true apprenticeship profession benefiting greatly from in-person mentoring and observation in ways which can't be replicated in remote work circumstances. While that belief may have held true in many past situations, cleaving to it when attorneys have a variety of work structures may risk leaving some attorneys behind. Kobre & Kim co-managing partner Steven Kobre echoed the sentiment of many partners and law firm leaders, saying that: "You can't put a price on being face-to-face. While Zoom works, Zoom works because everyone is on it." He reflected that those who continue to work remotely when offices reopen will have fewer opportunities.[63]

In hybrid environments, leaders at all levels must take proactive approaches to ensure equitable access to development for every attorney and professional – an issue which itself will pose new challenges to culture-building. The actions of partners, senior associates and others who lead teams will be decisive in determining how hybrid work circumstances impact those who they supervise.

(c) Fostering ongoing connection

An interesting paradox presented by the pandemic is that, while many attorneys have craved more opportunities to work remotely in the past, being forced to do so full-time resulted in a widespread sense of stress and isolation (amplified by personal struggles such as distance from loved ones, loss of childcare options, grief and illness). Regardless of future work arrangements, it has become clear that creating intentional spaces for connection among colleagues is critical for individual well-being and maintaining a sense of shared culture.

---

62 Joey Seeber, "6 Changes The Legal Industry Should Prepare For", *Law360*, 20 January 2021, www.law360.com/articles/1342683.
63 Dan Packel, "Law Firm Leaders Confront Return-to-Office Policies", *New York Law Journal*, 21 January 2021, www.law.com/newyorklawjournal/2021/01/21/law-firm-leaders-confront-return-to-office-policies/.

In addition to social activities like happy hours and team-building sessions, firms must continue to facilitate more informal, day-to-day interactions in both remote and hybrid work environments. *The Harvard Business Review* offered a variety of effective techniques from Mark Strassman, senior vice president and general manager at technology firm LogMeIn, who has led remote teams for two decades.

- Pair employees in different locations with colleagues for virtual co-working, in which colleagues can work independently for a set period with an open videoconference so they can easily ask questions and help one another;
- Create a 'hotwall' – a large monitor with a constant video connection in which remote workers can connect with those in the office at any time – in a central location in the office; and
- Ask leaders to hold weekly office hours in which anyone can drop in virtually to ask questions, get updates and engage in spontaneous conversations.[64]

One firm that was particularly successful in sustaining an ongoing sense of connection in 2020 was Latham & Watkins; Adrian Davis reflected: "Because Latham has long worked across offices, across practices and across borders, its existing culture of collaboration set us up well to move to work from home." He also said that an intentional approach to engagement was at the root of their efforts. "We repurposed and expanded trainings, and the commitment to engagement cascaded throughout the entire organization", he noted. The silver lining has been that people at the firm feel a tremendous amount of pride in how they've come together during the crisis, and this as cemented an ongoing commitment to welcoming 'bottom-up' ideas and continued innovation as the firm navigates the workplace landscape of 2021.[65]

8.4 Amplifying D&I

Many firms made weighty commitments to improving D&I in 2020, implementing a wide variety of programmes – training, mentoring, sponsorship, career advocacy – which have the potential to provide

---

64 Barbara Z Larson, "Give Your Remote Team Unstructured Time for Collaboration", *Harvard Business Review*, 27 October 2020, hbr.org/2020/10/give-your-remote-team-unstructured-time-for-collaboration.
65 Interview with Adrian Davis, Chief Attorney Development and Knowledge Officer, Latham and Watkins (6 February 2021).

real and lasting impact on their cultures. How firms carry out those commitments going forward will determine whether the positive changes they've ignited will fizzle out or build into ongoing success.

Firms must carry their efforts forward by focusing on:
- increasing representation of diverse attorneys and executives at the leadership level;
- ensuring diversity among new hires, including new associate classes and lateral attorneys;
- retaining diverse talent with robust professional development and D&I programmes; and
- ensuring that diverse attorneys and staff have not only a seat at the table, but also a meaningful voice in the firm.

By doing so, firms can not only create a more welcoming culture to members of historically underrepresented groups; they will also signal to all attorneys and staff that the firm is a place which provides equitable opportunities for all.

8.5 Emphasising wellness

The pressing need to support wellness during 2020 may pave the way to an ongoing understanding that wellness and work–life balance are a fundamental to productivity and performance. Firms which centred this priority during the pandemic laid the foundation for ongoing cultural improvements, and maintaining that focus will be crucial going forward.

As the pandemic stretched over many months in 2020 – with no clear resolution in sight – mental health struggles became an increasingly common issue worldwide. Mental Health America reported that the number of people in the United States reporting anxiety and depression symptoms reached an all-time high in September 2020. According to the data collected by the organisation, "anxiety screens were up by 634% from January and depression screens were up 873%".[66]

Those working in the legal industry already faced higher-than-average rates of mental health struggles and substance abuse. These issues will likely be compounded by the stressors of the pandemic and can disproportionally affect parents and young attorneys.

---

66 Mental Health America, "Number of People Reporting Anxiety and Depression Nationwide since Start of Pandemic Hits All-Time High in September, Hitting Young People Hardest", 20 October 2020, mhanational.org/number-people-reporting-anxiety-and-depression-nationwide-start-pandemic-hits-all-time-high.

Kristen Riemenschneider, a partner at Arnold & Porter, noted that the combination of her heavy workload and the responsibilities of caring for three children has always been a struggle, but it became especially onerous during the pandemic. "I think it's terribly sad that our profession is in a state where people are worried they're going to lose their jobs [because of their children]. That's really heartbreaking", she told *Law.com*.[67]

Attorneys in the first few years of their careers are less likely to have robust professional networks, and they often experienced more social isolation in 2020. Joel G Kosman, a former attorney who now practises as a psychotherapist primarily serving those in the legal industry, said that younger attorneys suffered from a lack of support during the pandemic: "Without having other people around them who are in similar situations, there's a void, and they're left wondering how they're doing. I don't think that can be replicated, even with a very caring and concerned and open spouse or partner."[68]

The cumulative impact of this stressful year, and its continuation into the future, may likely yield aftershocks for many months, if not years, to come. Firms began laying the foundations for sustainable wellness efforts last year, and they should continue to place accelerated focus on the import of wellness by increasing the range of benefits and programmes available to both attorneys and professional staff, as well as by inviting more open discussion about the importance of wellness and what that means for people working in law firms.

8.6 Building on successes from 2020

The COVID-19 pandemic isn't over, and in some sense it never will be due to the ways in which it has fundamentally changed many aspects of how we work and live. The success of vaccination programmes, the continued development of treatments and the evolution of the virus are all suffused with unknowns, and conversations about what the future of work will look like are ongoing and complex.

What we do know is that some law firms have sought to make rapid positive changes to support their people – attorneys and professional staff alike – in the midst of uncertainty and disruption

---

67 Jackson, *supra* note 56.
68 Anna Sanders, "Pandemic Fuels Mental Health Crisis For Young Attorneys", *Law360*, 25 January 2021, www.law360.com/articles/1346967/pandemic-fuels-mental-health-crisis-for-young-attorneys.

and that their efforts have resulted in stronger firm cultures. An overarching theme among firms that enhanced their cultures in 2020 is that being intentional about creating connections among people at all levels not only helped their culture thrive in the face of hardship, but also opened new opportunities for engagement that they will maintain once firmwide in-person work is once again possible.

Firms must remain vigilant in responding to change and continue to build on their efforts. Law firm leaders have an opportunity to learn from 2020 and capitalise on the silver linings which emerged, paving the way for continued cultural evolution.

Law firms which achieved the best business results during the pandemic are those which made a commitment to the core elements of culture – and those which continue to honour that commitment into the future will be best poised to navigate the future successfully.

The accelerated pursuit of racial equity in law firms

Tiffani G Lee
Holland & Knight LLP

1. Introduction

The year 2020 was unprecedented – a global health pandemic caused by the COVID-19 virus that disproportionately affected people of colour, an economic downturn, and racial justice issues sparked by the killing of George Floyd while in police custody. These events created a perfect storm that may make 2020 an inflection point in Big Law as it relates to diversity, equity and inclusion (DEI).

This chapter highlights some of the accelerating trends related to racial/ethnic diversity in Big Law and the pursuit of racial equity, specifically: (1) openly confronting race and racism; (2) embracing collaboration and coalition-building; (3) empowering and elevating DEI professionals; (4) engaging and equipping inclusive leaders; and (5) ensuring accountability through internal and external stakeholders.

2. Background: two phases of the pandemic

When assessing Big Law's focus on DEI, it may be helpful to bifurcate the pandemic between the early months of the pandemic, ie, before George Floyd was killed, and the later months of the pandemic, ie, after George Floyd was killed. In the early months, Big Law firms focused on figuring out how to promote inclusion and connection in a remote workplace, keep their DEI efforts visible, and provide support and resources to working parents and caregivers who were disproportionately impacted by having to juggle work with home responsibilities.[1] As firms began to make difficult decisions

---

[1] The impact of the pandemic on working parents and caregivers, especially women, has been well documented. See, eg, Dylan Jackson, "Big Law's Working Parents are Hurting. Money is Not the Answer", *The American Lawyer*, 26 January 2021; Whittney Bears and Malini Nangia, " 'My Career is Basically Over': Working Parents Offer Pleas for Empathy from Law Firms", *The American Lawyer*, 19 January 2021.

to furlough or terminate personnel, industry leaders worried that those employment decisions would disproportionately impact attorneys from traditionally underrepresented groups, specifically women and racial/ethnic minorities.[2]

Any concern that law firms' focus on DEI would stall in the pandemic abruptly changed on 25 May 2020. On that day, we experienced the traumatic horror of watching the eight minutes and 46 seconds during which George Floyd was killed while in police custody. The killing of George Floyd – preceded by the close-in-time killings of Breonna Taylor and Ahmaud Arbery – was a powerful accelerant that sparked an outpouring of grief, outrage, activism and sustained protests against police brutality and systemic racism. That killing also shifted law firms' attention to racial justice and racial equity as part of their DEI efforts.

After the killing of George Floyd, law firms were forced to openly confront issues of race and racism. They embraced the need to build coalitions to leverage their collective resources to drive change. DEI professionals emerged as strategic advisers, and the job market for such professionals exploded. DEI again became a leadership priority as law firm leaders had to attempt to evolve into more inclusive leaders. And clients continued to hold law firm leaders and their law firms accountable for DEI results. Each of these trends, which can accelerate transformational change in Big Law firms and the legal profession in years to come, is explored below.

3. Openly confronting race and racism[3]

After the police killing of George Floyd, law firm leaders and DEI professionals quickly realised the need to openly confront issues of race and racism. They recognised that a racial reckoning was also happening inside their organisations. Conversations about race and racism within law firms were never so openly and broadly

---

2 See, eg, Robert Grey, "Ten Ways to Avoid a Repeat of the Diversity Recession", *The American Lawyer*, 11 June 2020.

3 "Race" is a socially constructed system of categorising humans largely based on observable physical features such as skin colour, and on ancestry. There is no scientific basis for or discernible distinction between racial categories. "Racism" is a complex system of racial hierarchies and inequities, which operates at the micro or individual level and the macro or institutional/structural level. See "Equity v. Equality and Other Racial Justice Definitions", The Annie E Casey Foundation blog, 24 August 2020, www.aecf.org/blog/racial-justice-definitions.

had until after the killing of George Floyd. These topics were not new to DEI professionals and Black law firm leaders, and they were quick to amplify the significance of systemic racism and racial equity.[4]

Law firms embarked on a series of candid, courageous and uncomfortable conversations about difficult topics related to racial equity. Law firm leaders immediately scheduled town hall meetings to condemn racism and police brutality, express support and empathy for their Black employees, and reaffirm their commitment to DEI. Law firms also focused on education and learning on an individual and collective level by bringing in consultants and thought leaders to raise consciousness across the enterprise.[5]

Discussions about race and racism necessarily led to discussions about white privilege, white fragility, intersectionality, allyship and anti-racism.[6] Those conversations can become building blocks for cultural and structural change. They underscored the fact that just as racism is systemic, institutional and structural, racial equity must be pursued by removing systemic, institutional and structural barriers. Thus, these conversations were necessary but not sufficient to achieve racial equity in law firms.

If we apply Ibram X Kendi's definition of a 'racist policy' to law firms,[7] we can readily identify several law firm policies that create or

---

[4] See Maja Hazell, "The Crippling Impact of Anti-Black Racism, and How Allies Can Act Against It", *The American Lawyer,* 18 June 2020; Ayanna Alexander, "Black Firm Leaders Drive Big Law Social Justice Efforts", Bloomberg Law, 24 August 2020, https://news.bloomberglaw.com/social-justice/black-firm-leaders-drive-big-law-social-justice-efforts.

[5] Enterprise-wide learning and discussion about these root causes is critically important. Law firms often train on unconscious biases without addressing their root causes and the stereotypes upon which they are premised.

[6] See Peggy McIntosh, "White Privilege: Unpacking the Invisible Knapsack", *Peace and Freedom Magazine,* July/August 1989, at 10–12; Robin DiAngelo, *White Fragility: Why It's So Hard for White People to Talk About Racism* (2018, Beacon Press); Karen Catlin and Sally McGraw (editor), *Better Allies: Everyday Actions to Create Inclusive/Engaging Workplaces (2nd Edition)* (2020, Karen Catlin Consulting); Ibram X Kendi, *How to Be an Antiracist* (2019, Penguin Random House).

[7] Kendi defines a 'racist policy' as any measure that produces or sustains racial inequity between racial groups. His definition includes "written and unwritten laws, rules, procedures, processes, regulations, and guidelines that govern people". See Ibram X Kendi, "Ibram X Kendi Defines What It Means to Be an Antiracist", 9 June 2020, book extract available at www.penguin.co.uk/articles/2020/june/ibram-x-kendi-definition-of-antiracist.html.

perpetuate inequity between racial groups.[8] And if we think about the stereotypes about Black people that were developed to justify racism – all based on fabricated notions of intellectual inferiority, aggression or laziness – we can better understand and confront the well-documented biases that stall the development, retention and promotion of Black attorneys. We can then honestly interrogate and change the law firm processes, practices and cultural norms that consistently produce racial inequity.

Law firm leaders can no longer ignore the fact that systems of oppression and disadvantage as well as structural barriers to inclusion and equity exist within law firms. Just as they were created over time, they will have to be dismantled over time. Going forward, law firm leaders will need to play a key role in leading that transformational change. (See Section 6 below.)

4. Embracing collaboration and coalition-building

The global pandemic and racial reckoning provided unique opportunities for collaboration and coalition-building between law firms, law-related organisations and social justice organisations. Coalitions were formed to collaborate to support attorneys from traditionally underrepresented groups, to combat racial injustice in society generally, and to increase the pipeline of talent into the profession. By leveraging their collective power and resources, law firms made a significant impact within the pandemic and are poised to continue that impact in coming years.

4.1 The belonging project

Because the potential impact of the pandemic threatened the progress towards a more diverse legal industry, in early May 2020, Seyfarth Shaw LLP announced the launch of The Belonging Project, a first-of-its-kind nationwide collaborative initiative to proactively combat the effects of the pandemic on diversity in the profession.[9]

---

8   If we disaggregate law firms' "diversity" data and focus on the outcomes for Black attorneys, the inequity is stark. The percentage of Black attorneys at US law firms took a full decade to recover after the Great Recession of 2008/2009. See 2019 Report on Diversity in US Law Firms (NALP, 2019), www.nalp.org/uploads/2019_DiversityReport.pdf. In 2019, Black attorneys accounted for 4.76% of all associates, the highest level since reaching 4.66% in 2009. *Id.* at 5. Black attorneys account for less than 2% of partners among firms surveyed by NALP. *Id.* at 6.

9   See www.seyfarth.com/the-belonging-project.html.

The Belonging Project provides a virtual hub for industry organisations, law firms, diverse law students, diverse attorneys and their allies to focus on advancing DEI during the pandemic and beyond. It offers a comprehensive suite of professional development resources, including virtual one-on-one coaching and mentoring plus webinars focused on personal and professional development topics. Legal organisations that initially collaborated with Seyfarth on The Belonging Project included Diversity Lab, the Association of Corporate Counsel's ACC Foundation, Minority Corporate Counsel Association, National LGBT Bar Association, National Asian Pacific American Bar Association, Hispanic National Bar Association, Corporate Counsel Women of Color, and California Minority Counsel Program. By 31 December 2020, the project boasted 27 confirmed partners.

4.2 Law Firm Antiracism Alliance

Law firms also seized on the opportunity to leverage their collective resources to address systemic racism and racial injustice through *pro bono* work. In late June 2020, the Law Firm Antiracism Alliance (LFAA) was launched with 125 charter members.[10] LFAA's members are committed to using litigation and advocacy to overturn policies and laws that result in negative outcomes for people of colour. As outlined in the LFAA's charter, the group's aim is: "To leverage the resources of the private bar in partnership with legal services organisations to amplify the voices of communities and individuals oppressed by racism, to better use the law as a vehicle for change that benefits communities of color and to promote racial equity in the law." By bringing a racial justice lens to *pro bono*, the LFAA will tackle some of the broader issues that a single firm might be unable to tackle alone. As of 16 December 2020, 96 Am Law 100 firms have joined the LFAA (see Figure 1 below) and its total membership includes 287 law firms.

4.3 Thrive Scholars Law Track

Another accelerating trend is the focus on the pipeline of talent into the profession. In addition to long-standing programmes such as Just the Beginning – A Pipeline Organization and the NALP/Street

---

10 See Patrick Smith, "Over 125 Firms Have Joined the Law Firm Antiracism Alliance", *The American Lawyer*, 24 June 2020; Patrick Smith, "'We Have to Succeed': Law Firm Antiracism Alliance Holds First Summit", *The American Lawyer*, 31 July 2020.

Law Legal Diversity Pipeline Program, new pipeline initiatives were launched during the pandemic to target high-school students.

One new initiative is the Thrive Scholars Law Track Program.[11] Launched in October 2020, the Thrive Scholars Law Track Program aims to create a greater pipeline of Black and Latinx attorneys into the legal profession. Thrive Scholars will provide these students with the full range of support beginning in their junior year of high school. In addition to providing financial support, participating law firms agree to provide mentorship and internships during college to enhance the students' exposure to opportunities in the legal profession, and the law firms may choose to hire one or more of the students from law school. Explaining the creation of the programme, Steve Stein, CEO of Thrive Scholars, said: "Data from our 20-year experience ... shows the talent pipeline expansion starts at the high school level. We are committed to grow this program through partnerships with law firms that are seeking to increase diversity in their firms and in the profession."

Pipeline initiatives such as the Thrive Scholars Law Track Program won't immediately resolve Big Law's challenge with underrepresentation of attorneys of colour. However, such initiatives should continue for their future benefit.

5. Empowering and elevating DEI professionals

One trend accelerated by the pandemic and racial reckoning was the employment, empowerment and elevation of DEI professionals in law firms. By the mid-2000s, dedicated DEI professionals working in US law firms was commonplace.[12] Hiring of DEI professionals had been on the rise for years but accelerated sharply in 2020.

After the killing of George Floyd, the job market for DEI professionals exploded, with several firms announcing the hiring or promotion of DEI professionals. Rarely a week passed without one or more firms announcing new DEI leaders.[13] In the last two months of 2020 alone, nine law firms announced high-level DEI leadership appointments.[14] Importantly, many of these DEI leaders were hired

---

11 www.thrivescholars.org/.
12 See *Examining the Role of the Law Firm Diversity Professional* (Minority Corporate Counsel Association, 2009).
13 See, eg, Erica Silverman, "Fox Rothschild Adds Diversity Officer Role to C-Suite, Tapping IP Partner", *The Legal Intelligencer*, 10 June 2020.
14 See Dylan Jackson, "Morrison & Foerster Upgrades Diversity Leadership to Client-Facing C-Suite Role", *The American Lawyer*, 18 December 2020.

or promoted into C-suite roles. The shift elevates the position in a way that allows DEI professionals to have more clout in their law firms and greater opportunity to impact change by working side by side with other law firm leaders.

Having an executive-level DEI leader is a positive step that shows a firm's commitment, but it is not a guarantee of results. Potentially, it ensures that DEI is always a factor in a firm's decision making if the DEI leader has a "seat at the table" when important decisions are made and can have direct input into those decisions. The ultimate effectiveness of a C-suite DEI professional will depend on several factors, including but not limited to, the level of authority the person in the position holds, the strength and clarity of the commitment to DEI from the entire executive suite as well as senior management, appropriate reinforcement of the DEI leader's message by senior management, and the amount of dedicated budgetary and staffing resources.

Coming out of the pandemic, the continued empowerment of DEI professionals will be an important factor in law firms' ability to accelerate their DEI accomplishments.[15] Going forward, DEI professionals will need to be disruptors as well as change agents. They will need to focus less on implementing programmes and more on challenging and changing practices and processes. Most importantly, their relationships with senior management of law firms must be interdependent.

6. Engaging and equipping inclusive leaders

Leaders are stewards of a law firm's culture. Their behaviours and mindsets reverberate throughout the organisation. What leaders say and do makes up to a 70% difference as to whether an individual feels included.[16] Thus, it came as no surprise that law firm personnel

---

15   In addition to elevating the role of DEI professionals, law firms have also begun to value DEI work more generally. At the start of the pandemic, few law firms provided creditable hours for DEI work that was not *pro bono* work. See, eg, Patrick Smith, "Diversity Meets the Billable Hour at Dorsey Whitney", *The American Lawyer* (on law.com), 23 July 2019. Since the pandemic and racial reckoning, several firms have announced policies by which they will now give timekeepers creditable hours for DEI work. See, eg, Dylan Jackson, "Reed Smith Launches Diversity Billable Hour Credit for All Timekeepers", *The American Lawyer*, 27 January 2021; Meganne Tillay, "Hogan Lovells to Offer Billable Hour Credit for Diversity Efforts", *The American Lawyer*, 19 January 2021.
16   Juliet Rourke and Andrea Titus, "The Key to Inclusive Leadership", *Harvard Business Review*, 6 March 2020. The authors identified six signature traits of inclusive leaders: visible commitment, humility, awareness of bias, curiosity about others, cultural intelligence and effective collaboration. *Id*.

focused critically on their leaders' responses to the pandemic and racial reckoning.

6.1 DEI as a leadership priority

Judging by their responses to the killing of George Floyd and resulting social unrest, DEI and racial equity is now top of mind for law firm leaders. After the killing of George Floyd, they issued statements (internal and external), hosted town hall meetings, pledged financial support to fight racial injustice, and teamed up to form the Law Firm Antiracism Alliance (see Figure 1).[17]

In addition to the statements and pledges, senior law firm leaders were forced to look inward and give more attention to race equity issues within their own organisations, including the structural and cultural barriers to equity and inclusion. The impact of unconscious biases on key decision points, processes and practices could no longer be ignored. The lack of metrics around law firms' DEI efforts could no longer be ignored. And law firm leaders could no longer ignore their obligation to re-engage on an individual and organisational level to drive progress and change.

In October 2020, the Leadership Council on Legal Diversity, an organisation whose membership includes more than 300 managing

Figure 1. Am Law 100 firms' responses to racial injustice (2020)

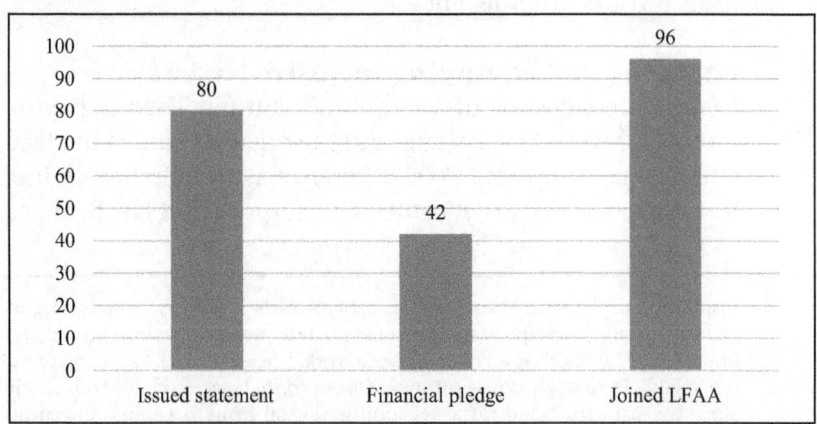

---

[17] Sources: "Law Firms Voice Support for Change – and Pledge to Donate and Take Action", *The American Lawyer*, 18 June 2020, with independent supplemental research by Holland & Knight's Research Services Department. Firms counted as having issued statements include those that issued internal and/or external statements. The amount pledged by the 42 firms who made a financial pledge totalled approximately $41,050,000 towards racial justice organisations and initiatives.

partners, chairpersons, general counsel and chief legal officers, launched its Leaders at the Front initiative to keep DEI at the top of each member's agenda.[18] As part of the initiative, members were asked to prepare what will become a public pledge that includes a personal commitment to improving diversity, an organisational commitment, and a set of metrics that can be used to annually evaluate progress. If a significant portion of the LCLD's law firm members follow through on their pledges, DEI and racial equity in law firms will be propelled forward in a meaningful way.

The organisational commitments made by these law firm leaders will be particularly important because senior leaders are best positioned to set the tone, pace and priority of cultural transformation and removal of structural barriers. They have the power and influence to ensure that DEI is a consideration in all major law firm decisions – from partner promotions to leadership selection or appointment to the allocation of work and business development opportunities. They have the power and influence to ensure that equity is woven into the fabric of the firm by regularly assessing all policies, practices and procedures, both formal and informal, to ensure they are equitable and bias-free. They have the power and influence to commit firm resources to assess and change key talent management processes, particularly recruiting, work allocation, performance evaluation and feedback, and education and training programmes, to interrupt bias, address systemic impediments to equity, and ensure fair and equitable outcomes.

6.2 Developing inclusive leaders at all levels of the firm

To fulfil their pledges and back up their bold statements with action, law firm leaders will have to develop inclusive leadership competencies themselves and develop inclusive leaders at all levels of the firm, particularly in middle management.

(a) *Inclusive leadership defined*

Inclusive leadership refers to the leadership traits and competencies required to activate and leverage diversity. While many definitions and studies of inclusive leadership exist, perhaps the most useful

---

18 Ruigi Chen, "Leadership Council on Legal Diversity Calls for Pledges", *Bloomberg Law Business & Practice,* 22 October 2020, https://news.bloomberglaw.com/business-and-practice/leadership-council-on-legal-diversity-calls-for-personal-pledges. See also www.lcldnet.org/leaders-at-the-front/.

Figure 2. Inclusive leadership model

Intrapersonal Dimensions	Inclusive Leadership Competencies	Interpersonal Dimensions
Reading Situations and Challenges	Innovative Collaboration	Leveraging Differences to Win
Reflecting with Empathy	Empowering Others	Developing with Feedback
Holding Self Accountable	Courageous Accountability	Holding Others Accountable
Identifying Motivation, Privilege & Acumen	Awareness & Clarity	Fostering Open Dialogue

definition and framework for the legal industry can be found in the Inclusive Leadership Model (see Figure 2) developed by Russell Reynolds Associates and used by the Minority Corporate Counsel Association (MCCA).[19]

The model is based on the finding that inclusive leaders excel in four key areas (the 'Inclusive Leadership Competencies') that operate on both intrapersonal and interpersonal dimensions: innovative collaboration; empowering others; courageous accountability; and awareness and clarity. Inclusive leaders bring awareness and clarity to problem areas in DEI, they practise courageous accountability to help resolve those problems, empower others, and foster innovative collaboration to unlock the unique contributions of each person in a group.[20]

(b) *Middle management: an area of opportunity*
Going forward, in addition to inclusive leadership at the top, law firms should focus equally on developing inclusive leaders in middle management. Middle managers such as practice group leaders and team leaders have important practice management roles in law firms. For example, they have a much greater role in hiring, work

---

19 Jean Lee, Sophia Piliouras, Cynthia Dow, Jacob Martin and Tina Shah Paikeday, *Unleashing the Power of Diversity Through Inclusive Leadership* (Minority Corporate Counsel Association and Russell Reynolds Associates, 2019), at 16. The Inclusive Leadership Model is reprinted here with the permission of the Minority Corporate Counsel Association.
20 *Ibid.*

assignments, feedback, evaluations and promotion decisions than does senior management. Thus, their decisions to distribute work equitably or to provide timely, constructive and actionable feedback is critically important to attorney development and ultimately attorney retention.

A manager's inclusive leadership behaviour has a direct link to an employee's sense of inclusion and belonging.[21] On the Inclusion Index, attorneys of colour are less likely to feel they belong than others.[22] The main factor behind those low belonging scores is the sense that law firms and corporate legal departments allow bias to impact hiring and promotion processes, thus limiting their opportunities.[23] A lack of inclusive leadership by team and practice group leaders will have a direct and detrimental impact on employee engagement, morale and motivation. Thus, equipping middle management to be inclusive leaders and holding them accountable is key. Law firms' senior leaders must hold practice group and team leaders responsible for developing inclusive leadership competencies and using them to recruit, retain and promote diverse talent.

Equipping law firm leaders to be inclusive leaders will be of utmost importance coming out of the pandemic and racial reckoning. Developing inclusive leaders at all levels of the law firm will increasingly become a competitive advantage. Without them, law firms will struggle to maintain and activate their diversity.[24]

---

21 Drika J Travis, Emily Shaffer and Jennifer Thorpe-Moscon, *Getting Real About Inclusive Leadership: Why Change Starts With You* (Catalyst, 2019). Catalyst's inclusive leadership model features two complementary dimensions – leading outward and leading inward – and six core behaviours: accountability, ownership, allyship, curiosity, humility and courage. *Id.*

22 Jean Lee, Sophia Piliouras, Cynthia Dow, Enrique Cabrera-Caban, Tina Shah Paikeday and Alix Stuart, *Leading Through Crisis (Executive Summary)* (Minority Corporate Counsel Association and Russell Reynolds Associates, Inc., 2020), at 3.

23 Jean Lee, Sophia Piliouras, Cynthia Dow, Jacob Martin and Tina Shah Paikeday, *Unleashing the Power of Diversity Through Inclusive Leadership* (Minority Corporate Counsel Association and Russell Reynolds Associates, 2019), at 8.

24 Law firms seeking to develop inclusive leaders can expect to encounter headwinds. Some will be based on the nature of most law firms, in which partners operate with a certain level of independence and autonomy. In addition, when it comes to intrafirm interactions, lawyers and law firm leaders can be surprisingly conflict-avoidant when conflict and discomfort is necessary in DEI work. Culture change is always daunting and difficult work given inertia, resistance to change and satisfaction with the status quo. And on an individual level, not everyone in a law firm will want to do the work of becoming an inclusive leader. He/she may exhibit resistance (passive or active), scepticism or even backlash. Overcoming these barriers and resisting these headwinds is the difficult but important work of the senior leader seeking to drive transformational change in a law firm.

7. Ensuring accountability through internal and external stakeholders

Now that law firm leaders have made bold statements about their commitment to DEI, racial justice and racial equity, expectations of their internal and external stakeholders are high. There are expectations of progress and not just pledges. These leaders will be held accountable for actions, outcomes and results because words of commitment are no longer enough.

7.1 Internal stakeholders expect action from law firm leaders

Law firms' internal stakeholders – their employees – are watchful and wary. Statements of commitment have been made before. If law firm leaders do not follow through on their bold statements, they risk losing talent at all levels, engagement and morale will suffer, and their credibility will be lost. The 2020 Inclusion Index Report found that attorneys rated their organisations lower on the Inclusion Index factors than they did in previous years, and all ratings were lower than those at other professional services firms.[25] Those lower ratings may indicate that those inside law firms are comparing their leaders' statements with their actions and finding them disappointingly unaligned.

7.2 Client pressures on outside counsel firms will increase

In addition to internal stakeholders, law firm leaders will increasingly be held accountable by key external stakeholders, namely clients and potential clients. In recent years, client pressure on Big Law to advance DEI became more insistent. For example, in January 2019, more than 170 general counsel and chief legal officers signed an open letter to Big Law firms urging them to take action to achieve diversity in the workplace and confirming that they would prioritise their legal spending with those firms that commit to DEI.[26] The general counsel signatories were motivated

---

25 Jean Lee, Sophia Piliouras, Cynthia Dow, Enrique Cabrera-Caban, Tina Shah Paikeday and Alix Stuart, *Leading Through Crisis (Executive Summary)* (Minority Corporate Counsel Association and Russell Reynolds Associates, Inc. 2020), at 2. The Inclusion Index factors include: working across differences, leveraging different perspectives, workplace respect, voice and influence, employee recruitment, development and retention, accommodating differences, organisational fairness and leadership commitment.

26 Christine Simmons, "170 GCs Pen Open Letter to Law Firms: Improve on Diversity or Lose our Business", *The American Lawyer,* 27 January 2019. More than 240 general counsel and corporate legal officers eventually signed the letter.

after seeing the lack of diversity reflected in some firms' partnership announcements the prior year. They sought to stress to law firm partners that they collectively control legal budgets in the range of hundreds of millions of dollars and were demanding accountability and change.[27]

Client pressure intensified during the pandemic. Early in the pandemic, clients expressed their concern that firms not use the pandemic and economic downturn as an excuse to "back-burner" their commitment to DEI.[28] In August 2020, Simon Zinger, then-Group General Counsel of the Dentsu Aegis Network, led an effort to launch "The General Counsel Oath" initiative, the goal of which was to leverage the collective power of in-house lawyers to make meaningful progress across the legal profession in the areas of DEI.[29]

Client pressure on Big Law firms will likely continue to accelerate. As one example, in January 2021, the then-general counsel of the Coca-Cola Company announced new diversity and inclusion requirements for its outside counsel firms requiring them to give a portion of work to Black attorneys and withholding a non-refundable 30% of fees from those that fail to meet certain diversity metrics. Outside counsel must staff new matters for the company with at least 30% of diverse lawyers, with at least half of them being Black.[30] Perhaps expressing the general sentiment of in-house lawyers, then-General Counsel Bradley Gayton said:[31]

The hard truth is that our profession is not treating the issue of diversity and inclusion as a business imperative. We are too quick to celebrate stagnant progress and reward intention. We have a crisis on our hands and we need to commit ourselves to specific actions that will accelerate the diversity of the legal profession ... We will no longer celebrate good intentions or highly unproductive efforts that haven't

---

27   Sara Deeter, "Michelle Fang is Disrupting the Legal Industry", *Modern Counsel*, 14 October 2019.
28   Jessica L Mazzeo, "In-House Perspective on Diversity, Inclusion and Equity During a Pandemic", *The Legal Intelligencer,* 14 May 2020.
29   Monidipa Fouzder, "General Counsel Oath Seeks to Promote 'Positive' Change", *The Law Society Gazette* (28 August 2020). The full text of The General Counsel Oath can be found at https://generalcounseloath.com/.
30   Phillip Bantz, "Coca-Cola General Counsel Says Diversity Efforts Aren't Working, Unveils New Guidelines", *Law.com Corporate Counsel*, 28 January 2021, www.law.com/corpcounsel/2021/01/28/coca-cola-general-counsel-says-diversity-efforts-arent-working-unveils-new-guidelines/.
31   www.linkedin.com/pulse/open-letter-commitment-diversity-belonging-outside-counsel-gayton/.

and aren't likely to produce better diverse staffing. Quite simply, we are no longer interested in discussing motivations, programs, or excuses for little to no progress – it's the results that we are demanding and will measure going forward.

While The Coca-Cola Company later moved Gayton out of the general counsel role and paused implementation of the diversity requirements he announced,[32] law firms should expect stricter requirements from other in-house counsel going forward. They will continue to call out the dissonance between what firms are saying and the results they are seeing. Some of them seem to have abandoned the "carrots" approach and are now opting for "sticks".

8. Conclusion

Pursuing racial equity will be an important aspect of diversity, equity and inclusion work in US law firms for the indefinite future. Whether law firms move closer to that goal will depend on what they do next. Will senior leaders continue to treat DEI as a priority? Will they continue to look inward to confront the systemic impediments to equity in their policies, processes and practices? Will law firms continue to develop inclusive leaders? Will they continue to embrace coalition-building? Will their DEI professionals continue to sit at the management table as strategic advisers? Or will they return to the status quo without backing up their bold words with equally bold action. Was 2020 a flashpoint or a turning point? Only time will tell.

---

32   Brian Baxter, "Coca-Cola Shakes Up In-House Legal Team, Swapping Out Gayton", *Bloomberg Law*, 21 April 2021, https://news.bloomberglaw.com/business-and-practice/coca-cola-shakes-up-in-house-legal-team-switching-out-gayton.

Building client relationships in a hybrid world

Michelle Holford
Slaughter and May

1. Introduction

The pandemic has changed everything and nothing.

The nature of work changed overnight when the pandemic took hold in 2020. For those in professional services, this largely meant a readjustment to working remotely almost 100% of the time. While the adjustment to be able to continue just 'doing the job' has been relatively straightforward and surprisingly successful, the adjustment needed to be effective at winning new business and developing client relationships is less obvious.

Anecdotal evidence from across industries shows that it is easier to win work from existing clients than it is to develop new ones in the virtual world, but even that is not a given if relationships have not been nurtured or weren't that strong to begin with. On top of that, there is a lack of clarity about this altered reality. Which changes are here to stay and what will revert back? What do these changes mean in practice? What new skills might be needed in this new, and possibly hybrid, world?

1.1 It all starts with strategy

Although this chapter examines what may be changing in relation to business development, there are some fundamentals which remain true. A business development strategy must clearly depict a target audience, identify the issues that audience is likely to care about and develop the right rhythm of interactions, to hit that audience with the right message, in the right way.

To be more precise, the audience identification must be specific and not vague – a clearly articulated client type or group, or persona, if you will, with similar characteristics. The issue can be almost anything – a change in legislation, a new industry trend, or the chance to network – but it should be a demonstration of understanding about the particular thing that a particular audience (or individual) is likely to care about at that moment in time. The third part, the rhythm of interactions is about getting the timing and method of communication right. This can be speed to market on a particular issue or a phone call with an idea that will resonate when shared – but picking the moment and delivery of the message are key.

Even before the pandemic, it was easy to get two out of the three correct but without achieving the third. However, business development is only ever truly effective when these three things, audience, messaging and timing, overlap. This overlap is a small space in a crowded world, but achieving it will yield results and the pandemic hasn't changed that.

To understand what has changed about business development you must understand what has changed for the client and then apply it in practice to the way that you operate. Therefore, what follows is an examination of the trends which are changing how this strategy might be executed. The strategy itself remains largely unchanged.

These trends include the increased reliance on virtual working, the digital transformation familiar in many industries, the explosion of data available to support effective business development, the drive for personalisation and greater empathy in professional services marketing as well as the impact that the environment, social and governance (ESG) agenda is having on the way business development is carried out. It also seeks to identify some of the responses to these trends, though these are not exhaustive suggestions and future ways of adapting will yet emerge.

Some of these trends were in train well before the pandemic took hold, and the effect of the last 12 months has been to accelerate their arrival. Given this accelerated arrival, time to delivery has been contracted and permanence remains unknown. Adjustments will inevitably need to be made. As a result, it is not possible to say today what the full outcome on business development behaviours will be over the longer term. What is certain though is that that remaining close to clients, alert to their needs and able to move quickly to adapt to their circumstances is essential. Not all can do this, not all realise it needs to be done, but those that can and do will find themselves in a position of competitive advantage.

2. **People are going to remain, at least partially, virtual**
The sudden explosion of video calling may reduce slightly once offices start to refill, but the reality is that most people expect to work

remotely at least some of the time. The McKinsey Global Institute estimates that more than 20% of the global workforce (most of them in high-skilled jobs in sectors such as finance, insurance and IT) could work the majority of its time away from the office, and be just as effective.[1] On top of that, office workers themselves want to be remote more of the time.[2]

Therefore, visibility, in essence, having a presence with clients such that they think of you in key situations where your services could be deployed, and which is vital to effective business development, must start to be achieved virtually.

For much of the past year, the only visibility has been virtual. New ways of working have been learned because the feedback loops previously relied on, the relationships maintained through face-to-face contact, the influence asserted by being able to be physically present at key moments is no longer as readily available. For those used to working in this way, the sensation of the loss of control can be alarming and disabling. This can also often cause a cessation in the activity necessary to remain visible. It shouldn't.

2.1 Building and maintaining relationships

When operating partly or wholly virtually, it can be easy to lose sight of the importance of continued building and maintaining relationships because it is that much harder. Working online, it is easy to regularly interact with the same small group of people on a piece of work. Often, those you know best are easiest to talk to online.

Being remote means that moments of serendipity that happen in physical encounters don't happen as frequently. Those moments, where you are able to share small points on which bigger things are built don't happen. The remote world therefore requires more communication than would normally be the case, not just a bit more but a lot more. This takes more energy and more time than usual and it might feel odd or forced or otherwise unnatural but it is vital.

It feels odd because engaging online is a more linear experience than in the physical world. It's harder to read someone's face

---

[1] McKinsey & Company, "What's Next for Remote Work: An Analysis of 2,000 Tasks, 800 Jobs, and Nine Countries", 23 November 2020, www.mckinsey.com/featured-insights/future-of-work/whats-next-for-remote-work-an-analysis-of-2000-tasks-800-jobs-and-nine-countries.

[2] Nielsen, "Balancing Act: With More Time at Home, Word Days and Media Habits", 13 August 2020, www.nielsen.com/us/en/insights/article/2020/balancing-act-with-more-time-at-home-work-days-and-media-habits-merge/.

online, building trust and rapport is harder and, combined with an occasional poor internet connection, this can sap the will of even the most committed relationship builder. As a result, it can be easier to win work from existing clients when working remotely. They know you well, you don't have to prove yourself as much and they may be more likely to have a need for your services, so you keep busy servicing them. And it is true, the best form of business development is doing the work and doing it well. Therefore, it's hard to stray from this comforting way of working. However, the new client pipeline needs to be filled and while developing newer and less established relationships and winning work online is undoubtedly harder, it cannot and should not be ignored. A list of contacts that you have not spoken to in six months is a good place to start and then being bold and calling them. It is worth noting that clients and contacts will remember who picked up the phone to them during challenging times. Clients can be feeling isolated too and a call, a piece of advice or simply the fact that you have told them you are thinking about them can go a long way. It doesn't matter that they won't have immediate work for you and nor should you expect that.

Many will seek to put off this truly hard form of business development, persuading themselves that they should wait until they can be back in the office or working more normally or whatever other form of procrastination is available. The truth is that it should not wait. There is no reason to delay. This is absolutely the time to figure out a new way of doing something.

2.2 Widening networks

Satisfying existing clients is one thing but winning work from entirely new clients in a largely virtual world is quite another. It is very hard to do it from a cold start. Warm introductions are very helpful and for that reason relationships with other advisers are key. Bankers, financial advisers, etc who can validate your introductions can aid new relationships enormously. Don't underinvest in these in the new world just because your usual ways of doing the 'leg work' of relationship building are not available to you. Find new ways because you are going to have to do it.

Plug those individuals into your network and see if you can help them. Find out who they are connected to. Ask your contacts for endorsements. A positive word from another can be an enormous aid to demonstrating credibility, particularly when it comes to a pitch situation. The new way of working might even create opportunities because the pandemic has changed the rules. Some more introverted personality types can find building new relationships personally very daunting. Those who struggled before might find this new environment for business development better suited to them. No networking in a room full of unknown people, no late evening events or endless small talk. You can build relationships based on the expertise you have, engaging with people who may be interested to hear from you, and you can do it all from behind your computer screen in the comfort of your remote working surroundings. The possibilities are endless, as we shall see.

2.3 **Matching virtual presence to offline impression**
While the immediate face-to-face and screen-to-screen interactions are important, wider market visibility is also important. That means having a presence online. A website and social presence are the minimum requirements as platforms which enable engagement with a target audience. Such a presence needs to be actively curated and developed over time so that it remains current and visible and care and consideration should be taken as to how to achieve this.

Individuals should develop their own online networks, working through platforms such as LinkedIn. By sharing content through networks, range and visibility to those who are most likely to be receptive to what you have to say can increase significantly. As well as firm generated content, lawyers can produce and share personally created content on related points, such as a short video filmed and uploaded from a phone, or a blog post, even commenting on an issue via social media. This starts to develop and curate a presence online which will be found by prospective clients. It is important to understand how to use these platforms effectively rather than simply reporting or resharing content from a central firm website. It can take a degree of confidence to do this, and many will observe on social media long before joining the fray but it is worth the investment over time.

The key to doing this well is being authentic. A consistent position in terms of how you present yourself and what you do will help grow your profile and start to mark you out as someone worth listening to and following. It's ok for some of this to be personal as well, in fact, I'd recommend it and it doesn't need to be perfect and polished either. People follow people and you can cultivate an online presence that marks you out as an expert in a particular area, if you are consistent and regular with the content that you produce and share. This is also an opportunity for more junior professionals to create themselves a recognisable brand, within their own area of expertise.

2.4 Pitching and winning work

Pitching online is hard. The video call is an unforgiving medium and only allows for linear chat, where one has to wait not only until another finishes speaking entirely before speaking but also to establish no one else wishes to speak before speaking. This is tiring and hard work and the richness of the in-person experience is not possible to recreate fully. It is not possible to know when a pitch situation might again permit several people together in the same room, therefore it is best to assume that at least for now, winning new work through pitch processes will require some form of online meeting. Much of the process should remain the same, in terms of information gathering and understanding client requirements fully, before beginning to draft a response. However, the meeting will need some thought and coordination. There are some ways in which you can deliver a better experience.

- It is an old adage that no plan is ever followed in the heat of battle but it is in the planning that you do which will help you land on the three things you absolutely need to deliver while in the meeting. As long as you focus on doing that, the plan won't matter too much.
- To achieve that, prepare beforehand what you want to say and then halve the number of words you use to do it. That will get you closer to the succinctness you need to achieve online that the in-person experience is more forgiving of.
- Ensure you have someone who is chairing the meeting from your side and be prepared to accept that should that person appear to cut you off mid flow, it is because they have picked up from your audience that it is time to move on, in a way that you might not have been able to do while screen sharing or speaking.
- Have some questions for the client and turn it into a conversation so you hear as much from them as they do from you.
- Observe your audience and try to maintain eye contact, look at the screen and respond to the reactions as if it were physical. Capturing an audience on screen is difficult, but done well, it can be all the more memorable.
- Send your document in advance if you can. While you can share a screen, technology remains generally poorly used in live pitches online and being able to read the faces of those you are

pitching to is more important than sharing your document in the moment.
- Confidence with technology – practise with the technology beforehand. It may sound obvious, but the pressure of an online pitch can be made worse if you don't know how to use the platform you are delivering it from. Work out what you will be using and find and practise with it in advance.

2.5 Getting back to face to face

We are not going to remain remote forever. In the future, we are likely to operate in a more hybrid way, where people are physically available some of the time. While the need to get together for a specific piece of work or project may drive availability, for the more casual catch up, or relationship-led conversation, matching the times when you might be available to when a client might be available may be harder, take longer and as a result be more infrequent. Remaining methodical and persistent in your approach to these encounters is really the only way to ensure that they happen. When they do occur, the opportunity will be valuable and the quality of the interactions high. Visibility is always worth investing in.

3. **Digitisation of everything**

The trend to digitisation is not a new one. It was happening before the pandemic but the reliance people now have on the digital experience has grown exponentially. According to research undertaken by McKinsey in mid-2020, five years' worth of digital adoption for both consumers and business was achieved in around eight weeks.[3] More than half the world's population is now using social media.[4] Many are consuming nearly all their content online[5] and over 40% of internet users use social media for work.[6] Most

---

[3] Aamer Baig, Bryce Hall, Paul Jenkins, Eric Lamarre and Brian McCarthy, "The COVID-19 Recovery Will Be Digital: A Plan for the First 90 Days", McKinsey Digital, 14 May 2020, www.mckinsey.com/business-functions/mckinsey-digital/our-insights/the-covid-19-recovery-will-be-digital-a-plan-for-the-first-90-days.

[4] Simon Kemp, "More Than Half of the People on Earth Now Use Social Media", *DataReportal*, 21 July 2020, https://datareportal.com/reports/more-than-half-the-world-now-uses-social-media.

[5] Heather Jordan, "COVID-19 Changed the Advertising Playbook. Now What?", Nielsen, 25 February 2021, www.nielsen.com/us/en/insights/article/2021/covid-19-changed-the-advertising-playbook-now-what/.

[6] Kemp, *supra* note 4.

people expect to continue to do more online even as the pandemic recedes.[7]

This trend appears irreversible and will lead to greater expectations of how easy working and communicating online for work will be in future. In practice, this means choice and use of channel and platform are vital when engaging with clients, whether meeting for coffee, running an event or doing a pitch. It means organisations will need to think about how their content is going to be consumed before they produce it. It means the online client experience must be seamless. Most of all it means organisations need to be nimble in the implementation of new technologies and the investment required to track and deliver them.

3.1   The online client experience

This online client experience is an important one to get right. Many will think that this is a less relevant part of legal business development but, in fact, the experience clients have online will impact what they expect their experience to be in the offline world. Understanding your client personas, and being able to create an online journey that meets their needs and expectations, is likely to now hold greater significance than it might have done previously. A reputation for delivering a high-quality service should be matched by the quality of the online experience, as it is highly likely that a client will have had the online experience before a meeting. They will have looked for you online, they will have read your content and they will have started to form a view.

3.2   Platforms for everyday use

Collaboration platforms such as Zoom, Teams and Googlemeets have undergone significant investment recently and have an increasing range of functionality to replicate the offline experience – breakout rooms, white boarding and audience polling are some of the newer functionalities and more are added daily. It is also possible to federate with clients (where individual domains are connected) allowing ease of access to teams, project documents and shared files. These platforms have been used with relative ease over the last

---

7   Arun Arora, Peter Dahlström, Eric Hazan, Hamza Khan and Rock Khanna, "Reimagining Marketing in the Next Normal", McKinsey & Company, 19 July 2020, www.mckinsey.com/business-functions/marketing-and-sales/our-insights/reimagining-marketing-in-the-next-normal.

12 months. The challenge is to continue to maintain the advances that we made in the move to using these platforms 12 months ago so the client experience remains outstanding.

3.3 Channels

Using multiple channels can double or triple the reach of a brand and its content over a website or email campaign alone. It also means content can be reused, but it will need to be repackaged for different channels. For example, podcasts are chatty and light and often benefit from several different voices, including some external ones, such as a client, a recognised industry voice or industry body. A video on the other hand can tackle a more detailed point, creating visual effects as necessary to supplement the understanding of a point. A blog post needs to be short and pithy and written quickly. It can point towards a longer briefing if one is needed, but the point of the post should be brief.

Content should also be regularly produced, not every day but each channel has a rhythm. For example, there is no point starting a blog if there aren't a number of people committed to posting regularly. A LinkedIn page should be used instead.

Another way to repackage content is to use it to deliver a conference speaking slot. Taking elements of the content that has already been put together to create a talk or point of view that can be delivered to different audiences throughout the year. This might also be less fear inducing online than doing it in person! Conference sponsorship can also be a way to highlight involvement and brand presence to a wider range of potential targets, than would be reached through other channels alone.

3.4 Digitising events

Online events can be a challenge because you can't directly digitise them, ie you can't convert directly what was done in the real world, online. There are any number of categories of event – conferences, round tables, webinar/seminars and so on. All are different and even for those organisations used to doing webinars and other online events before the pandemic, the new world in which we are all working and living means new rules apply. Timescales are shorter, preparations more intense. And this is unlikely to change as we emerge into a hybrid world either, where both the offline and the online may need to be catered for as part of the same event.

(a) **Forethought with formats**

There are several different types of event that can be run and a number of different platforms that can be used but it remains important to understand what the aim of the event is, along with the audience and overall message. From there, format and platform can be established.

A round table event can be run on several platforms. The key is to use a platform that allows for effective interaction between participants and that will fit, ideally, all participant faces on screen. Common platforms are Zoom and Teams. Typically, there is a facilitator, who does not need to be a content expert, but who needs to keep the conversation moving along, asking questions and bringing in less vocal participants where necessary. Round tables will be very hard to recreate in a hybrid sense, where intimacy and participation are key drivers of success.

If the event is more about imparting information to an audience, then a broadcast format may work better and these are often the more traditional webinar platforms, many of which were in use long before the pandemic. The difference this time round is understanding your audience, which is different to the pre-pandemic audience. They work and live differently and may have different preferences about timing and length of willingness to engage online. You may have an idea of your clients' preference but otherwise, an early morning session before the day gets going can work best. If you are working across time zones, offering a choice of slots can be an effective way of achieving greater engagement. There are many platforms which can deliver this experience, such as Webex, ON24, Webinartogo etc. This type of event is likely to be the most easily replicable in a hybrid sense. With a good broadcast set-up, you can share the same information to an online and offline audience. You can also have in-person and remote contributors. Asking a question should be as easy from a remote audience as the in-person one. The key to the success of this will be a good chair for the event who can manage both audiences.

It might not be a single event, but a whole day you are trying to replicate. You won't be able to take the day online. People won't have the desire or the capacity to sit through a series of online sessions. But you can work out what it is about the event or session that they would have benefited from in the real world and then try and recreate that online. It might be hearing from a particular speaker, it might be a topic or networking opportunity. There are platforms which will give you a more interactive experience, allowing you to replicate networking in some form, or to continue speaking with speakers and panellists once the main session has come to an end in breakout rooms. Networking though, is extremely hard to replicate in a hybrid way and if that is a main driver of such an event, consider format options to ensure you achieve the outcome you seek.

(b) *Making it successful*

Starting early to gain momentum will help and often you will need several pieces of content to achieve this before the main event. In terms of the content of the message, these can all be variations on a theme and lead up to the main event. Perhaps a briefing, a podcast and a video call can all be released at varying times in the run-up to an event. Personalisation is also important and you might find that personal follow-ups, from the person who knows the contact best at the client, will get more engagement.

People also want more information about online events. They want to know about the platform, the speakers, the topics etc. They expect information to be available to them online and they want to be able to find it. Don't hold it back from them. The more you give them the more interested they will become. A 'save the date' might have been good enough in the old world, it isn't in the new one.

This ensures that you are sharing sufficient information with people to give them a good flavour of the event and whether it will be worth their investment of time.

Post event, continuing the engagement with those attendees is likely to lead to greater returns over the longer run. Send videos with edited highlights of the day, send footage of the speakers not seen before or send related content which has relevance to the topics. The aim is to try and have a further conversation and you have a greater chance of doing that if you follow through post-event with something which your attendees relate to. This is also true of those attendees who could not attend, and in the new world, many may assume that you will make event materials available to them online, whether or not they were able to attend on the day.

Ultimately, you have to work harder to capture and retain attention online. This means your speakers must be captivating, the platform fit for purpose and the content well pitched. You are likely to spend less on an online event than you might have done on a physical one. However, don't scrimp on content. If you need to pay for a speaker that is higher cost than you would normally pay for, do so. The content will be what draws your clients to your event.

(c) **Hybrid events**

As the world returns to something more recognisably normal, it will be possible to conduct events again with an in-person element. Some events, particularly those with very senior people, for whom the networking is the key priority should remain a wholly offline experience. However, many events will be able to be run in a hybrid way, where both remote and in-person speakers and audiences can attend. Much of the learning from above will need to be deployed and technology and IT infrastructure will need to enable high-quality broadcast and remote participation as well as in-person participation. To date, this has only really been done well by television studios and high-end events production companies. Going forwards, it is going to need to become the domain of all those who are trying to ensure they have the greatest possible chance of connecting with their more widely dispersed client base.

Despite the fact that many of the benefits from events are hard to recreate online, and will require learning to achieve successfully, building and maintaining a sense of community amongst your client base will have long-term benefits.

3.5 Digital touch points

In the offline world, the number of 'touch points' you have with a client can be a good indicator as to relationship health. There should be no difference in the online world, and replicating that and giving clients reasons to interact is important. Clearly, a digital interaction is not as effective as a physical one but clients are increasingly online – they will seek digital interactions and you should provide them.

A client portal can provide clients with the means to access information and services you provide to them online. Real-time matter and transaction data and financial reporting data is likely to be the most highly prized, but access to key value add services such as learning and development materials or premium client content can also drive engagement. These digital touch points must be easy and intuitive and give clients something they value.

There are other ways to do this too. Chatbots and live chat functions can be used to support lead generation and social customer relationship management (CRM) can actively enhance prospects.

Recent McKinsey research has shown that B2B buyers are now comfortable with spending significant sums online and that more businesses are using a live chat function to generate leads and sales.[8] This might not sound very professional services like, where e-commerce is not a feature of the sales cycle, but the approach can lend itself well to someone looking for a particular insight or piece of content on a website. It is not as easily dismissed as some might think.

3.6 Digital acceleration

The pandemic has accelerated the use of digital in many sectors and law has been digitising for many years. However, few sectors will have had to put their pilot projects, proof of concepts, new marketing channels etc into practice quite as fast as many law firms will have done. The success of these projects has surprised many and demonstrated what can be achieved when there is a push factor as well as a pull factor for innovation. This ability to move with speed and fail fast, where necessary, should be one of the factors that law firms hang on to coming out of the pandemic.

4. Empathy and engagement – the personalisation of the client experience

We have spent the last year peering into each other homes, understanding more about the lives we lead outside work and sharing concerns about health and happiness. This is not going to change overnight. People have enjoyed the informality and getting to know each other better. This requirement for the human connection and the empathy that comes with it has long been an important feature of B2B marketing but it is not always recognised or acted upon. A 2016 study, published in the *Psychology and Marketing Journal*, looking at empathetic relationships in professional services showed that within such relationships emotional concern is the strongest driver for commitment.[9] In other words, showing your clients that you care about them can enhance their commitment to you.

There are several consequences of this greater knowledge and empathy. Deeper insights will lead to greater expectations. Clients

---

8   Arnau Bages-Amat, Liz Harrison, Dennis Spillecke and Jennifer Stanley, "These Eight Charts Show How COVID-19 Has Changed B2B Sales Forever", McKinsey & Company, 14 October 2020, www.mckinsey.com/business-functions/marketing-and-sales/our-insights/these-eight-charts-show-how-covid-19-has-changed-b2b-sales-forever.
9   I Weißhaar and F Huber, "Empathic Relationships in Professional Services and the Moderating Role of Relationship Age", *Psychology and Mark*et*ing*, 9 June 2016, 33: 525–541, https://doi.org/10.1002/mar.20895.

are more likely to expect their advisers to understand their issues better. In doing so, they are becoming more engaged and will care about what you know, and how that relates to them. Clients are humans first and foremost and being able to connect with people, to share thoughts and views which are valued will become increasingly important.

4.1 Greater expectations in relation to issues client care about

There is a lot of noise out there. Almost every professional services firm is trying to help their clients interpret the world they are living in right now and you should avoid simply being another voice adding to the fray.

Content should be meaningful and based on issues you know clients are facing. The best way to do this is to talk to your clients about the concerns that they have and what will help them as they seek to address these issues. Talk to others in your field about the work they are doing and what is at the forefront of addressing some of these issues. The issues that keep clients awake at night are rarely focused on a single area of expertise and likewise, the best solutions are often found at the intersection of different practice areas. Teasing out these issues and applying cross stream solutions creates opportunities for the most meaningful content.

Content should also be human, even if you are writing a technical briefing on a specific point. This means changing the way you think about content. A lot of law firm content can be dreary and dull. It commends itself to the regular insomniac. However, legal content does not need to be written that way. Clients are human and in-house lawyers work closely with businesspeople in their organisations. They want an interpretation that can be shared easily without being rewritten and content that will address a commercial point rather than simply point out the technical elements. Ideally, you will repurpose the content you create for different channels to increase visibility, which we explore below, and this means you will need to further adapt the way you are communicating. Legal training does not often cover how to write in this way, but the result is worth the effort.

4.2 Recognising the opportunity

When creating content there is often a trade-off between speed and insight. A piece that you can get out quickly may not have the thought or insight that a piece over which more time is taken can have. Before you create a piece, know which you are going for, so as to avoid achieving neither. In the fast-moving pandemic, many lawyers were producing content simply to help clients understand what was happening. This content was being produced at breakneck speed and contained limited insight. The main benefit was to provide clients a fast interpretation of the latest announcements. This was helpful and many will have found engagement of these pieces was high if the piece came out speedily after an announcement was made. Engagement will have been much lower if the piece arrived several days later, when clients will have found other sources for the same content. By contrast, a piece which arrives after the usual melée has subsided, but which (while still short and pithily written) contains an insightful view of the subject in hand, interpreting the information from a different perspective or with an overlay which may aid understanding, can be valuable to clients and is likely to be welcomed. At all times, however, the perfect should not become the enemy of the good enough.

One must also look out for fatigue on a particular subject. While it may hold fascination for the author, it might not for the client! Engagement rates should be monitored to spot the point at which the drop-off might suggest a different tack. This can be seen in some COVID-19-related content now and the wise author will pick carefully from the plethora of topics available before engaging with clients.

4.3 Empathy

It's not always necessary to tell people how much you know, or even to have all the answers. Sometimes the best conversations are had by simply asking questions and listening to the answers. Given the informality with which business has been conducted over the past months, it is important to try and find ways of bringing that approach into the next phase of working. You can start by asking how someone is and really listening to the answer, ask about how they are managing professionally and personally, ask about their business or their plans. People can be fearful of these conversations, and unsure what to do with the answers, but it is not necessary to be. It may, on occasion, require you to suspend belief for a while, but in doing so, see if you hear something new in what people tell you.

4.4 The value of asking what clients think

The virtual world that the pandemic has thrust us into and the hybrid world that we may emerge into will have fewer feedback mechanisms than before. The ways in which feedback is normally received, through regular, every-day interactions with others, do not exist in the same way. It's much harder to have a revealing, casual conversation or a quiet word which identifies a problem. Therefore, proactively seeking client feedback is more important than ever. It is also the case that clients' businesses have been through a significant period of change themselves and they may not look the same as they did before the pandemic. This may have affected how they see the relationship with you, as an adviser, so the assumptions and norms that you previously relied on are no longer as valid. The lawyer who has not picked up the phone to a client during the crisis may not find themselves as well positioned as the crisis recedes and the client is looking to the future.

There are a number of mechanisms for doing this: face to face (remotely or physically), an online survey or via a third party administered approach. All are valid and have different pros and cons, which are outside the scope of this chapter, and you will have a view on what is most suitable for your firm or clients but the key is that you do it and, most importantly, act on the result.

It is worse to solicit feedback and not act on it than it is not to solicit feedback in the first place. The pandemic is also likely to be changing the way in which you work and deliver your advice. Talking to your clients about those changes, what they are seeing in their own businesses and their changing expectations of advisers is an important part of the conversation. The information they yield will enable you to determine which changes you can make that may enhance your relationships as well as which may negatively impact them. There has never been a better time to ask "How are we doing?".

4.5 Two-way engagement

At a time when clients are being bombarded with webinars, seminars and other online experiences designed to sell a company's wares, it pays to think about how you can generate more meaningful connections. The Deloitte Marketing Trends 2021 survey identified participation as a key trend in 2021.[10] A two-way dialogue can create more meaningful engagement and if clients can see the purpose behind what they are doing, it can increase their commitment to you and your organisation.

---

10   Deloitte Insights, 2021 Global Marketing Trends, www2.deloitte.com/content/dam/insights/us/articles/6963_global-marketing-trends/DI_2021-Global-Marketing-Trends_US.pdf.

This can be achieved through participation and joint creation. Rather than sending clients your content, get them involved in creating your content, to record a video with you or to discuss a particular topic on a podcast. Rather than inviting your clients to a webinar, invite them on the panel to discuss. Rather than telling them about your associate training programmes, ask them to present alongside you or ask them to talk to your employees about a topic that is close to their heart, which might have nothing at all to do with their business. In creating opportunities for them to engage with your business and give their opinions, you achieve a continual stream of feedback. Clients like to be asked what they think and will want to tell you more than you realise.

5. **Data and more data**

All law firms hold a ton of data. Few use it well. While the use of data and insights to analyse marketing performance is nothing new, it is something that law firms are only latterly getting to grips with. The shift to almost entirely online marketing overnight for such firms has meant they now have access to much more data that can help evaluate performance. It is also largely real-time data and it can be used to identify potential clients at key moments in their buying journeys.

The availability and volume of this data is going to increase as more and more channels open up and more content is created and shared. The challenge is to be able to gather the data from the variety of sources and present it in a way that is meaningful and capable of being acted upon. Firms should seek out the skills necessary to this. The data can also be enriched with information from existing internal sources and acquired third party sources, all of which can help to build up a picture of a client's preferences and behaviours and point to how to improve engagement levels going forwards.

5.1 **Client preferences**

Client contact data is a critical starting point for marketing. That data needs to be held in accordance with the relevant regulations to which you are subject. For those in Europe, this may be the GDPR. The US is taking a state-by-state approach. This chapter presupposes that those reading are familiar with the appropriate regulations and their requirements.

Understanding clients' preferences and having a way to capture them is important and ideally an online web form can achieve this in a compliant way. The other way of capturing this data is for partners and other fee earners to identify their clients' likely preference based on their knowledge of them. The benefit of the former is that it can act like a marketing tool in and of itself, as your clients can express their own preferences and tell you what they want to know about. It also has the added benefit of being more likely to collect correct data. This data, once captured, should be regularly reviewed to ensure that it is responsive. Data decays very quickly unless it is looked after.

Ideally, a firm would have an automated way of capturing, monitoring and updating this data. Many professional services firms will have this capability as part of their CRM solution but law firms are notoriously bad at doing it, even if they have the relevant software in place. It is most likely you will have some form of process that relies in part on a manual input at some point. Overall, you are aiming to get a picture of the value of marketing a particular product or service to a particular contact, and once delivered, the performance of that piece of marketing. However you do it, active management of contact data will lead to greater accuracy in targeting and greater engagement as a result. It will also lead to better quality content being produced if used correctly.

5.2 Real-time feedback

When all marketing is being done online, an enormous amount of data is created. It can offer real-time feedback which is valuable. However, understanding the data and generating the insights takes time. Done properly, it can show which target audiences engage with which pieces of content. It can show the best time to send content and it can show which messages people are most receptive to. Most law firms will have an email marketing channel and that will be the largest provider of feedback but there are other sources too and being able to integrate those sources to tell a more complete picture will yield results. Many law firms are not well set up to understand this data but engaging with it is vital.

It can be as simple as looking at which clients opened a mailing and have engaged with the content and finding an appropriate way to follow up with them. This follow-up is key – speaking to clients quickly, and while the issue is fresh in their mind. Follow-up can take many forms. For example, offering a conversation with an expert in that area, providing training on a particular subject. The focus of a subsequent piece of content can be changed to reflect where the highest levels of engagement came from. It is, in effect, intelligently steering the car based on what you can see in front of you, rather than blindly driving on, based on what you think might be. The data must be seen and discussed and then acted upon.

The next step is to report on that data in a meaningful way, at an aggregate level. That means having a reporting function in your CRM system that is set up to provide you with the data you need, at campaign or client level. Many firms will have a team doing this, but it is important that those teams engage with the end user of the data, so that they understand how the data is going to be used and which analysis will be most valuable. The data can be used to effect change but it is surprising how many times this data can be provided with no knowledge of its ultimate purpose. Therefore, can we see that certain sectors are most engaged on a particular topic? Which segments are not engaging with the content? In this way, you can use the data to improve the effectiveness of your content and messaging.

In short, measure your results and respond accordingly.

5.3 Creating the 'single view of the client'

It is likely that many law firms will already have programmes underway to bring together the data it already holds in different systems. This works towards the 'single view of the client' perspective, where data including client financials, relationships across the firm, pitch track record etc is accessible in one place and able to be viewed together, giving a complete picture of the client. The business development perspective should be prominent in the thinking around how these systems are developed and implemented. This data can be used in combination with the marketing activity data, giving a more complete picture of client activity. It can also then be used at an aggregate level to identify trends and aid the performance of marketing. Consideration should also be given to supplementing the data with external sources, which can help segmentation of the data for analysis.

While a single view of the client approach has been in use in other professional services firms for some time, it is not a very 'law firm' type label and many firms actively recoil from pooling their combined knowledge on a client. However, the availability of data to understand a client journey is now widespread. It doesn't need huge amounts of time spent on analysis, but understanding a basic picture of your client across the organisation can be an enormous aid to focusing in on how to achieve further growth in that relationship. Those that can achieve this, and use it well for business development, will create a significant competitive advantage.

6. **Travel**

The pandemic saw travel stop and all meetings conducted online. While this has proven effective, it was also the only option. Once business travel is an option again, what will happen? There may be less choice for advisers than you think.

Spending the pandemic communicating virtually with clients and prospects means that everyone is more familiar with this way of engaging. This means it won't be a surprise when you wish to do it again, even once the pandemic begins to recede and travel opens up again.

The pandemic, in this sense, has been a great leveller because no one has been able to travel. The benefit that might have been bestowed by a boots on the ground approach is less effective in current circumstances. Virtual trips can be an effective approach. A series of client visits based in a particular region or country over a short period of time allows for consolidated learnings and the dedicated time is well used.

However, the Citi Hildebrant 2021 Client Advisory report on law firm trends expects to see a greater focus on business development this year noting that while lawyers have not been able to travel, they have found their clients more accessible than ever before leading to deeper relationships being developed.[11] This also means that for those who have not perhaps been as generous with their time during the pandemic, those clients have also been accessible to others.

Therefore, the pressure to travel again once it is possible to do so is likely to be high as firms find themselves competing with others prepared to do so. It is true that the strengthening sustainability agenda is putting downward pressure on the travel and this is only going to continue. However, for the adviser selling only time, nothing quite says to a client "I care" as much as being physically present.

McKinsey observes that business travel took two years to recover after the 2008/9 financial crash and predicts that it might take as many as five years to recover this time.[12] However, for those with

---

11 Citi Private Bank and Hildebrandt Consulting, 2021 Client Advisory, www.privatebank.citibank.com/ivc/docs/2021CitiHildebrandtClientAdvisory.pdf.
12 Kevin Sneader and Shubham Singhal, "The Next Normal Arrives: Trends that Will Define 2021 – and Beyond", McKinsey & Company, 4 January 2021, www.mckinsey.com/featured-insights/leadership/the-next-normal-arrives-trends-that-will-define-2021-and-beyond.

clients now more accessible to other firms and whose competitors might be hopping on a plane to visit them as soon as they are able, travel is likely to return more quickly.

There are, though, careful choices to be made. Professional socialising is likely to be lower down the priority list than personal socialising for a period of time, people may be wary of meeting others where vaccination status is unknown and hotspots for new variants of the virus are likely to continue to emerge. Therefore decisions about where and with whom time is spent in future will need to be wisely made.

7. What does the ESG agenda mean for business development?

A focus on the ESG agenda was growing before the pandemic with Larry Fink's 2018 annual letter to CEOs exhorting a focus on social purpose, followed by the Business Roundtable letter in 2019, which sought to shift the focus from solely shareholder benefit to the benefit of all stakeholders.[13] Many initially thought the ESG agenda might suffer in an economic crisis. In fact, the pandemic has shown there is a strengthened interest in sustainable and responsible business from a corporate perspective.[14] This agenda will place a spotlight on service providers as corporates ultimately seek to extend their behaviours through the supply chain.

Professional services firms should expect to have their purpose and ESG credentials examined. Going forwards, many clients see the success of home working as having achieved a mind-set shift in remote working in their own organisation. It is likely that these same clients will assume that their advisers are baking these changes into their way of working once the return to the office begins. So, what does this have to do with business development?

Clients are asking more questions about diversity, sustainability and environmental impact. To start with, these questions might appear as part of panel pitches. Often innocuous sounding, they shine a spotlight on a firm's own behaviour towards its employees or supply chain. Already clients are asking for details of, for example,

---

13 Business Roundtable, "Business Roundtable Redefines the Purpose of a Corporation to Promote 'An Economy That Serves All Americans'", 19 August 2019, www.businessroundtable.org/business-roundtable-redefines-the-purpose-of-a-corporation-to-promote-an-economy-that-serves-all-americans.

14 Half of FTSE 100 companies link executive pay to ESG targets, www.ft.com/content/609eae5e-1576-4081-9340-5d5001b5b02e.

the way in which employees were treated during the pandemic. Such questions can be considered by some to be rather 'fluffy' in nature and can often be ignored or downplayed in the desire to present as fulsome a picture of one's credentials as possible. However, these questions carry increasing weight in awarding work. The questions can then progress to a specific requirement in relation to a piece of work or an expectation of future changes and before too long it is feasible to conclude that an organisation may have overlooked the changes occurring in their client base and be in an altogether more challenging position when it comes to their ability to win work.

7.1 To take a position?

Much work has been done to demonstrate the link between having a clear purpose and, for example, improved productivity, greater profitability or enhanced client relationships. For the professional services community, while these links may be true and rational, the knowledge itself may not be enough to be the ultimate driver of change. There are many reasons for this. Articulating a social purpose for an advisory B2B business is much harder than for a consumer brand B2C business. Firms may fear taking a position for fear of alienating clients not as far along the journey. A partnership structure means such approaches will need to be achieved through a high level of consensus and, ultimately, advisers will feel their position is to be led by their clients and changes will occur in response to client need.

This is an understandable position to take and, therefore, it is not a point that can be remedied immediately in order to win more work, nor should it be. But, law firms and other professional advisory businesses will have to decide when that tipping point comes and, when it comes, to have done enough work prior to that point to make the necessary change possible and convincing. Achieving this is an art but it is essential to remain competitive and will be a genuine contributor to effective business development in the long run.

8. Conclusion

The trends examined here don't fundamentally change the basics of a business development strategy, but they do change the speed of time to market, the delivery of initiatives based on real-time data, and client expectations. At the same time, they create greater opportunities for engagement, for deeper relationships and the demand for a more client-centred experience.

These opportunities are hugely exciting and if grasped well can create significant competitive advantage. It is not just the job of a chief marketing officer to realise these advantages, but of the firm's leadership and management as well as its individual lawyers and professionals. To deliver well will take investment, communication and drive. Putting the client experience at the heart of the changes will yield results for the firm that recognises what is necessary and delivers.

The new normal: remote working, billing and law firm activism

Alex Dimitrief
Zeughauser Group

Count me among the pundits who rushed in early 2020 to volunteer advice to law firms and legal departments about how to survive the pandemic. In hindsight, few foresaw how well most law firms would fare, and even fewer predicted that the elite firms would earn record profits. So, as lawyers and their clients begin to return to the office in meaningful numbers, what's next? In my view, the new standards set for client service and interaction by lawyers during the pandemic will by and large become the 'new normal'. But I also believe that there are several even more profound changes afoot insofar as inclusion and hourly billing.

1. **Developing business and relationships remotely**
It was never anything personal, but even before the pandemic, few clients genuinely enjoyed more than an occasional business outing – and the shorter and more convenient, the better. At many companies, heightened conflicts of interest standards increasingly precluded extravagant meals or expensive entertainment. In other words, schmoozing has always been overrated.

    Now that Zoom and its competitors have proven their mettle, there is no going back to the default of in-person meetings. The pandemic established that few tasks performed by prospective or existing outside counsel require an on-site presence. Most of a law firm's business can be conducted effectively by thoughtful emails and crisp online presentations. The few exceptions – eg, preparation sessions to gain the trust of a critical witness, meetings with clients who want to be able to test the confidence of their lawyers on a critical issue – prove the rule. Don't resist the cost and time savings afforded by today's ever-improving technologies.

    How, then, should lawyers go about cultivating new relationships and strengthening existing ones?

1.1 Discerning client alerts

Provide concise but compelling updates that set you apart. Avoid dwelling on the obvious. For example, do not 'alert' a sophisticated client that the US Supreme Court's decision to grant *certiorari* in an abortion case could spell trouble for *Roe*[1] and *Casey*.[2] Rather, focus on why pro-life advocates pushed a particular case for review and elaborate on a potential pro-choice wrinkle or two. In my experience, only unique and practical insights prompt recipients to hire their authors for advice.

1.2 Websites

Clients and prospective clients visit them, but their quality remains decidedly mixed. Websites should be searchable so that visitors can readily access material related to the lawyers, issue(s) or types of matters that prompted the visits. And be careful not to exaggerate your experience or oversell your credentials and talents. (For instance, I've generally found that most litigators who stress how much they like going to trial are trying to compensate for how few cases they've actually taken to a final verdict.) It's worth having a friend or relative give you candid feedback about whether your page may be over the top.

1.3 Results and references

Few things speak louder than factual descriptions of excellent results, save for clients or other disinterested parties who are willing to vouch for the quality of the work that generated those results. Marketing departments should focus less on 'best lawyers lists' and more on landing deserved mentions in "Big Deals" or "Big Suits" or profiles in *Law360*, *Corporate Counsel*, the *Financial Times* or the *Wall Street Journal*.

Never underestimate the power of the network among general counsel and their teams. Pick your spots, of course, but ask your clients to make introductions for you and serve as references. They will be doing (and seen as doing) their counterparts a solid by recommending you in the right circumstances.

---

[1] *Roe v Wade*, 410 US 113 (1973) (establishing in a 7–2 decision that the right to privacy under the Due Process Clause of the US Constitution protects a woman's right to choose to have an abortion).

[2] *Planned Parenthood of Southeastern Pennsylvania v Casey*, 505 US 833 (1992) (reaffirming *Roe* in a sharply divided 5–4 decision but upholding restrictions in 1988 abortion control law pursuant to a new 'undue burden' standard).

1.4 Reach out, but wisely

When contacting prospective new clients, credibly highlight why *you* are interested in working for *them* (eg, their lines of business, the types of transactions they do, the legal issues presented by their operations, the countries in which they operate) and focus less on why they should be interested in hiring you.

Touch base with existing clients periodically, but do so in ways that are helpful to them (ie, making sure they have everything under control) and not a pretext to ask for more business. You know the difference and so do they. General counsel frequently tell me how surprised they always are by how few lawyers ever ask open-ended questions about where a company and its legal team need help the most. By focusing exclusively on securing business for themselves in their areas of expertise, lawyers regularly miss out on potential opportunities for their partners in other areas where clients are thinking about trying someone new or simply had not encountered much of a need before. This issue is especially pronounced at law firms that have disavowed lockstep compensation schemes.

1.5 Online events

When done well, online symposiums are far more convenient and, if you pick the right topics, should generate larger audiences. But be sure that the presentations are about the issues and *not* about how your firm is positioned to address the issues (which is a huge turn-off).

Zoom cocktail hours and other online social gatherings are a closer call. Some (like superb magic shows) can be a huge hit with families gathered around on the couch. When in doubt, don't overdo them and also make sure that associates are on board. Generally speaking, they have a better filter than partners for what works virtually and what doesn't.

1.6 Feedback

It is always safe (and valued) to ask clients to evaluate your work. Remarkably few lawyers do this enough. You can solicit feedback in any number of ways via in-person meetings or remote communications – personally, through another lawyer at your firm or using an outside consultant. Why wouldn't you want to know what's on a client's mind, whether they're happy with your work and what else you might be able to do to lock in repeat business?

2. Remote work

The great aplomb with which lawyers have remotely practised high-quality law over the past two years has also permanently changed internal law firm dynamics. But the pronounced shift to remote work raises issues more fundamental than how much to invest in technology, whether to renegotiate leases and how to optimise office space. Managing partners who are hoping to entice and/or require lawyers to return to the office on a regular basis will need to come up with credible and compelling reasons for face time requirements.

This will be challenging. Before the pandemic, more and more lawyers were already working from remote locations for at least a couple of days per week. (Full disclosure: when I was in private practice, I started working from home when dial-up modems became all the rage.) I am sympathetic to the concerns voiced by leaders of law firms that time in the office can be helpful (and sometimes is necessary) for training new lawyers, facilitating informal communications, promoting intellectual spontaneity and inter-lawyer creativity, building camaraderie, maintaining a firm's culture and, perhaps most importantly, mitigating the downsides of too much isolation. Insurance carriers would also point to data suggesting that allowing remote work leads to a higher number of malpractice claims. But I remain thoroughly unpersuaded by the argument that remote workers are less effective and/or committed, as belied by the record performance of law firms during the pandemic and associated economic downturn.

Most firms will land on a hybrid model in which lawyers will divide their time between the office and home (or other remote locations), and a significant number will allow lawyers the option to work remotely full time (or, more precisely, yield to the expectations of the up-and-coming generation of lawyers that they should be able to). Here's the rub: the leaders of a law firm owe it to their professionals to be brutally honest about all of this. If face time is required for someone to advance within the firm and remote lawyers will confront higher hurdles in career advancement, then say so. The worst outcome would be for a law firm to pay lip service to the notion that lawyers may work remotely but then, even with the best of intentions, nevertheless view time in the office as a proxy for a lawyer's dedication to work, the firm and clients. *Sub rosa* office time standards devalue the careers of lawyers who believed it when they were told they could work remotely. It also doesn't take a degree in rocket science to see how such hypocrisy would disproportionately affect women who also believed it when they were told they could capitalise on the flexibility of remote work in making their work/life/family choices.

For all these reasons, firms that choose to allow remote work should monitor their review processes vigilantly to ensure that lawyers are not penalised, consciously or subconsciously, for availing themselves of this option. Nor should such firms designate high-visibility cases or transactions as matters available only to lawyers who are coming into the office four or five days a week. In particular, don't presume to make work/life choices for women of the sort that are rarely ever made for men. Leave it to female professionals to make their own informed choices, in consultation with their families, about whether to take on challenging and time-consuming assignments with extensive office-time and/or travel requirements that might ultimately prove to be valuable career-enhancing opportunities.

Caution is also merited in at least two other respects.

- I am surprised at how many firms are singling out administrative personnel for less flexible office time requirements even though they also proved during the shutdown that they can effectively discharge their responsibilities from remote locations. There are exceptions, of course, such as meeting centre coordinators, but firms should think twice before relegating everyone except the lawyers to what will inevitably be regarded as second-class citizenship.
- Mentoring will have to become much more proactive. We partners have always been a tad naïve about the degree to which associates have truly felt welcome to stop by our offices when they had a moment to spare, but the transition to remote work puts the onus squarely on partners to initiate the types of informal interactions that all of us took for granted when working at the office was more the norm. Firms will also need to be more thoughtful and creative about respectful ways to monitor the emotional well-being of lawyers who are working remotely, an increasingly important topic that I address more fully below.

3. Improved billing hygiene

Remarkably, it took a pandemic for most lawyers to come around to honouring the basic principles of Billing 101 – recording time in meaningful detail at the end of each day, not delegating this important task to assistants who aren't privy to the details of the work that was done, respecting requirements for task-based billing and submitting bills on (and often ahead of) time. Yet many lawyers who got this religion during the dark days early on in the pandemic when anxieties about establishing one's worth were running high are already regressing to bad pre-crisis habits. Don't make this mistake, which will not go unnoticed.

Also remember that in-house legal teams have a variety of targets (both substantive and procedural) to meet. During the crisis, timely and accurate bills were important tools for clients to determine whether they and their outside counsel remained on track. Post-crisis, there is no excuse for invoices that fail to provide meaningful and timely updates about matters in ways that are simple for clients to absorb and act upon. During the crisis, bills (as opposed to, say, 'COVID-19 alerts') were the most anticipated and closely read 'marketing communications' that clients received from their outside counsel – was a firm being sensitive to the client's challenges, were outside counsel delivering the types of value and results required for the company to succeed during the pandemic, and, more generally, did the law firm 'get it' (which meant different things for different companies across different industries)? Post-crisis, fewer companies will settle for anything less than timely, informative and analytics-driven billing, meaning that law firms simply can no longer afford to relegate billing to backroom personnel as a necessary administrative evil.

4. Diversity and inclusion

It would be difficult to overstate how much time and attention law firms devoted for many years before the pandemic to diversity and inclusion programmes. (One of my very first meetings at Kirkland & Ellis back in 1986 was about reprioritising gender equality.) Yet, despite all of the good intentions, it would also be challenging to understate the success of most of these initiatives, save for a few exceptions at some law firms. I won't belabour the data. We all know and have experienced this.

Yet the depth, breadth and urgency of the grief, concern and anger aroused by the killings of George Floyd, Breonna Taylor, Ahmaud Arbery, Tony McDade and Rayshard Brooks in the midst of the coronavirus crisis brought a new sense of urgency for racial equity in a profession whose noblest credo is a commitment to equal rights under law. Having the courage, sensibility and grace to address and interact on discomforting topics like racism and inequality in authentic, empathetic and reassuring ways has become a litmus test for today's law firm leaders.

As the months have passed since last year's widespread protests, some firms appear to be losing their focus on anti-racism. This would be a huge and unfortunate mistake. To many, what was especially discomforting about last year's tragedies was their similarity to spates of deaths of Black Americans at the hands of police officers and vigilantes over the past decade and how little had changed in response to their accumulation despite the outpourings of grief and plethora of promises to do better. This time around, law firms cannot content themselves with platitudes against racism and inequality and will be judged harshly in the future unless they continue to take concrete actions on at least three fronts.

4.1 Supporting equality initiatives

Most law firms have already made visible commitments to anti-racism initiatives through statements by their leaders, significant financial contributions to leading non-profit organisations, increased *pro bono* activities and recognising Juneteenth as a holiday. This is all great, so long as the uptick in *pro bono* work sticks, but it's also honestly the easy part.

4.2 Expanding the pipeline

Many firms have also undertaken to expand the pool of prospective lawyers from Black and other minority communities by funding scholarships for minority students and donating to historically Black law schools. Others are participating in ground-breaking programmes (like Thrive Scholars out of Boston[3]) to provide students of colour from low-income communities opportunities to succeed at top colleges and thereby qualify for admission to top law schools.

An even more fundamental change is required. Historically, law firms have put far too much stock in the ranking of law schools and grades as predictors of future success. Instead of lamenting inadequate pipelines, firms should hire more students from a broader spectrum of law schools, including historically Black law schools. Hiring committees should also look beyond grades to consider a student's overall circumstances – eg, were there financial or other reasons why a student attended Howard rather than Harvard, did the student need to sacrifice studying to earn money to pay for school, and are there other extenuating considerations *vis-à-vis* traditional hiring criteria? As author Rita Mae Brown so

---

3   For information about the Thrive Scholars programme, see www.thrivescholars.org/.

aptly put it: "Insanity is doing the same thing over and over again but expecting different results."[4]

4.3 Self-critical analysis

Law firms must also find meaningful ways to connect with their Black stakeholders to hear, understand and constructively discuss how racism and inequality have affected them and their families. They must make it safe and valued for Black employees to raise concerns about being treated differently and being afforded unequal opportunities. Firms must also use metrics (both objective and subjective) to weed out conscious and unconscious biases that result in people of colour being treated differently. And leaders of all colours must commit to improve the training, retention and promotion of people of colour by establishing concrete and measurable goals for which leaders will hold themselves and partners accountable (eg, attrition rates of Black lawyers, number of partners and clients for whom lawyers of colour have worked). Creativity, experimentation and courage in devising new anti-racism metrics will go a long way. To those who say this is hard and fraught with peril, my answer is that law firms have a long history of finding numerous ways to assess themselves in virtually every other aspect of their performance.

Taking an honest look in the mirror at how a law firm treats its lawyers of colour is the hardest part. But let's face it. Ours remains a profession in which, despite overwhelmingly positive intentions, race continues to matter in ways that ought to concern all of us. Law firms can no longer afford to be places where people do not speak openly and candidly about our differences or the potential consequences of those differences. All of us need to do more – including, it bears emphasis, clients who deserve to be called out by relationship partners when they do not back up their diversity requirements and rhetoric by making professional and business development opportunities available to lawyers of colour.

Review processes merit especially careful consideration. Are lawyers of colour being afforded the same candid feedback as white lawyers on a timely basis? Too many Black and Hispanic or Latino associates receive sugar-coated reviews that do not empower them to focus on weak spots (which all of us have) and thereby improve their performance as their careers progress.

---

4   This famous definition of insanity is often misattributed to Albert Einstein and sometimes even to Benjamin Franklin or Mark Twain. See www.news.hypercrit.net/2012/11/13/einstein-on-insanity/.

5. **Law firm activism**

The anger and unrest spawned by the George Floyd tragedy have not only boosted demand for environmental, social and governance (ESG) practices, but have also heightened expectations among stakeholders that law firms will join corporations in taking more visible stands on social and political issues like election integrity, voting rights and climate change. Truth be told, it is not surprising that students at elite law schools have recently begun to mount protests against Paul Weiss because of its longstanding representation of ExxonMobil.[5] I still remember the boycotts of firms that represented South African companies back when I was in law school. What's more novel is pushes like the one we just witnessed to withhold business from law firms that represented parties who, in the view of other clients and other stakeholders, were on the wrong side of the 2020 US election disputes.

Some of this is inevitable in today's world of Twitterdom and 24/7 echo chambers on cable news channels. In the end, the leaders of law firms will be accountable primarily to the women and men who work there and who can choose to take their practices elsewhere if they cannot square their personal views and values with those of the firm's clients. But I hope this won't go to extremes. To be sure, I readily acknowledge that no company is entitled to be represented by a particular law firm. But even the most challenging clients will always be able to find alternatives, and, on balance, I'd prefer that harder-edged clients be represented by law firms constrained by mainstream sensibilities. It was precisely for this reason that, when I was at General Electric, I liberally granted conflict waivers, often over the objections of my team. I took considerable comfort in knowing that our adversaries and counterparties would be represented by high-quality lawyers at principled law firms.

6. **Towards value-based billing**

Perhaps the most difficult and frustrating conundrum facing law firms is that, even after lawyers have stepped up and delivered great service during a crisis, many clients come to resent the firms' profitability as having come at the clients' expense. Some firms are fortunate to have developed strong relationships with clients who are not as cost-sensitive (eg, private equity firms). Others

---

5   See, eg, Emily Pontecorvo, "Calls for Law Firm to #DropExxon Go National with Law Student Boycott", Grist, 10 February 2020, https://grist.org/climate/calls-for-law-firm-to-dropexxon-go-national-with-law-student-boycott/.

have savvily focused on profitable niches where clients are always happy to pay premium rates for superb work in essential areas (eg, bet-the-company trials, multi-jurisdiction transactions, enterprise-threatening investigations, capital markets). But most law firms are constantly being challenged by their clients to find more ways to deliver more value for less money. This becomes a vicious cycle for less successful firms because the law firms that are able to charge the top rates can afford to pay top salaries that draw the best talent (from law schools and, increasingly, from competitors) who, in turn, enable these firms to continue to command the top rates and earn the highest profits.

I sympathise with lawyers who believe that they are unfairly singled out for criticism of their financial success, especially when compared to expensive investment bankers, management consultants and Big Four partners. From where I sit, law firms deserved every penny of the record profits they earned by working so hard and so well during the coronavirus crisis. So why, then, is success of the sort that Big Law enjoyed in 2020 viewed by many law firm leaders as a mixed blessing and resented by so many of the clients who made it possible?

To me, the root cause is hourly billing, which remains prevalent despite years and years of sharp criticism. Can't you just hear the conversations that must have taken place in legal departments across the country when Covington & Burling LLP disclosed the rate that Eric Holder was charging Oregon Health & Science University to investigate the school's handling of sexual misconduct and discrimination complaints?[6] "Yes, I realise that he was the Attorney General of the United States and I'm sure he's great, but is anyone really worth $2,295 per hour?!"

The honest and fair answer is yes, great lawyers do indeed deliver this much value to clients, who require the expertise and services of world-class lawyers to conduct their businesses with integrity in today's increasingly challenging world. (I also suspect that the hourly rates effectively paid to senior partners at firms like Goldman Sachs, McKinsey and KPMG, to name a few, dwarf those of the lawyers who work alongside them.) But many clients and other critics of hourly billing cannot get past the perception that, even when a law firm delivers high-quality results, hourly billing

---

6 Mike Scarcella, "Covington's Eric Holder Bills at $2,295 Hourly, New Contract Shows", law.com, 16 April 2021, www.law.com/nationallawjournal/2021/04/16/covingtons-eric-holder-bills-at-2295-hourly-new-legal-services-contract-shows/.

incentivised the firm to recommend, do and bill for more work than was genuinely necessary. On this view, it is *always* in the hourly biller's interest to do (and be paid for) more work.

For now, I will resist revisiting the great and mostly one-sided debate about whether the hourly rate promotes inefficiency over the long term (although I can't help but notice the dearth of "expert analysis" of the extent to which abusive hourly billers do not win repeat business). I've become far more concerned about the corrosive effect on lawyers and law firms of constantly being on the clock, particularly in remote working environments where days blend into nights and so many people are no longer constrained from working by the boundaries of traditional business hours or commuting to the office.

Honestly, why else would lawyers who are making good livings singularly distinguish themselves among those in the professional services with such constant complaints about professional misery? We've all read the multitude of surveys over the years reporting that high percentages of lawyers would not choose to be a lawyer again, don't want their children to become lawyers and don't have enough personal time to "have a life". We've also seen the alarming studies documenting the struggles of lawyers with drinking, addiction, depression and anxiety. In this respect, the pandemic has not helped. Indeed, a study by Justin Anker and Patrick Krill released in May 2021 reports that 25% of female lawyers are seriously considering exiting the legal profession because of mental health issues, burnout or stress.[7] (To be clear, though, I cite this data point with the belief that it says nothing about the fitness of women for legal careers and everything about the overall state of our profession.)

Yes, much of this self-loathing is undoubtedly directed towards the tedious, mind-numbing and adversarial nature of what lawyers do at law firms, especially as associates. We lawyers also tend to be perfectionists who hold ourselves to absurdly high standards and feel personally responsible for the consequences to our clients when a matter does not turn out well. Still, last time I checked, much the same could be said of most of the nature and pressure of the work performed at banks, private equity firms, hedge funds

---

[7] Justin Anker and Patrick R Krill, "Stress, Drink, Leave: An Examination of Gender-specific Risk Factors for Mental Health Problems and Attrition among Licensed Attorneys", PLOS ONE, 12 May 2021, https://journals.plos.org/plosone/article?id=10.1371/journal.pone.0250563.

and consulting firms, especially in entry-level positions. To me, the difference has always been that lawyers alone are compensated based principally on the number of hours that they work. I remember wearing 3,000 billable hours per year as a badge of honour when I was in private practice, and I'll never be able to thank my family enough for bearing with me as I made this mistake.

This needs to change, at long last, if nothing else for the well-being of our profession. Devising alternative valuations of legal services will not be easy, but the starting point should be in-depth conversations with clients about how much value they ascribe to securing and/or avoiding various types of outcomes in legal matters. Several years of experimentation and risk-taking will be required for both sides of the attorney–client relationship to gain the knowledge and experience necessary to strike fair and mutually beneficial deals that are not based principally on the number of hours worked. But it's eminently doable; at GE, I was often struck by the contrast between the unwillingness of law firms to commit to fixed fees for matters because of their "unpredictability" and the confidence with which the leaders of our aviation business were prepared to commit to fixed prices for incredibly complicated jet engines that remained in the early stages of design and development. In the end, most clients will not care how much lawyers make per hour as long as the clients receive the desired outcomes at prices that they consider fair. Stated differently, value-based billing would highlight value and breed less resentment.

The pandemic has also brought home (indeed, literally) how much de-emphasising the number of hours worked and focusing instead on the value created by lawyers will improve the quality of life at law firms. Imagine a world where talented women and men are rewarded (financially and otherwise) instead of penalised for finding creative ways to avoid burdening clients with bills for the drudgery of big and seemingly endless cases and deals? Can you think of another profession that is more sceptical about the net benefits of time-saving advances in technology? It should never be against a firm's best interests to invest in predictive coding and other types of artificial intelligence that will spare clients the cost (and a firm's associates the pain) of hours of mundane legal work.

7. **The (deserved) staying power of Big Law**
There are already rumblings out there that the success being enjoyed by law firms is not sustainable, with one expert going

so far as to warn that there is a "freight train coming down the tracks".[8] But I am confident that dire warnings such as these about Big Law's supposedly inevitable demise will again prove to have been unfounded. Law firms will continue to succeed because, by and large, there is great value in the important work that lawyers do for their clients.

Still, reorienting the economics of the legal industry toward this value and away from the number of hours required to deliver that value would reduce stress on both sides of attorney–client relationship and, in the process, help make our work as enjoyable as it is rewarding. If nothing else, the pandemic ought to have reminded us that life is simply too short to bill 2,500+ hours year after year or to give in to what the critics have always naysaid about what remains a noble profession.

---

[8] S Reisinger, "Huge GC Survey Sees Legal 'Freight Train' Looming", *Law360*, 7 April 2021, www.law360.com/articles/1372335/huge-gc-survey-sees-legal-freight-train-looming (reporting that 75% of general counsel say their budgets will not keep pace with growing workloads).

Pro bono post-pandemic: our evolving commitment to serving others

Sara Andrews
Lisa Dewey
Anne Geraghty Helms
DLA Piper

1. **Introduction**
    This chapter examines the legal profession's deep-seated commitment to providing *pro bono* legal services on behalf of others, a commitment evidenced by the institutionalisation of *pro bono* programmes and the presence of full-time *pro bono* lawyers in law firms around the world. It begins by looking at how *pro bono* has changed since the start of the global COVID-19 pandemic and considers how, as we begin to move towards the future, we may not feel the same urgency to respond to health and economic crises, cries for racial justice, rising food insecurity, the "shadow pandemic" of violence against women, or fairness in our election systems, as we did in 2020 and beyond. But, even as we return to a "new normal", we know that the urgency will still be there and our profession and our approach to serving others will never be the same.
    After looking at how the pandemic has changed *pro bono*, we discuss how those changes have underscored the business case for *pro bono*. Finally, we examine these *pro bono* trends in a global context and consider the path forward.
    The lessons we learned during the pandemic are likely similar to those we have learned in other aspects of the profession and in everyday life. During the COVID crisis, we changed by necessity. We adapted to new technologies and found that those technologies enabled us to work more efficiently and often to serve our clients better. We found that lawyers truly wanted to help, and we were able to engage volunteers, both within law firms and in corporate legal departments, in new ways. In the United States, we walked our clients through online court, we reached out to small businesses,

and we gave critical thought to our existing commitment to racial justice and how we could do more to stand up for the principles of equality and fairness in our country. Around the world, lawyers assisted charities and low-income clients with issues related to the pandemic, including housing, employment and questions about how to access government emergency assistance.

As we re-imagine *pro bono* going forward many of the lessons we learned will be worth keeping. Remote technology has provided us better and more efficient ways to serve our clients. *Pro bono* has offered us opportunities to stay connected and engaged even while physically apart. Remote court allows us to attend hearings without having to leave our offices and without our clients having to take time off work or to find childcare.

Law firms have long been committed to *pro bono*, and since the start of the pandemic, we witnessed a deepening of that commitment across the legal profession. Moving forward, we must maintain the sense of urgency we felt during that tumultuous period. As with any natural disaster, our clients will continue to feel the ripple effects of the pandemic for years. We must continue to keep our clients front of mind, even as our lives become more normal, and we must bring lessons learned into the future. So, we present this chapter with great optimism, tempered with a note of caution. We know that the legal profession is unique in its commitment to helping others, and we must retain our sense of urgency and resolve even when it feels that the world is no longer in crisis.

2. Evolution by necessity: how *pro bono* changed during the pandemic

The pandemic has transformed the way we approach *pro bono* in three major ways. First, technology has created a seismic shift in how we connect with clients and deliver services. Second, we have seen an acceleration in the trend towards serving more clients by delivering brief services. Finally, we have seen increased collaboration in tackling access to justice issues – not only between and within law firms, but also with legal services agencies and NGOs, with corporate legal departments, and with civil society.

2.1 Transformation through technology

The move to online court and the increased use of technology to deliver remote legal services was well underway prior to 2020, but the pandemic fast-tracked these developments – a shift which will have profound implications for the ability of poor and marginalised populations to access justice. Law firms also are delivering *pro bono* legal services in fundamentally different ways.

Prior to the pandemic, there were efforts to use technology to further *pro bono*. The Legal Services Corporation held an annual conference dedicated to the use of technology in legal service delivery and gave grants to legal services organisations for this purpose.[1] Pro bono Net was founded in New York in 1999, to expand access to legal rights information and refer *pro bono* matters to law firms via technology.[2] Tech start-ups like Paladin[3] and organisations like Justice Connect[4] help link legal teams with *pro bono* opportunities and make their progress and impact easier to track. During the pandemic, Paladin created a portal to help lawyers find *pro bono* opportunities to assist people affected by COVID-19 and other natural disasters.[5]

There were also creative efforts underway to automate legal processes for people who cannot afford a lawyer. For example, a non-profit start-up called Upsolve[6] helps low-income families file for bankruptcy using an online web app. Another mobile app, JustFix.nyc,[7] provides renters with information about tenant issues and helps them assert their rights against negligent landlords. The app Formally[8] enables users to fill out US immigration forms online and helps them through the process. These types of applications are not solely directed at laypersons; they also help guide lawyers providing *pro bono* assistance.

During the pandemic, law firms have shifted to serving *pro bono* clients in the same manner as billable clients: virtually. We now appear in court on behalf of *pro bono* clients remotely, submit court filings via email, meet with clients via video conference, and organise online legal clinics to provide advice on issues like immigration and housing.

---

1 See Technology Initiative Grant Program, LSC – Legal Services Corporation: America's Partner for Equal Justice, www.lsc.gov/grants/technology-initiative-grant-program.
2 See About – Pro bono Net, www.probono.net/about/.
3 See www.joinpaladin.com/.
4 See The Gateway Project – Justice Connect, https://justiceconnect.org.au/about/digital-innovation/gateway-project/.
5 Connie Loizos, "A New Pro Bono Portal Just Launched for Lawyers Looking to Help People Hit Hard by the New Pandemic", *TechCrunch*, 30 April 2020, https://techcrunch.com/2020/04/30/a-new-pro-bono-portal-just-launched-for-lawyers-looking-to-help-people-hit-hard-by-the-pandemic/.
6 Upsolve, https://upsolve.org/.
7 JustFix.nyc, www.justfix.nyc/en/.
8 Formally, https://formally.us/home.

Virtual engagement and representation have benefited both lawyers and clients in many ways. It may be easier for *pro bono* lawyers to take on matters involving court appearances when they do not need to travel to the courthouse and wait for their matter to be called, taking precious hours away from a busy workday. As Jim Sandman, President Emeritus of the Legal Services Corporation (LSC), the United States' largest funder of civil legal aid programmes, put it:

> *The pandemic has created the capacity for technology to eliminate an important barrier to justice: the requirement of the in-person court appearance. In the past, having to pay for transportation and childcare, and to take time off from work to attend a hearing in person, meant that many people just did not make it to court. This was a huge reason for the many default judgments in eviction and consumer debt cases. With remote appearances by Zoom now common, we are seeing reports from across the country of increased participation in court proceedings and fewer default judgments. Many people also are more comfortable in remote hearings. Zoom court feels like just another online meeting rather than an imposing court process, and this can make court feel less intimidating both for litigants and pro bono lawyers.*[9]

Beyond convenience, there are indications that remote court proceedings may be less traumatic for participants, particularly for domestic violence survivors.[10]

The use of technology has also helped to reach clients in rural areas where there are fewer lawyers. Tiffany Graves, *pro bono* counsel at Bradley, who is based in the US state of Mississippi, noted that pre-pandemic, it was nearly impossible for her to place matters in the rural areas of the state.[11] The use of technology has made it possible for her to mobilise lawyers located in major cities to help serve those clients who would not otherwise have access to legal counsel.

However, there are some challenges presented by the move to online *pro bono* services. Not everyone has ready access to computers, the internet or broadband. According to the United Nations, at the

---

9   Taken from an interview between the authors and Jim Sandman on 8 March 2021.
10 Ashley Carter and Richard Kelley, "Remote Court Procedures Can Help Domestic Abuse Victims", *Law360*.com, 18 October 2020, www.law360.com/articles/1315788/remote-court-procedures-can-help-domestic-abuse-victims.
11 Taken from an interview between the authors and Tiffany Graves on 25 February 2021.

end of 2019, 47% of the world's population did not use the internet.[12] The 'digital divide' is particularly pronounced in rural areas,[13] which are less likely to have large numbers of lawyers. In the United States, income is a major determinant of who has internet access, meaning those who qualify for *pro bono* legal services may not be able to access them using technology.[14] People of colour in the US are disproportionately impacted by the digital divide.[15] There are efforts underway to address these issues, in part by providing computer and internet access in public places like courts and libraries, or by offering free digital hotspots.[16] However, these efforts have been made more difficult by the need for social distancing in public spaces.

In addition, using technology can create security and privacy concerns. As with any matter, lawyers need to maintain their ethical obligation to keep information related to a client's *pro bono* representation confidential. This can be a challenge when conversations take place in a public space via video conference over a public WiFi connection or when written communications are sent via unsecured email, text or social media platforms.[17]

Finally, there are times when in-person service is simply better. Clients may have difficulty communicating via a remote platform, either due to lack of language or technological proficiency, for example. And it can be more difficult to build trust with a client via video or over the phone, especially where the lawyer needs

---

12 *Measuring digital development: Facts and figures 2019*, ITU, www.itu.int/en/ITU-D/Statistics/Documents/facts/FactsFigures2019_r1.pdf.
13 *Measuring digital development: Facts and figures 2020*, ITU, www.itu.int/en/ITU-D/Statistics/Documents/facts/FactsFigures2019_r1.pdf.
14 Camille Ryan and Jamie M Lewis, "Computer and Internet Use in the United States: 2015", United States Census Bureau (issued September 2017), www.census.gov/content/dam/Census/library/publications/2017/acs/acs-37.pdf. Monica Anderson and Madhumitha Kumar, "Digital Divide Persists Even as Lower-income Americans Make Gains in Tech Adoption", Pew Research Center, 7 May 2019, www.pewresearch.org/fact-tank/2019/05/07/digital-divide-persists-even-as-lower-income-americans-make-gains-in-tech-adoption/.
15 See *The Lewis Latimer Plan for Digital Equity and Inclusion*, National Urban League, https://nul.org/sites/default/files/2021-03/NUL%20LL%20DEIA%20033021%20Latimer%20Plan_vFINAL_11AM.pdf.
16 For example, the DC Superior Court in Washington, DC has created several sites across the city where people can use a computer and WiFi to connect to an online hearing in court. See District of Columbia Courts, "DC Courts Provide Remote Sites for People to Use to Appear for Court Cases", 29 September 2020, https://newsroom.dccourts.gov/press-releases/dc-courts-provide-remote-sites-for-people-to-use-to-appear-for-court-cases.
17 See *Providing legal services remotely: a guide to available technologies and best practices*, DLA Piper/New Perimeter, Open Society Justice Initiative (OSJI), Legal Empowerment Network, www.newperimeter.com/our-work/legal-institutions/assisting-legal-services-providers-to-work-remotely.html.

the client to communicate openly about trauma or uncomfortable topics. These are important caveats to keep in mind as we continue to build remote service delivery models in the future.

2.2 Increased interest in brief services

Like technology, the idea of offering brief or unbundled *pro bono* legal services is not new. Law firms and legal services providers have successfully hosted legal clinics and provided limited services to clients for years. We have conducted research assignments to support larger policy initiatives, or, for example, in the US, represented death row clients in a single appeal or clemency petition, rather than taking on an entire case. But the interest in brief services has taken on a new meaning during the pandemic, as online technology platforms have made it easier for lawyers to drop in to meet a client for a few hours online, provide research assistance to an NGO, or offer brief advice to a client appearing at an eviction hearing without leaving home.

Take, for example, a legal clinic that DLA Piper and Legal Aid Chicago ran in the Woodlawn Community of Chicago for nearly a decade prior to the pandemic. For each clinic, volunteer lawyers would leave their downtown offices and drive to a community centre about 30 minutes away. They would arrive to a waiting room full of people who had come for the chance to discuss an eviction, a family law problem or an issue with their social security benefits with a lawyer. After their client meetings, volunteers would gather with legal aid lawyers in a central room to discuss the clients' legal issues, with sandwiches and cookies as sustenance through what was often a long evening. The clinic never ended before the last client was seen.

Enter the pandemic. For the first time in 10 years, the clinic closed its doors. Within a month, Legal Aid Chicago had brought the clinic online. Rather than holding it once per month, the online platform allowed the organisation to schedule clinics every other week, booking appointments via phone or video. Lawyers could now log on from home and serve a client in under an hour, rather than spending an evening travelling to and from a clinic. The clients no longer needed to take public transportation or find childcare to meet with a lawyer. Indeed, they need not be from the neighbourhood at all, and might be from an area that was previously underserved because of the lack of transportation and access. On the flipside, the virtual version of our clinic now sees far fewer homeless and elderly individuals, and we have worried about our continued ability to find and serve those populations in a virtual world.

This clinic example is just one of many in which lawyers have been enabled by the pandemic to help in discrete ways, providing valuable advice without a long-term commitment and, thanks to the support of legal aid lawyers, without the need for ongoing specialised knowledge. *Pro bono* lawyers have held similar remote clinics to help people prepare immigration paperwork, apply for child support, clear a person's criminal record or to seek protective orders. Though not always ideal, these models help expand access to justice for clients who would otherwise have no ability to consult with a lawyer.

2.3 Increased collaboration

People come together in times of crisis. Crises can bring out the best in people, and that is certainly what we saw during the pandemic, both within and across law firms, legal departments, and service providers, and among other institutions within civil society. There are many benefits to a collaborative approach: collaboration prevents duplication of effort, increases the number of people served and promotes solidarity among the legal profession.

To provide just a few examples, when the pandemic hit, the American Bar Association quickly put together a COVID-19 task force[18] to assess the legal needs arising from the pandemic, promote collaboration and help mobilise *pro bono* resources. US state access to justice commissions and some state bar associations, including New York's,[19] convened COVID-19 *pro bono* task forces to mobilise *pro bono*[20] and address looming crises, such as the rise in evictions and domestic violence. Lawyers from DLA Piper have been fortunate to serve on a couple of these task forces.[21]

Lawyers also worked together to address systemic issues. For example, the Law Firm Antiracism Alliance[22] is a group of over 280

---

18 The ABA Coronavirus (COVID-19) Task Force, www.americanbar.org/groups/legal_services/the-aba-coronavirus--covid-19--task-force/.
19 COVID-19 Pro Bono Recovery Task Force – New York State Bar Association (nysba.org).
20 See eg, https://dcaccesstojustice.org/dcrepresents/; www.marylandattorneygeneral.gov/Pages/A2JC/default.aspx. See also LA Represents, COVID-19: Keeping Los Angeles Safe (corona-virus.la).
21 See eg, www.marylandattorneygeneral.gov/A2JC%20Documents1/AG_Covid_A2J_TF_Report.pdf (Guy Flynn, Partner, DLA Piper served as co-chair of the Pro Bono and Reduced Legal Fee Services working committee); https://dcaccesstojustice.org/dc-access-to-justice-commission-covid-19-task-force/ (Lisa Dewey, Partner, DLA Piper, co-chairs the DC Access to Justice Commission COVID-19 Task Force subcommittee focused on mobilising *pro bono* with Rebecca Troth, Executive Director of the DC Bar Pro bono Center).
22 See Patrick Smith, "'We Have to Succeed': Law Firm AntiRacism Alliance Holds First Summit", *The American Lawyer*, 31 July 2020, www.law.com/americanlawyer/2020/07/31/we-have-to-succeed-law-firm-antiracism-alliance-holds-first-summit/?slreturn=20210308073259.

law firms that has come together with legal services to dismantle structural and systemic racism. In addition, some of the biggest law firms and corporations in the US are partnering with advocacy groups to provide *pro bono* legal services to Asian Americans who have suffered hate crimes through the Alliance for Asian American Justice.[23]

In many ways, the *pro bono* community and access to justice ecosystem has grown closer during the pandemic, supporting one another as we responded to the multiple challenges posed by the crisis. Members of the Association of Pro bono Counsel (APBCo) also are meeting regularly to discuss how we can do more to help. Paul Lee, *pro bono* counsel at Steptoe, observed:

> *We, as a profession, have come together more – pro bono and serving people in need is the soul of law and the legal profession. I feel like so many of us have really stepped into this moment. My hope for our future is that we continue to feel fired up and translate this energy into service and constructive work.*[24]

As Tiffany Graves, APBCo president, similarly notes:

> *A silver lining of the past year is our pro bono counsel community. As a leader of APBCo, I see everyone checking in on each other more frequently and talking about secondary trauma and the stress of the job. For many of us, this past year has been our busiest time to date. Our APBCo community is supporting one another and helping each other to avoid burnout.*[25]

(a) **Teaming with our corporate clients**

Another trend that seems to have accelerated during the pandemic is the number of in-house departments working with law firms on *pro bono*.[26] Our *pro bono* team heard from in-house counsel more

---

23 Sameer Rao, "BigLaw, GCs Lead New Effort To Fight Anti-Asian Violence", *Law360*, 15 April 2021, www.law360.com/articles/1375562.
24 Taken from an interview between the authors and Paul Lee on 2 March 2021.
25 Taken from an interview between the authors and Tiffany Graves on 25 February 2021.
26 Law firms and in-house departments have been teaming on *pro bono* for many years. The Pro Bono Institute's Corporate Pro Bono Project® as well as the Association of Corporate Counsel chapters have provided support for these collaborations. See Corporate Pro® Bono®, www.probonoinst.org/projects/corporate-pro-bono/. Since 2003, the Corporate Pro bono Project has recognised "innovative *pro bono* collaborations of in-house legal departments with law firms and public interest organizations" with its CPBO Pro Bono Partner Award. See Corporate Pro Bono Awards, www.cpbo.org/initiatives/awards/.

than ever during the pandemic about teaming on *pro bono*, and we work with several clients at any given time on *pro bono* projects.[27]

In-house lawyers are motivated to do *pro bono* for many of the same reasons that law firm lawyers are, including strengthening connections among colleagues and teams, as well as responding to the crises caused by the pandemic and calls for racial justice. In-house counsel also look to share knowledge with law firms concerning *pro bono* as they begin to structure their own internal programmes. This may involve input on making the business case for *pro bono* or aligning with their corporate missions, philanthropic practices, corporate social responsibility (CSR) and environmental, social and governance (ESG) programmes. Our *pro bono* team (with over a dozen full-time *pro bono* counsel with decades of experience around the world) meets regularly with in-house departments about substantive projects, *pro bono* interests and infrastructure issues.[28] Nicolas Patrick, Partner and Head of Responsible Business at DLA Piper International, commented:

> *Many companies and in-house departments are increasingly focused on the spectrum of ESG risks and want to better understand and measure the social impacts of their business operations, products and services – historically social impact was viewed more narrowly and considered only in respects of philanthropic or volunteer programs. There is renewed focus on corporate purpose and values, and many companies are beginning to look for law firms that align in these areas.*[29]

A few in-house departments also now have full-time *pro bono* counsel, including Microsoft and Entergy.[30] Patricia Graves at Goldman Sachs and Valerie Farkas at Bloomberg recently founded the Association of Corporate Pro Bono "for attorneys and

---

27 See North American Pro Bono: Overview, DLA Piper LLP (US), www.dlapiper.com/en/us/focus/probono/overview/.
28 See *Beyond Elite Law: Access to Civil Justice in America*, 626–27 (Samuel Estreicher and Joy Radice, eds, Cambridge University Press, 2016).
29 Taken from an interview between the authors and Nicolas Patrick on 23 February 2021.
30 Beth Henderson currently serves at Microsoft's full-time *pro bono* counsel. See www.law.com/corpcounsel/2020/11/03/how-microsofts-legal-department-is-combating-evictions-during-a-pandemic/; Christy Kane serves as Entergy's full-time *pro bono* counsel. See www.entergynewsroom.com/article/entergy-names-first-pro-bono-counsel-leader/.

non-attorneys who run in-house *pro bono* programs".[31] And over 180 companies have signed onto the Pro Bono Institute's Corporate Pro Bono Challenge®.[32] According to Eve Runyon, President and CEO of the Pro Bono Institute:

> *We have seen great strides in the development of in-house pro bono over the past several years; 2021 marks the 15th anniversary of the Corporate Pro Bono Challenge® initiative, which was launched by PBI's Corporate Pro Bono project to encourage increased participation in pro bono by in-house legal staff. During this past year, in particular, many in-house legal departments have doubled down on their pro bono commitment by developing and expanding their efforts and by focusing their services in more intentional ways. Other departments that had not previously engaged in pro bono have moved to establish pro bono programs for their attorneys and legal staff. Pro bono has provided a meaningful opportunity for lawyers and legal staff within companies to use their skills to play a positive role in addressing the unique challenges of today, which, at times, have felt overwhelming. Pro bono has helped in-house volunteers to feel a part of the solution.*[33]

(b) *Furthering our diversity and inclusion efforts*

Another important area where we have seen increased collaboration is at the intersection between *pro bono* and diversity and inclusion (D&I). The COVID-19 pandemic has had a disparate impact on Black and Brown people, and the economic crisis is also disproportionately impacting people of colour. In addition, a number of regions have experienced a horrifying increase in anti-Asian hate crimes and discrimination. Efforts to bring attention to these issues, raise awareness about systemic racism and the experiences of our diverse colleagues, and educate many about why so many *pro bono* efforts have always been about racial justice has brought *pro bono* and D&I professionals together in ways that we have not seen before.

---

31 See Association of Corporate Pro Bono, https://acpbinc.org/.
32 See List of CPBO Challenge® Signatories, Corporate Pro Bono, www.cpbo.org/cpbo-challenge/about-the-challenge/list-of-challenge-signatories/. About the Challenge, Corporate Pro Bono®, www.cpbo.org/cpbo-challenge/about-the-challenge/.
33 Taken from an email communication between Eve Runyon and Lisa Dewey on 6 April 2021.

Although at some firms, the D&I and *pro bono* efforts are managed by the same team,[34] many have two separate departments. For those firms the pandemic and the global calls for racial justice and a renewed racial reckoning have resulted in closer collaboration.

Many firms in the US have shifted their *pro bono* work to prioritise the fight against systemic racism. Steve Schulman, Pro Bono Partner at Akin Gump, notes, "We will continue to see more alignment with D&I efforts and our affinity groups who want to engage in *pro bono* related to racial justice."[35]

The same is true at DLA Piper, where advancing racial and gender equality is one of our focus areas. In 2020, DLA Piper's US *pro bono* team came together with the firm's D&I team to host town hall meetings. Our people wanted to know how we were responding to the calls for racial justice during cascading crises, and it was meaningful to be able to speak together on these issues. As we think back on this period, one of the silver linings will be the relationship that has blossomed between our *pro bono* and D&I teams. Many of our D&I resource groups also are using *pro bono* to come together as a group while also serving the larger community.

Raymond Williams, DLA Piper's National Diversity & Inclusion partner reflected:

As we strive toward a more just world, it is imperative we consider the intersectionality between Diversity and Pro Bono teams. These common goals include working within our communities and collaborating with our clients to champion social justice. Through seamless collaboration, we have been able to quickly marshal our firm resources to take action to address social unrest, voter rights, education and housing deltas, among other issues. I have no doubt, addressing these issues so quickly, with boots on the ground, would have been impossible without our Pro Bono team.[36]

---

34 Lamin Khadar, Manager, Positive Impact (*Pro bono*, ESG, D&I) for Dentons Europe, explained in an interview with the authors on 4 March 2021:

> *Our pro bono, diversity & inclusion and ESG work is led by the same team. We think of our pro bono work outside of the United States organisationally through the lens of these other efforts. Historically, in Europe, there has been more of a focus on corporate responsibility, so these efforts led to creating a more integrated approach.*

35 Taken from an interview with the authors and Steve Schulman on 1 March 2021.
36 Taken from an email communication between Ray Williams and the authors on 1 April 2021.

Finally, many corporate clients are asking their firms for information about D&I initiatives and *pro bono* efforts. Appreciating and leveraging the synergies between *pro bono* and D&I will result in greater and more sustained impact both internally and externally.

3. **_Pro bono_ is good business – now, more than ever**

For many years, law firms have recognised that, beyond our ethical obligations as lawyers, engaging in *pro bono* is good for business. The pandemic has only emphasised how *pro bono* can further law firm goals,[37] including by helping with connection, integration and wellness among lawyers during a time when we have been isolated in our remote work environments. There are many other ways in which *pro bono* helps us achieve law firm goals: by creating opportunities for professional development, deepening corporate client relationships, helping with recruitment and by creating a purpose-driven institution. When *pro bono* is aligned with a law firm's goals, every aspect of firm life is improved, and lawyers are more likely to feel personal and professional satisfaction.

3.1 **_Pro bono_ gives us opportunities to connect**

During a time when most lawyers worked remotely, *pro bono* helped law firms and their lawyers stay connected to one another, to their communities and to their clients. We heard from many of our colleagues in corporate legal departments that the same was true for them. The desire to reach out, assist someone in need, and realise that "we're all in this together" has helped us maintain a sense of connection that we lost when our physical offices closed. Claire Donse, Partner and International Head of Pro Bono, DLA Piper, observed:

> Pro bono has been important to our sense of purpose during the past year and has provided a fulfilling way to help people. Many lawyers have been doing pro bono across countries and offices – it has led to cross-pollination in an important way during a time when haven't been able to be physically together.[38]

Many lawyers joined new law firms during the pandemic when we were not regularly in the office and helping them to integrate remotely

---

37 See *Beyond Elite Law: Access to Civil Justice in America*, 622–24 (Samuel Estreicher and Joy Radice, eds., Cambridge University Press, 2016) (citing Reena N Glazer, *Revisiting the Business Case for Law Firm Pro Bono*, S. Tex. L. Rev. 563 (2010); Esther Lardent, *Making the Business Case for Pro Bono*, Pro Bono Institute Law Firm Pro Bono Project (2000), www2.nycbar.org/mp3/DoingWellByDoingGood/pbi_businesscase.pdf).
38 Taken from an interview between the authors and Claire Donse on 23 February 2021.

has been challenging. *Pro bono* provides lawyers an opportunity to meet their colleagues, not only within their own office but from a diverse array of practice groups and offices. While this has always been true, the internal connections that *pro bono* can foster within firms have been particularly important during the pandemic.

Angela Vigil, *pro bono* partner at Baker McKenzie, observed:

Pro bono is community. We miss seeing each other and attending meetings with practice groups and offices at a regional and global level, and that sense of community has been missing during this time. Pro bono has been soaring, including by laterals joining the firm who are reaching out to learn about pro bono opportunities.[39]

Pro bono has always brought us together in new ways, and that has never been more true than during the pandemic.

3.2 *Pro bono* provides professional development opportunities

Pro bono has always provided associates with meaningful opportunities to develop as lawyers, by offering opportunities and leadership roles that they otherwise may not have had on billable matters until they were more senior, if at all.[40] This trend has continued during the pandemic, and we expect it will remain a key aspect of our *pro bono* practice going forward.

In addition, there is a growing emphasis on including topics like cultural competence and humility, as well as trauma-informed counselling, as part of professional development. Training on these topics is important not only for our *pro bono* clients, many of whom have experienced trauma, but for all of our clients in an increasingly global and diverse business world.

3.3 *Pro bono* promotes wellness

Well-being within the legal profession has been a growing focus of the American Bar Association[41] as well as within law firms across

---

39 Taken from an interview between the authors and Angela Vigil on 9 March 2021.
40 See *Beyond Elite Law: Access to Civil Justice in America*, 622–24 (Samuel Estreicher and Joy Radice, eds., Cambridge University Press, 2016).
41 "Well-Being in the Legal Profession", American Bar Association (2021), www.americanbar.org/groups/lawyer_assistance/well-being-in-the-legal-profession/. See Grace Maral Burnett, Jacquelyn Palmer and Mindy Rattan, "Analysis: Lawyer Well-Being Critical During Pandemic", Bloomberg Law, 25 March 2020 ("Survey results show that large law firms have been leading the way in making changes in response to the lawyer well-being movement"); Georgetown Law Center on Ethics and the Legal Profession and Thomson Reuters Institute, *2021 Report on the State of the Legal Market*.

the country. Studies have shown that volunteering has a positive impact on well-being and mental health.[42] Helping others keeps us connected and offers a sense both of community and of larger purpose.[43] These connections, the ability to provide access to justice to those who might otherwise go without, and the opportunity to be a part of something larger than ourselves improves our overall outlook.[44] This has been especially true during the pandemic when most of us have been physically apart from our colleagues, extended family and friends. We have heard from many lawyers that assisting on a meaningful *pro bono* project, such as advancing racial justice, combating hunger, protecting the right to vote or helping those struggling to provide for their families, has been especially gratifying during a period when we all felt alone and helpless at times.

Dani Morrison, DLA Piper associate, recently reflected about her recent involvement in a voting rights case:

> *I cannot begin to express how honoured I feel to have been a part of this team, at this firm, while fulfilling our responsibility to protect the integrity of the democratic process during this moment in history. In one of the most polarising and tumultuous times in our nation's history we were able to defend the right to vote – not in support of a particular group, political agenda, or cause – but, as one, in the common defense of our fundamental right.*[45]

---

42 See Nancy Levit and Douglas O Linder, "Happy Law Students, Happy Lawyers", 58 *Syracuse L. Rev.* 351, 366 (2008) ("and doing good, which can lead to more lasting happiness, and a life with meaning. People who have a richer sense of happiness are … those who embrace a larger sense of civic engagement."); Anne M Brafford, "7 Reasons To Do Pro Bono Work", *Law360*, 21 March 2013, www.law360.com/articles/424004/7-reasons-to-do-pro-bono-work. See also Arianna Huffington, *Thrive*, 240–45, Harmony Books (2014).

43 See Paula Davis, "Money Doesn't Lead to Happiness in Law – Here Is What Does", *Forbes*, 8 October 2020, www.forbes.com/sites/pauladavislaack/2020/10/08/money-doesnt-lead-to-happiness-in-law--here-is-what-does/?sh=10dc36804c81 (noting Kennon Sheldon and Larry Krieger's study on lawyer motivation that "revealed that autonomy, belonging and competence were most strongly correlated with motivation and well-being – all of which have been called into sharper focus by the pandemic"). See also Daniel H Pink, *Drive – The Surprising Truth About What Motivates Us*, Riverhead Books (2009).

44 See Emily Drake and Todd Conner, "How Are We Managing Pandemic Stress?", Crain's Chicago Business, 10 February 2021, www.chicagobusiness.com/chicago-comes-back/how-are-we-managing-pandemic-stress ("I think about wellbeing as something requiring more connection – more about a sense of belonging, that basic fundamental need that is so hard to create but getting easier to measure").

45 Taken from an email communication between Dani Morrison and the authors on 10 April 2021.

Lawyers have also expressed that the firm's *pro bono* commitment made them feel better during a difficult time. Melissa Sampson, DLA Piper associate, noted:

This last year with the pandemic was rough, and we were busy. Pro bono gave our lawyers an opportunity to get involved in election protection or immigration work and to help people with so many of the problems they faced because of the economic downturn. Being able to help also helped us cope with the things happening around us that can feel overwhelming – and even if I couldn't take on a particular pro bono matter, knowing that the firm was engaged and helping made me feel good and hopeful.[46]

3.4 *Pro bono* and the growing focus on environmental, social and governance (ESG) strategy

ESG, often referred to as "doing well by doing good",[47] has increased in relevance and importance for companies and law firms during the pandemic and global crises.[48] *Pro bono* is an essential part of an ESG strategy for any law firm or legal department. There is an access to justice crisis in the US[49] and around the world.[50] In the US, we operate in a complicated legal system, and most litigants do not have a lawyer. The majority of people worldwide cannot afford to hire legal counsel, and legal aid organisations only have capacity to help a small percentage of those in need. The pandemic has exposed and increased inequality, and many believe that the access to justice gap has widened dramatically over the past year.[51]

As part of an integrated ESG strategy, *pro bono* contributions will likely continue to grow. ESG strategies often refer to the Sustainable

---

46 Taken from an email communication between Melissa Sampson and the authors on 12 April 2021.
47 See Andrew Cohen, "Will ESG Go MIA Amid COVID-19? Two Berkeley Law Experts Weigh In", *Berkley Law*, 29 April 2020, www.law.berkeley.edu/article/will-esg-go-mia-amid-covid-19-two-berkeley-law-experts-weigh-in/.
48 See E Leigh Dance and Anna Livia Mazzoni, "Six Essential ESG Lessons for General Counsel from COVID-19", Law.com Corporate Counsel, 7 December 2020, www.law.com/corpcounsel/2020/12/07/six-essential-esg-lessons-for-general-counsel-from-covid-19/.
49 See *Legal Services Corporation By The Numbers The Data Underlying Legal Aid Programs* at 2019 LSC By The Numbers.pdf | Powered by Box; www.lsc.gov.
50 It is estimated that at least 5.1 billion people around the world have legal needs that are not being met. See Access to Justice for All | World Justice Project, https://worldjusticeproject.org/world-justice-challenge-2021/access-justice-all.
51 See World Justice Project Policy Brief, *The Global Pandemic and the Global Justice Gap*, October 2020, https://worldjusticeproject.org/sites/default/files/documents/Global%20Justice%20Gap-11-02.pdf.

Development Goals (SDGs), 17 calls to action adopted by all United Nations member states in 2015 to address critical global challenges through 2030. For the first time, these universal goals include a focus on justice for all in Goal 16. *Pro bono* projects frequently align with and support the Sustainable Development Goals,[52] especially Goal 16.

Going forward, we will likely continue to see the intersection between ESG strategies and *pro bono* work. Jesse Medlong, Sustainability and ESG Lead for DLA Piper's Consumer Goods, Food and Retail Sector, explained:

Stakeholder capitalism – often used interchangeably with ESG – has emerged as a durable and transformative trend in global business. ESG is fundamentally reordering how businesses identify and address stakeholder impacts from their operations. For the legal industry, these stakeholder impacts include its monopoly over the levers of justice even as a historic crisis in access to justice continues to worsen. Pro bono is the profession's response. Any for-profit organisation that employs lawyers can use pro bono to help address the access to justice crisis. This is precisely how stakeholder capitalism is intended to work. And with its manifold benefits for business, pro bono resembles other ESG efforts that show what's good for stakeholders is often good for the bottom line, especially over the long term.[53]

4. Adapting *pro bono* to an increasingly global profession

The emergence of global law firms has been accompanied by the development of *pro bono* programmes that are equally global in scope and reach. A growing number of firms have full-time *pro bono* lawyers located in different countries and engage in *pro bono* projects in the multiple jurisdictions where their lawyers are based. In addition, some firms have expanded their *pro bono* focus to include projects in countries or regions where they might not have

---

52 See United Nations, Department of Economic and Social Affairs, "The 17 Goals", https://sdgs.un.org/goals.

53 Taken from an email communication between Jesse Medlong and the authors on 28 March 2021. See also Pilita Clark, "ESG Strategies Still Buoyant Despite COVID, Say In-House Lawyers", *Special Report Financial Times*, 15 June 2020, www.ft.com/content/6621918c-a3e8-11ea-a27c-b8aa85e36b7e; Andrew Cohen, "Will ESG Go MIA Amid COVID-19? Two Berkeley Law Experts Weigh In", Berkeley Law, 29 April 2020, www.law.berkeley.edu/article/will-esg-go-mia-amid-covid-19-two-berkeley-law-experts-weigh-in/.

a presence. This could include undertaking multi-jurisdictional comparative research projects, advising a non-profit organisation with a global footprint, assisting a government in a developing region on legislative reform or providing skills-based training to law students or practising lawyers in countries with limited access to resources.[54] The broadening of the geographic scope of *pro bono* programmes was well underway prior to the pandemic. Although the inability to travel during the pandemic has placed limitations on this type of work, creative use of technology has made some efforts to engage in *pro bono* across borders easier in ways that will likely be preserved moving forward.

4.1 New Perimeter

One example of a global approach to *pro bono* is New Perimeter, a non-profit affiliate DLA Piper created in 2005 to deliver long-term *pro bono* assistance in under-served regions around the world.[55] Through New Perimeter, teams of DLA Piper lawyers from across the firm's global offices work with charities, governments and academic institutions on projects to support access to justice, social and economic development, sound legal institutions and women's advancement. Many of the matters are focused in countries where DLA Piper does not have an office, and they frequently involve international travel. As the COVID-19 pandemic grounded flights, New Perimeter's full-time staff was forced to think creatively about how to continue to work on projects with a global reach without the ability to travel.

New Perimeter was able to transition some projects, particularly those providing training to build local capacity, to a remote format. For example, during the first year of the pandemic, DLA Piper lawyers, through New Perimeter, delivered online trainings to local lawyers and law students in Colombia, The Gambia, Kenya, Mexico, Laos, the Philippines, Rwanda, Tanzania, Uganda and Zambia. The trainings were originally scheduled to take place in-person in those countries. Although the participants missed out on the many benefits and cultural exchange that in-person interactions and travel bring, the remote format generated other benefits. It was much easier to

---

54 "Global Due Diligence Manual: Navigating the World of Pro bono", Pro bono Institute, www.probonoinst.org/wpps/wp-content/uploads/Global-Due-Diligence-Manual.pdf.
55 www.newperimeter.org.

recruit international teams of lawyers and to mobilise them quickly when they did not need to block off a full week of travel. It was also more cost effective. We will likely be more strategic in the future about incorporating remote visits and trainings into our projects, as opposed to travel being the default.

In addition to moving projects to a remote format, the New Perimeter team spent time thinking about how desk-based global research could be targeted, timely and impactful. We undertook multi-jurisdictional research projects related to the pandemic that provided information that was needed and likely to reach a broad audience. For example, collaborating with two major international organisations, a New Perimeter team researched and published a guide for legal services providers around the world on how to transition to remote legal work.[56] This was followed up by an online event that provided training on the guide and discussion among legal services providers from multiple regions. In addition, New Perimeter published a review of the global response to the rise in intimate partner violence during the pandemic.[57] We will likely increase our involvement in these types of projects moving forward.

4.2 DLA Piper's global *pro bono* team

DLA Piper has more than 15 full-time *pro bono* lawyers located around the world. In any given year, we are developing opportunities and managing projects resulting in over 200,000 hours of *pro bono* time contributed by the firm's lawyers across the globe. The use of remote technology has made it easier for the global team to communicate, collaborate and connect across borders and time zones.

In North America, for example, we can instantly log onto a video conference with our *pro bono* colleagues in Hong Kong and Australia to talk through issues related to a project in Southeast Asia. That type of communication not only makes it easier to successfully execute our projects, but it promotes solidarity among a far-flung team. Before the pandemic, the North American *pro bono* team, which has members across the US, had a weekly conference call. Now, we see each other's faces on our computer screens at least once a week and often several times a day. We can also attend

---

[56] See New Perimeter, DLA Piper LLP (US), www.newperimeter.com/our-work/legal-institutions/assisting-legal-services-providers-to-work-remotely.html.

[57] See New Perimeter, DLA Piper LLP (US), www.newperimeter.com/our-work/access-to-justice/responding-to-intimate-partner-violence.html.

conferences and webinars every week that are being hosted around the world.[58]

In addition, the increased use of remote technology to carry out *pro bono* legal services has meant that it has been easier for the team to include participating lawyers from diverse regions in *pro bono* matters.

5. Looking to the future

It is a wonderful aspect of our human nature to ask what we can do to help in times of crisis. That is certainly what we saw during the pandemic, and what we know we will see again when crises inevitably strike in the future.

We have an opportunity, now, to emerge from the crisis better than before. We will bring with us new approaches to *pro bono* that remote technology has offered, and continue to collaborate in new ways, all with the goal of serving even more clients than we could before.

As always, we must listen to and learn from those who understand the evolving needs of our communities and remain vigilant, because the problems caused by the pandemic will not just disappear. Bryan Stevenson, in his book *Just Mercy*, tells how his grandmother taught him that: "You can't understand most of the important things from a distance. You have to get close."[59] The *pro bono* needs in our communities were present before the pandemic – the pandemic has only worsened and increased those needs. We must continue to keep those needs in our hearts and minds as we emerge from the pandemic and into a new world.

---

[58] While working and connecting remotely with so many people on such a regular basis is wonderful and has many benefits, it can also be tiring and overwhelming. We will no doubt come back to a balance of more phone calls, and intentional decision making on what conferences, webinars and videos to attend and watch in any given week. See Jeremy N Bailenson, "Nonverbal Overload: A Theoretical Argument for the Causes of Zoom Fatigue", *Technology, Mind and Behavior*, 23 February 2021; Hannah Roberts, "Zoom and Gloom: Lawyers Getting Fatigue from Endless Video Calls", Bloomberg Law, 22 July 2020.

[59] Bryan Stevenson, *Just Mercy: A story of justice and redemption*, Spiegel & Grau, 2014, p14.

How firms are leveraging technology and data to drive strategy, efficiency and client relationships

David Cunningham
Reed Smith

1. Introduction

The work-from-home mandate of 2020 forced the immediate adoption of some technologies, lowered long-held resistance and opened the legal market to a faster pace of tech-driven progress.

Until 2020, the progressive NewLaw label was applied only to newly formed law companies[1] and the Big 4 because of their intrinsic use of technology, data and processes. Now, the adoption rate of technology and data-driven business leadership (called legal operations or 'legal ops') in legal departments and law firms is surging forward. NewLaw can now reflect leadership style rather than how recently the business was founded.

This chapter addresses some of the areas where technology supports transformational change in the business and practice of law. Across these areas, several themes are evident.

- With work-from-home, office hoteling and video meetings the long-term norms, even complex transactions rely on technology to get parties together.
- Leaders who use metrics to evaluate law firms' performance are changing the nature of how legal services are selected, priced and valued.
- The business models of legal departments, law firms, law companies and the Big 4 are blurring and integrating. Good execution of the business model can be as important as the quality of the legal services.

---

1   The term 'law company' is used in this chapter, although some prefer the term 'alternative legal service provider' or 'ALSP'. In either case, the term refers to companies providing legal-oriented services to legal departments that are not traditional law firms practising law. These services can include e-discovery, document review, due diligence, consulting and other areas.

- Rather than keeping technology solutions internal, firms are seeking a competitive edge by providing their solutions directly to clients, which requires engagement with client leadership beyond the classic partner-only relationship.

The following sections provide high-level perspectives of technologies that illustrate these themes.

2. Technology stands in for the office

2.1 Current state

Working outside the office was the most prominent and fastest change caused by the pandemic. When the offices were suddenly not available, technology became the only way for a firm to deliver clients and recruits its brand experience. A firm's prowess in providing an online experience is now fundamental to its identity and perception of quality.

The pandemic forced firms to evolve how they leveraged technology throughout the year. In realising the duration of work-from-home needs, many firms invested in becoming all-mobile, software workflows replaced paper-based processes like the review of pre-bills, and few partners were still using traditional office phones.

2.2 What's accelerating

- *'Virtual event platform' services:* Firms had to adopt technology to become professional online event organisers. Virtual event software allows for keynotes, workshops, concurrent events, attendee collaboration, role-based experiences and sophisticated sign-up experiences and analytics.
- *Recruiting:* Associate recruiting was a big hero of the transition. Firms saved most of their historical travel costs while still recruiting to their expectations.
- *Collaboration:* Group chat platforms struggled to gain traction in law firms for years until the pandemic and then became ubiquitous overnight.
- *Hoteling and hybrid meetings:* For many firms, hoteling has become the new assumed standard for post-pandemic planning. It is a welcomed change helping to reduce real estate costs once the market recovers, although another area where technology must adapt. Attendees outside a conference room should have an experience as visual and collaborative as attendees inside the room. Long video shots down a

conference table will not be acceptable. Multiple cameras and on-table camera systems, in some situations, will be necessary to make hybrid meetings more interactive and personal.
- *Matter teams working from anywhere:* Large tech companies have already begun to release employees from previous geographic expectations for working from an office. Regardless of whether law firms maintain or relax geographic expectations for their lawyers and staff, without consideration for local bar requirements, parties involved in a matter may not be in an office building and may not be willing to come to the firm's office building. Whether for daily online discussions or completing complex transactions, software-based collaboration systems are gaining traction as to where work gets done.

3. Legal ops metrics and dashboards

3.1 Current state

Over the last five to 10 years, legal departments have been growing their sophistication in measuring their outside counsel's performance. Progressive legal departments are investing in legal operational ('legal ops' is the common shorthand) leadership roles, technology and metrics to provide more business insights to their general counsels. However, many law firms remain unaware of how their clients measure their performance beyond the bills getting paid. Although law firms have been increasing their partner dashboards' sophistication, these dashboards focus on financial metrics.

3.2 What's accelerating

Legal departments track billing rates, spend, and budgets and dozens of non-financial matter aspects as outside counsel metrics. Examples of other metrics include:
- ratios of work done in-house to work done by outside counsel;
- diversity of the law firm; involvement of diverse lawyers in firm leadership roles;
- diversity of the leaders and timekeepers of the matter teams;
- time to complete a matter;
- the complexity of a matter;
- strategic vs commodity work;
- the risk associated with the matter;
- billing compliance and timeliness;
- budget and scope accuracy;

- value of the results of the matter; and
- after-matter survey feedback, which can focus on perceptions of quality, responsiveness, expertise, value adds, project management, and other factors.

These departments may have three types of tools to support their needs for data-driven decisions.
- *Request for proposal (RFP) software:* Software to help automate the creation and sending of RFPs and then comparing responses from outside counsel.
- *Matter management:* Software to open and manage matters, budgets, and spend.
- *Spend analytics:* Software that uses artificial intelligence to analyse billing data for further efficiencies and find time entries that are out of compliance with Outside Counsel Guidelines.

Law companies, including the Big 4 legal business services, have similar expectations to the legal departments for legal operations metrics and dashboards and their use of underlying software to manage matters.

Therefore, the highest amount of transformation is still to come as more law firms turn towards metrics in various ways.
- *Managed services:* As dozens of law firms launch their own managed legal services businesses (generally focused on e-discovery), whether in-house, as a 'captive business', or a spun-off business, they are more likely to measure their performance.
- *Legal ops leaders:* A transformative trend in law firms is hiring or promoting legal operational leadership who directly focus on the client's perspective and apply business principles to the legal practices.
- *Client's metrics:* Some firms, through legal ops leaders or another leadership trend – client service leaders – explicitly focus on understanding the metrics tracked by their customers and prospective customers.

The legal market is maturing by working towards data-driven decisions and understanding the importance of measuring and improving performance. These insights, benchmarked over time, will provide the transparency firm leaders need to improve the business and practice of law.

4. Data-driven outside counsel selection

4.1 Current state

The processes of creating and responding to RFPs are still generally low-tech and hugely time-consuming on both sides of the buying decision. Data-driven technologies in law firms and legal departments are gaining acceptance, and sweeping changes are likely in the longer term.

4.2 What's accelerating

Within legal departments, two key areas are growing in use.

- *RFP automation and analysis:* RFP automation software allows the legal department to define the scope, cost and timing expectations and provide outside counsel with this information on which to bid. The law firms can submit their responses through the same software rather than provide glossy PDFs. Department gains a simpler, more visual and more comparable review process. The software can show RFP responses side-by-side and rate and rank the responses from each firm. Departments use these systems for existing panel firms, so each firm's expertise and overall relationship guidelines are already known.
- *Provider matching service:* Other technology solutions exist to take a different approach – working to match a department to pre-evaluated providers. These replace rather than streamline an RFP process. Corporate legal departments in need of help can use such a service to compose scope and expectations as a simple Boolean-type request rather than a lengthy RFP. Both the tech provider and the legal department assess pre-vetted attorneys' responses and select who will win the work. This approach is certainly the exception rather than the norm and is not fit for many types of work, but this type of matching is similar to trends in other industries.

Law firms may not always appreciate further automation of legal buying decisions. Still, they should recognise that progressive legal departments are already making data-driven buying decisions. Law firms generally do not understand how they look to departments using internal metrics or RFP analysis services. Fortunately, many departments are willing to share this information if a law firm partner or leader asks to understand it.

It is also common for firms to leverage RFP response drafting software. These systems are focused on the assembly of pre-written expertise and biographical material. However, the most advanced software also makes experience information available within a firm automatically by continuously updating itself with data from the firm's accounting, marketing, conflicts and HR systems.

5. Pricing and resourcing analysis

5.1 Current state

Like the Outside Counsel Selection section above, the scoping and pricing of matters has evolved to become more sophisticated and data-driven. However, there are still significant capabilities to be improved over time.

- Legal departments have software to evaluate the value of a matter, and law firms have software to determine their fees and costs, but these systems rarely share information.
- Pricing analysis software used by law firm Pricing Teams is rarely in the hands of the partners responsible for the matters.
- Partners generally allocate timekeepers to matters without the support of information to identify firmwide industry experience, subject matter experience, relationships, availability, diversity and other factors.

5.2 What's accelerating

The ongoing evolution of the pricing and matter staffing functions may be some of the most intriguing on the business side of law practices. Innovations can including the following.

- Providing partners with direct access to scoping, pricing and staffing software to draft matter plans and budgets (with advanced support from the Pricing Team).
- Today, some firms utilise standalone resource management (eg, work allocation) systems. Partners, or perhaps only staffing partners, can identify skills, availability, an associate's desired areas of involvement, diversity and other attributes.
- Legal departments track an array of information about matters, such as rates and total cost expectations, complexity, timing needs, priority, risk levels, diversity expectations and business unit allocations. It is feasible that legal departments provide this information to law firms so that the law firm's budgeting system considers this information when planning and pricing a matter.

With the build-up of data in both law firms and legal departments, it seems inevitable that AI-based systems will be applied in the coming years to provide firm and team recommendations based on all the attributes previously mentioned. Such insights cannot replace a partner's expertise or the value of a long-running relationship but can provide complementary insights in a fast-moving market.

6. Automated time entry

6.1 Current state

Few processes have changed as little as time entry in law firms. Ironically, the processes that could speed and improve the collection of fees – time entry, pre-bill review, billing and collections – have made only incremental improvements at large firms over the past decade. So, it is especially compelling when innovation in time entry becomes available.

6.2 What's accelerating

Automated time entry provides two elements that keep a timekeeper from facing a blank timesheet at the end of the day. It monitors a timekeeper's activities in critical systems, notably word processing, document management, email, research, work websites and some phone activities. The more advanced systems use AI to apply client/matter codes automatically, determine research areas, identify sections of documents being edited and understand the work context. As a result, the system drafts time entries throughout the day with no effort on behalf of the timekeeper. The timekeeper's role is to review these draft time entries, assumedly at the end of each day, to revise, if necessary, and approve.

For those willing to overcome the discomfort of a system monitoring their activities, the results are worthwhile and improving over time. These systems are still maturing but are on track to:
- create reasonably accurate narratives;
- assign reasonably accurate matter and task codes;
- establish more specific time allocations and less 'block billing' than a timekeeper may normally type manually; and
- provide the same or incrementally more (ie, higher accuracy) total time than a timekeeper would remember on their own.

Having a day's worth of entries to tweak rather than remember from scratch (or spend time scanning email, documents and calendars) can help timekeepers meet daily time entry expectations. More specific and granular time entries should show value down the road as firms evaluate the impact on billing and collections. These systems may find more billable time but, with the prevalence of fixed and alternative fee arrangements, the most significant value to a firm can be the time saved by each timekeeper and the detailed collections of time data from which the firm can analyse its efficiency. When a firm knows everything that is happening with its timekeepers in near real-time, it creates a long-term asset to assess matter staffing, experience management, training needs, hiring needs and financial planning.

7. Billing analysis

7.1 Current state
The analysis of time narratives and bills is becoming an arms race – law firms and legal departments are both doing it, but with different weapons and different objectives in mind. The more diligent and informed party can impact millions of dollars to their bottom line. But, there are still inconsistencies, inefficiencies and duplications of effort in the market, which are lost opportunities for all involved.

7.2 What's accelerating
In law firms, the pre-bill review process is typically a senior partner's assessment of write-offs and discounts. While this is still the dominant protocol (likely transitioned from paper to electronic workflow by the pandemic, if not well before), many firms have added one or both additional automated review capabilities.

- *Time entry analytics:* This type of AI-enabled software automatically reviews time narratives and time allocations to identify patterns, categorise phases and tasks, break down block billing, and perform other analyses, primarily for budgeting and profitability insights.
- *Outside Counsel Guidelines (OCG) compliance software:* Many of the expectations outlined in Outside Counsel Guidelines documentation affect billing rules. Managing these rules across hundreds of clients and millions of time entries is challenging, and thus software is available to manage compliance with OCGs proactively. Over time, these tools plan to provide alerts at both the entry of time and the review of bills to recognise deviations from compliance.

Either of the above systems should help alert a firm to issues that would later cause a client to push back on bills that are out-of-compliance or deviate from their value expectations. This analysis can save months-long delays on getting bills paid and allow a firm to address compliance and value issues before providing invoices.

But focusing only on the improvement of collections is a bit short-sighted. The longer-term value realises the client's perceptions of the bills since legal departments are doing their own "spend analysis". Each law firm should assume that clients use AI to scrutinise every word and number on their bills for compliance, value and other metrics, and then benchmark them against other firms. Increasing realisation by 3% is a positive result for a firm but could fail to meet general counsel expectations due to other intrinsic measures of success. This failure may result in falling substantially lower on a department's preferred provider chart due to the general counsel's measurement of efficiency and value of outside counsel.

8. Experience and relationship analytics

8.1 Current state

Technology that identifies experience and relationship information across a firm can be a strategic differentiator, at least for large firms. There were no common third-party experience management systems 10 years ago, and now the majority of the Am Law 200 law firms have installed such a system.

It is easy to understand the need. At any given time, a firm may have hundreds of lawyers who have worked on thousands of matters across companies, industries, geographies and practices. And this experience evolves from every angle – new matters are opened each day, lateral partners join the firm with their own 20 years of experience, and other lawyers are leaving the firm. And every matter has its own universe of co-counsel, opposing counsel, banks and other companies involved in transactions. Experience management systems store all of this information and make it searchable. Equally valuable is tracking relationships over time as friends take leadership roles in companies or as lawyers change firms, become general counsels, or become judges.

8.2 What's accelerating

For most firms, experience management systems remain a behind-the-scenes system for the marketing team to search to address RFP or questions from partners. Most partners in firms do not have direct access to this information. This model is already transforming and will evolve more quickly in the coming years. The goal, already in sight for some, is two-fold.

- A search or voice-friendly query provides a partner with an instant profile of a person or company, so they have this information when the phone rings, when they are running out for a meeting or perhaps even sitting at dinner.
- A proactive prompt about a person or company with information that the lawyer or other professional didn't realise they needed to know. Examples can include a lateral partner who started yesterday and knows a key person at a company to which they are marketing or a newly opened matter for an industry in which they have experience.

There are significant hurdles before a firm can achieve practical experience and relationship analytics. Most notably, it can take years to have good quality data on which to search. Sources of this information can be unstructured (email, documents, marketing data), structured (conflicts, docketing), third party (relationship and court databases), *ad hoc* (spreadsheets and contact lists maintained by individual lawyers) and well-intentioned but perhaps not well-maintained collections of data (the firm's customer relationship management (CRM) or various practice-specific databases).

It is challenging to compel busy timekeepers to write down their experiences and relationships. Fortunately, improvements have happened at the data level as well. Systems can now automatically scan email and calendars to identify relationship patterns, correlate information across the firm's data sources, bring together outside sources, track timekeeper activity during the day and more. These automated data collection systems are the key to having real-time, complete and meaningful data.

9. Practice workflow, automation and collaboration

9.1 Current state
AI may get headlines, but streamlining lawyers' everyday activities can be among the most useful technologies gaining adoption in law firms. It is not cutting-edge technology but can be transformative to the efficiency of a timekeeper and a firm.

It is interesting to contrast legal departments to larger law firms in this regard. Over 5,000 legal departments are customers of the most prominent matter management and workflow vendors in the market. Smaller law firms have all-in-one matter management software available to them, addressing the opening and status tracking of matters, customer contact management, billing and other processes.

However, it is rare for larger firms to track matters with software. Matter management or project management systems can be seen as hindrances to the fast-paced, constantly changing nature of legal work, especially for litigators. And that has been understandable since standard project management systems have only offered a blank slate for users to type in and maintain task information manually.

9.2 What's accelerating

New practice-specific matter management systems are now gaining adoption, notably in larger firms. These systems do not generally focus on capturing and managing every aspect of a matter. Instead, they address the inefficiencies of how the work usually gets done. An M&A transaction is a useful case study. A complicated transaction has multiple companies, banks, insurers, lawyers and other experts, dozens of documents in numerous waves of redlined versions, and sets of signatories. Handling a complex transaction via email and without being in the same conference room is a challenge and potentially confusing. Streamlining this work, organising the content and ensuring all parties are on the same page is an excellent use of matter management or at least extranet technology.

Three different approaches are evolving through acquisitions by leading software companies.
- *Extranets:* Extranets are the traditional and most common approach, whereby documents are uploaded to a shared repository and tracked there to completion.
- *Practice automation and collaboration:* Practice-specific software has some unique assets. It can act as a specialised matter management system from the beginning of matters and provide collaboration capabilities when all parties need to come together.
- *Shared matter management:* New systems are emerging that allow all the parties to use software of their choice (document management, collaboration, etc) in their own businesses but

then work together with all shared matter parties during transactions, using the shared matter management system as an inter-company bridge with a common set of dashboards.

10. Managing contract lifecycles

10.1 Current state
The management of a contract through its stages, from initial drafting to final signatures, has become one of the hottest tech investment areas. Contract lifecycle management (CLM) software can provide efficiencies in review and approvals and tracking commitments after the signatures are complete. CLM software in legal departments is still in the early stages and is generally not yet a focus for law firms.

10.2 What's accelerating
CLM software can lighten the burden on in-house lawyers currently managing the workflows via email and tracking down status. And can set off a change in expectations for law firms to participate in the workflow rather than share via email or cloud storage sites. And it can shift some control to the party who licenses the CLM software (whether department or firm) since it provides a treasure trove of ongoing contract knowledge.

But workflow automation is just the beginning. Two other aspects of contract management are emerging.
- *Contract negotiation:* A critical bottleneck in completing contracts is the cycle of negotiations across parties. AI-enabled software exists that can help bridge gaps, identify compromises and recommend paths forward.
- *Contract as data:* As these tools break contracts down from long free-form narrative documents into distinct assets (eg, clauses, timelines, commitments) to be managed, it becomes foreseeable that contracts become another collection of data. The evolution from a document to a database of clauses is not around the corner, but CLM and AI-enabled negotiations are certainly fuelling the change.

11. Client solutions and no-code platforms

11.1 Current state
Law firms are no longer dependent on IT to develop software. The IT departments of law firms did not create most custom software

solutions offered to clients by firms. Similarly, IT departments are not who win most hackathons. Solutions that allow the creation of software without manual programming, called 'no-code' platforms, are the difference in many of the cases. No-code solutions will not replace sophisticated programmed software and casual software creators will not replace professional developers. But, for many purposes, quickly developed solutions are meaningful and engaging. They can make the difference between hitting or missing an opportunity in the market.

11.2 What's accelerating

These no-code platforms are far from new, so their availability is no longer transformational. But the growth in the number of law companies, innovation leaders, law firm-supported consulting businesses, and legal ops leaders creates a substantially larger base of people identifying needs in the market to which they can be applied. So, the market's real changes are the sources, precision and pace of software solutions now available from law firms. They also allow rapid prototyping without great hassle for any person or start-up.

Fortunately, no-code development also has great use for professional developers in or outside the IT department. Notably, it is a common approach for enhancing the Microsoft Teams environments many firms customise to be their workspaces.

12. Chatbots and other natural interfaces

12.1 Current state

In some ways, chatbots seem to have already peaked. Pop-up windows that offer to help answer questions when no human is available can be so simplistic that they are more irritating than helpful. But, done well, in a practice-specific context to solve a targeted problem, chatbots can offer comfortable dialogue to learn quickly from an expert.

12.2 What's accelerating

Combined with or part of no-code and workflow solutions, chatbots can be created when a topic is hot in the market and then get more advanced over time. It is easy to see how an always-on chatbot can help a lawyer or practice suddenly scale up to address hot topics. During such situations, lawyers can consider if their time is better spent writing an article or creating a chatbot interface to market their expertise.

13. **Conclusion**

This chapter covers only a small number of technology changes happening in the legal market. And that represents one of the biggest challenges. While new technology is indeed capable of delivering efficiencies and insights and legal providers are, in general, more open to acquiring technology, timekeepers are struggling with all the change expected of them. Technology has to make pivotal, not just incremental, improvements to be worthy of the time it takes to stop, learn and adopt all these new ways of working.

COVID-19's impact on lawyer innovation and decision making

Randall Kiser
DecisionSet®

1. Introduction

Law firm leaders generally underestimated the magnitude, duration and impact of the COVID-19 pandemic. Like other experienced but untrained decision makers, many law firm leaders were excessively optimistic about their firms' prospects. Affected by the recency and availability biases, they overweighted recent years of increasing revenue and profits per partner and, influenced by the planning fallacy and the inside view, they underestimated the pandemic's persistency.[1]

Law firm leaders and executives surveyed in May 2020 expected the economy and the workforce to "return to full operations" within 4.1 months. In September, four months later, the total number of COVID-19 deaths in the United States had reached 206,882, only one-half of the total COVID-19 deaths reported by 23 January 2021.[2] The surveyed law firm leaders expected their own firms to "return to full operations in a range of five- to eight-months with the average landing at 6.7".[3] Not a single surveyed leader anticipated a return to normal operations "more than 10 months out".[4] If the law firm leaders had been reliable forecasters, the COVID-19 pandemic would have been a minor blip on the chart of law firm operations and performance, and you probably would not be reading this book.

---

1   See Daniel Kahneman, *Thinking Fast and Slow*, Farrar, Straus and Giroux, 2011.
2   This data is derived from the University of Washington's Institute for Health Metrics and Evaluation (HME). It is available at https://COVID19.healthdata.org/.
3   The Mad Clientist, "Clients Expect Full Return in 8 Months, Law Firms 6", BTI Consulting Group, 20 May 2020, https://bticonsulting.com/themadclientist/clients-expect-full-return-in-8-months-law-firms-6.
4   *Ibid.*

To gain a better understanding of the long-term effects of the COVID-19 pandemic on law firms, this chapter addresses three questions.

1. Do law firms and other organisations become more innovative in crises like the COVID-19 pandemic?
2. How will the COVID-19 pandemic affect the quality of decision making by law firm leaders and attorneys?
3. Will the public health response to COVID-19 in the United States and the United Kingdom change the location of the world's major conflict resolution centres?

Before addressing those questions, this chapter provides a critical perspective by describing the pandemic's financial impact on law firms and trends in US legal services trade balances.

2. COVID-19's financial impact

2.1 Law firm financial performance in 2020

In 2020, profits per equity partner (PEP) in Am Law 200 firms are projected to increase by more than 15%.[5] Demand for their legal services, however, declined by 2.9%, as measured by billable hours. This decline in demand follows 12 years of declining or flat demand growth and was accompanied by a 3.7% drop in associate attorney productivity.[6]

Magic Circle firms did not achieve similar increases in profitability. Net profit at Freshfields Bruckhaus Deringer, for instance, was £685 million, slightly below the prior year's net profit of £688 million, and PEP was £1.82 million, a decrease from £1.84 million.[7] At Allen & Overy, another Magic Circle bellwether, profit decreased by 2.5%, and

---

[5] Georgetown Law Center on Ethics and the Legal Profession & Thomson Reuters Institute (2021), *2021 Report on the State of the Legal Market* (p11); Hugh A Simons and Joe Blackwood, "The Lessons and Implications of Big Law's Stunning 2020 Profitability", *The American Lawyer*, 25 January 2021, www.law.com/americanlawyer/2021/01/25/the-lessons-and-implications-of-big-laws-stunning-2020-profitability/.

[6] Dan Packel, "Most Big Firms Are Increasing Revenue, But Performance Gap Steadily Grows", *The American Lawyer*, 2 December 2020, www.law.com/americanlawyer/2020/12/02/most-big-firms-are-increasing-revenue-but-performance-gap-steadily-grows/; Georgetown Law Center on Ethics and the Legal Profession & Thomson Reuters Institute (2020), *2020 report on the state of the legal market* (p4).

[7] Ben Rigby, "Freshfields' Profits Remain Stable as Magic Circle Firm Pushes Ahead with US Expansion", *The Global Legal Post*, 23 July 2020, www.globallegalpost.com/big-stories/freshfields-profits-remain-stable-as-magic-circle-firm-pushes-ahead-with-us-expansion-86050054/.

PEP fell by 1.7% to £1.63 million.[8] The performance of Magic Circle firms, however, must be placed in a broader economic context: gross domestic product in the United Kingdom plummeted by 9.9% in 2020. The US economy contracted by 3.5%.[9]

The profitability of US law firms in 2020 was largely dependent on pedestrian measures displayed earlier in the Great Recession. Faced with declining demand and productivity, law firms turned to the usual suspects to goose profitability: expenses, employees and rates. Expenses were cut by 6% from Q2 2020 to Q4 2020, attorney headcount decreased by 4%, and rates increased by 5%. "The lion's share of firms' revenue increases," states *The American Lawyer* journalist Dan Packel, "stemmed from rate increases."[10] Some 73% of law firm leaders intend to impose another round of rate increases in 2021.[11]

Apart from rate increases, the efforts to increase profits per equity partner are attributable to simple changes in operations: "Firms across the industry have told us that they now require their lawyers to enter time on a daily basis," states Gretta Rusanow, the Managing Director of Citi Private Bank's Advisory Services Law Firm Group. "Recorded time is subsequently reviewed on a weekly basis."[12] Law firm partners also increased their scrutiny of client payments and decreased their tolerance of delinquent accounts. "The focus on billing and collections has probably been the most common trend we have seen across the industry," states Rusanow.[13]

Law firms' financial performance in 2020 has been hailed as "a tribute to the innovation and resiliency of law firms and their leaders".[14] This is peculiar because, outside of the legal services industry, price increases, expense reductions, layoffs and timely billing and collection practices generally are not considered to be innovations or signs of resilience. Although law firms point to the

---

8	Rose Walker, "Allen & Overy Posts Drop in Profits and PEP", *Law.com*, 16 July 2020, www.law.com/international-edition/2020/07/16/allen-overy-posts-drop-in-profits-and-pep/.
9	Jason Douglas and Paul Hannon, "UK Economy Suffers Biggest Slump in 300 Years Amid COVID-19 Lockdowns", *The Wall Street Journal*, 12 February 2021, www.wsj.com/articles/u-k-economy-suffers-biggest-slump-in-300-years-amid-covid-19-lockdowns-11613118912.
10	Packel, *supra* note 6.
11	Thomson Reuters (2020), *2020 Law Firm Business Leaders Report* (p12).
12	Citi Private Bank and Hildebrandt Consulting LLC, *2021 Client Advisory*, p9.
13	*Ibid*.
14	Thomson Reuters, "2021 Report on the State of the Legal Market: An 'Inflection Point' for Law Firms", 12 January 2021, www.legalexecutiveinstitute.com/state-of-the-legal-market-2021/.

"seamless" transition to remote work as an innovation, this, too, is neither a substantive change nor an innovation. Most professionals in other domains worked remotely for at least half of every week before the COVID-19 pandemic, indicating that innovations acclaimed in law firms are sometimes commonplace in other professions.[15]

The shift to remote working complements many attorneys' personalities. Attorneys tend to prize autonomy and their personality profiles, in general, are more consistent with individual contributors than group collaborators and leaders.[16] Many attorneys have been working remotely at their law firm's offices for years, and the shift to their homes is more corporeal than psychological. If attorney personalities were incompatible with remote work, the abrupt transition from the law firm office to the home office would not have been as seamless as law firms report.

2.2 Legal services trade balances

Many Big Law firms seem to assume that the declines in domestic demand can be offset by international demand and that US firms will always be the predominant international players. Although US firms now capture about 50% of the global market, that share may well decrease due to competition from European and UK firms, presently holding 25% of international market share, Asia-Pacific firms, garnering a 12–15% share, and other increasingly nimble, responsive law firms.[17] Under the Trump presidency, the US also has sustained major reputational damage in international markets, and the negative financial effects resulting from that diminished reputation may be severe and prolonged.

It is difficult to understand why US law firms expect to maintain hegemony in international legal markets. This confidence, in part, may be based on the historical record of US trade surpluses in services. As shown by Figure 1, the balance in services had grown for 15 years, but it started a serious decline in 2018 when President Trump's America First policy manifested as America Burst in the international services context.

---

15 Danielle Braff, "Thanks to the COVID-19 Pandemic, Law Firms Are Starting to Embrace Virtual Offices – But Will it Last?", *ABA Journal*, 1 February 2021, www.abajournal.com/magazine/article/thanks-to-the-covid-19-pandemic-law-firms-are-starting-to-embrace-virtual-officesbut-will-it-last.
16 See Randall Kiser, *Soft Skills for the Effective Lawyer*, Cambridge University Press, 2017, pp62–67.
17 Paul Hodkinson, "Which Law Firms Best Reflect the Global Marketplace?", *The American Lawyer*, 13 February 2020.

Reliance on historical trade surpluses in all services also is misplaced because the trends in professional and business services are unfavourable to US law firms. When professional and business services are separated from all services, it becomes evident that US exports of professional and business services peaked in 2019. As shown by Figure 2, US firms are not increasing their share of the international market in professional and business services, and

Figure 1. Balance on services, millions of dollars, quarterly, seasonally adjusted (IEABCS)

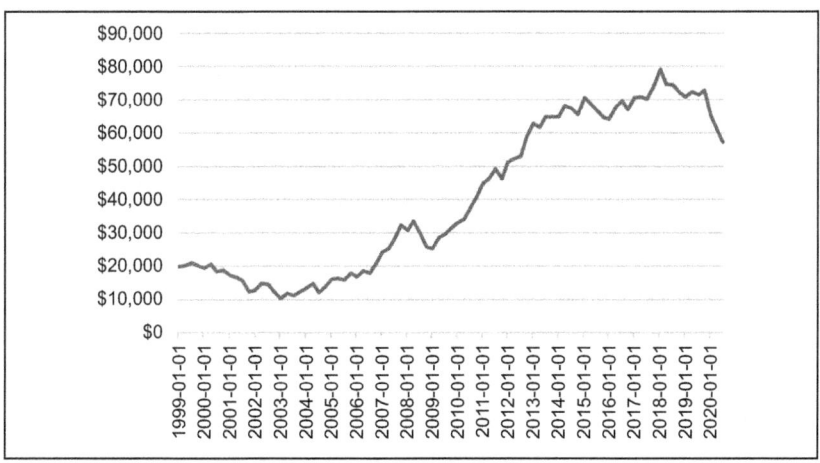

Source: Author's creation based on US Bureau of Economic Analysis. Federal Reserve Bank of St. Louis.

Figure 2. US import/export trends in business/professional services, 2018–2020 (in millions of dollars)

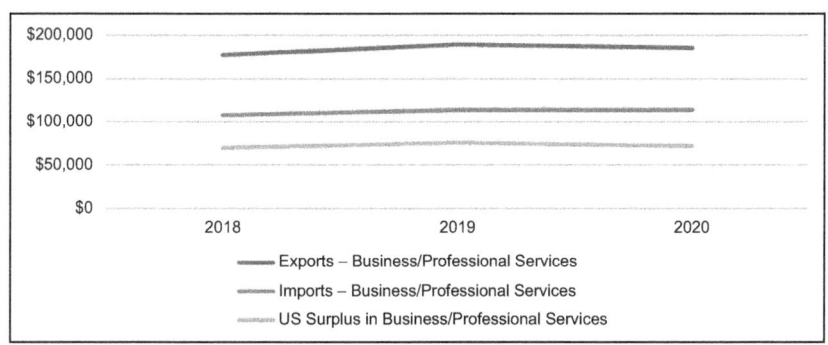

Source: Author's creation based on US Bureau of Economic Analysis.

Figure 3. US import/export trends in all services, 2017–2020 (United Kingdom only, in millions of dollars)

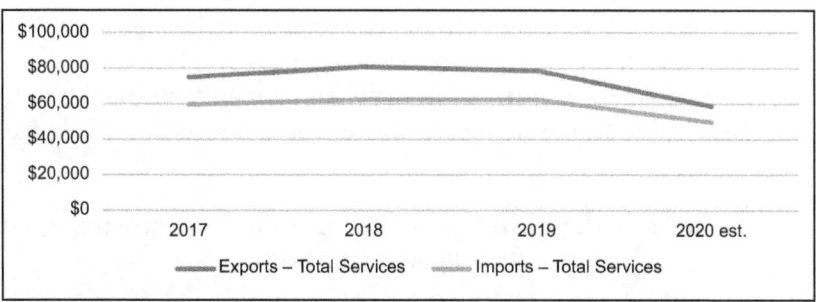

Source: Author's creation based on US Bureau of Economic Analysis.

they are unlikely to gain market share, especially considering the increasingly negative perception of the US in the 2016–2020 period.

The outlook for US firms exporting services to the United Kingdom is clouded. As shown by Figure 3, the US has a trade surplus with the United Kingdom in services, but the amount of this surplus is steadily dwindling.

The takeaway from the international services data is that US law firms may be overly confident about their international market share, and future financial dislocations resulting from the COVID-19 crisis probably will not be offset by revenue from non-US sources. Between 2008 and 2019, the percentage of international lawyers in Am Law 50 firms grew from 24% to 35%.[18] This expansion of international offices has been a "drag on firm-average profitability" and seems to overlook the reality that international clients may "have no particular incentive to use a newly grown US firm whose name has no brand resonance".[19] The lack of brand resonance is exacerbated by a more conservative approach to legal expenditures in the global market: "US companies spend nearly twice as much of their revenue on legal services as the global average."[20]

3. Innovation in crises

The early stages of crises provoke optimistic predictions of imminent change and innovation. These predictions stem from the

---

[18] Hugh A Simons and Nicholas Bruch, "Big Law's International Tilt Has Gone Too Far: A Restructuring Beckons", *The American Lawyer*, 23 April 2019, www.law.com/americanlawyer/2019/04/23/big-laws-international-tilt-has-gone-too-far-a-restructuring-beckons/.

[19] *Ibid*.

[20] Paul Hodkinson, "Which Law Firms Best Reflect the Global Marketplace?" *The American Lawyer*, 13 February 2020.

conviction that "necessity is the mother of invention and driving change is much easier in times of adversity than times of plenty", as expressed by Bill Mooz, a Senior Fellow at the Silicon Flatirons research centre.[21] "Logic dictates," Mooz asserts, "that the even greater adversity of the coronavirus calamity will produce an even greater wave of change."[22]

Although logic dictates that innovation should expand in crises, people are not logical, and innovation does not reliably emerge from crises. The acute needs and sense of urgency evident in crises do not result in a commensurate level of innovation. More often, crises simply generate anxiety, reduce creativity and reinforce old, maladaptive behaviour patterns. Necessity, in theory, is the mother of invention, but the perception of necessity, in reality, scares people and stifles innovation.

In June 2020, McKinsey & Company surveyed executives in 200 organisations ranging from financial services companies to industrial manufacturers. McKinsey found that the COVID-19 crisis had stalled and sometimes terminated innovation efforts:

Executives must weigh cutting costs, driving productivity, and implementing safety measures against supporting innovation-led growth. Unsurprisingly, investments in innovation are suffering. The executives in our survey strongly believe that they will return to innovation-related initiatives once the world has stabilized, the core business is secure, and the path forward is clearer. However, only a quarter reported that capturing new growth was a top priority (first- or second-order) today, compared to roughly 60% before the crisis hit. [exhibit]. This decline in focus on innovation is evident across every industry we surveyed; the sole exception is pharmaceuticals and medical products, where we see an almost 30-percent increase in the immediate focus on innovation.[23]

Making seemingly short-sighted decisions, the surveyed executives reported that they are "deprioritizing innovation to concentrate on four things: shoring up their core business, pursuing

---

21 Bill Mooz, "Will the coronavirus calamity lead to the next wave in legal innovation?", *Legal Evolution*, 19 April 2020, www.legalevolution.org/2020/04/will-the-coronavirus-calamity-lead-to-the-next-wave-in-legal-innovation-148/.
22 *Ibid.*
23 Jordan Bar Am, Laura Furstenthal, Felicitas Jorge and Erik Roth, "Innovation in a Crisis: Why It Is More Critical than Ever", McKinsey Insights, 17 June 2020, www.mckinsey.com/business-functions/strategy-and-corporate-finance/our-insights/innovation-in-a-crisis-why-it-is-more-critical-than-ever.

known opportunity spaces, conserving cash and minimizing risk, and waiting until 'there is more clarity'".[24]

Law firm leaders, like the executives that McKinsey surveyed, generally placed innovation on hold while they focused initially on financial survival and then, as the financial strains eased for some firms, shifted their attention to increasing profits per partner. Altman Weil's 2020 Chief Legal Officer Survey asked Chief Legal Officers "what actions their outside law firms had offered proactively to assist law department during the COVID-19 crisis".[25] The survey responses display a stunning lack of responsiveness and innovation: "Only 12% of firms offered to collaborate on new alternative fees, 10% proactively offered additional discounts, and 7% suggested new process efficiencies to reduce costs." After studying the responses, Altman Weil concluded: "There were opportunities available to build loyalty and cement client relationships that were left on the table in 2020." For most law firms, the COVID-19 crisis evidently functioned more as a distraction and diversion from innovation, not as an impetus and inducement for innovation.

The Altman Weil survey results are consistent with Thompson Hine's surveys of in-house counsel and other senior business executives. Those surveys assess "the gap between what law firms say they are trying to do and what buyers experience".[26] Comparing the results of its 2017 survey with the 2020 survey, Thompson Hine "found that 72% of respondents believed their law firms had not done anything to alleviate the pressures faced by in-house legal departments in that three-year span". Focusing specifically on progress within the one-year period that included the COVID-19 crisis, Thompson Hine reports: "More than two-thirds of our survey respondents said their primary outside firms had made no progress in innovation." The overall survey results are epitomised by a general counsel's remark: "While the firms we use are trying to appear to be moving toward more technology-based services, in reality, not much has really changed."

The McKinsey, Altman Weil and Thompson Hine data indicate that, despite our intuitions and aspirations, innovation does not

---

24 Ibid.
25 Altman Weil Inc., *2020 Chief Legal Officer Survey*, www.altmanweil.com/CLO2020/. All quotations in this paragraph appear on page iv of the survey.
26 All data and quotations in this paragraph appear in "The Innovation Gap Persists", Thompson Hine, December 2020, www.thompsonhine.com/uploads/1135/doc/TH_InnovationGapPersists_2020.pdf.

increase during crises. This data is consistent with earlier research showing that "the opportunities for reform in the wake of crisis are smaller than often thought. The prime reason is that the requisites of crisis leadership are at odds with the requirements of effective reform".[27] The "crisis dividend" presumed to include rapid and substantive innovation turns out to be more conceptual than real.

4. Decision-making quality

The quality of decision making by law firm leaders and attorneys likely deteriorated during the pandemic. This deterioration, if it occurred, would have resulted, in part, from two factors correlated with poor quality decision making: a lack of rich cues normally obtained through in-person interactions and decreased creative thinking. These factors are discussed below.

4.1 Lack of rich cues

An antecedent to catastrophic decision making is the lack of rich cues in communication. When decision scientists examine events like the Challenger and Columbia space shuttle disasters, they detect a paucity of in-person communications and an abundance of email, telephone and written communication. The nuances that distinguish in-person communication – facial tension, fake smiles, nervous hand gestures, momentary eyebrow raising, voice irregularities and muted affect – are absent or at least not detected in the electronic communications that characterise remote working. This leads to ultra-hazardous decision making because humans are notoriously inaccurate in understanding another person's feelings, beliefs, and intentions in direct, personal interactions, and they descend to an even lower level of empathic accuracy in their electronic communications.

The tone-deaf nature of electronic communications is exacerbated by the fact that people are not aware of their impaired effectiveness in understanding and relating to other people electronically. As psychology professor Vanessa Bohns notes, people "are largely oblivious" to the fact that their impact on other people varies with the means of communication – in person or by email, for example. Based on her studies of 14,000 people, Bohns reports that they are more likely to comply with requests made personally and less likely

---

27 Arjen Boin and Paul 't Hart, "Public Leadership in Times of Crisis: Mission Impossible?" *Public Administration Review*, September/October 2003, 63(5), 544.

to comply with requests made by email.[28] The people making the requests, however, are oblivious to the medium and inaccurately predict compliance rates for both in-person and email requests. They underestimate the number of people who will comply with their in-person requests and over-estimate the number of people who comply with their email requests. Stated differently: "Those in the face-to-face condition underestimated their persuasive powers while those in the email condition overestimated their success rate."[29]

For lawyers, Bohns' research suggests that perceptions of colleagues' cooperation and collaboration on critical client assignments or law firm management responsibilities, derived from email and other electronic communications, may turn out to be distressingly inaccurate. We are not as persuasive in electronic communications as we think we are, and our colleagues are not as malleable and compliant as we perceive them to be.

The superiority of face-to-face conversations over electronic communications is reiterated in studies conducted at Beijing Normal University's Cognitive Neuroscience and Learning Laboratory. Using an optical topography system to measure neural synchronisation in the left inferior frontal cortex, the researchers found that face-to-face communication "involves more continuous turn-taking behavior between partners". They confirm our intuition that:[30]

> the human brain is evolutionarily adapted to face-to-face communication. However, such technologies as telephone and e-mail have changed the role of traditional face-to-face communication. The current study showed that, compared with other types of communication, face-to-face communication is characterized by a significant neural synchronization between partners based primarily on multimodal sensory information integration and turn-taking behavior during dynamic communication. These findings suggest that face-to-face communication has important neural features

---

28 VK Bohns, "(Mis)Understanding Our Influence Over Others: A Review of the Underestimation-of-compliance Effect", *Current Directions in Psychological Science*, 2016, 25(2), 119. MM Roghanizad and VK Bohns, "Ask in Person: You're Less Persuasive than You Think Over Email", *Journal of Experimental Social Psychology*, 2017, 69, 223.

29 Association for Psychological Science, "You're Less Persuasive than You Think Over Email", 7 December 2016, www.psychologicalscience.org/news/minds-business/youre-less-persuasive-than-you-think-over-email.html.

30 Jing Jiang *et al*, "Neural Synchronization During Face-to-face Communication", *Journal of Neuroscience*, 7 November 2012, 32(45), 160–64.

that other types of communication lack, and also that people should take more time to communicate face-to-face.

Other studies have demonstrated that non-verbal behaviour in face-to-face interactions is so rich that we can predict human behaviour simply by measuring the frequency and duration of face-to-face interactions, total conversation time, physical distance between conversing partners, and body motions. Massachusetts Institute of Technology professor Alex Pentland and his colleagues discovered that "unspoken social signals – who's talking, how much, in what tone, interrupting or not, facing toward whom and away from whom, gesturing how – told them all they needed to know about the performance of a group".[31] Face-to-face interactions contain so many non-verbal signals, Pentland reports, that "usually we can completely ignore the content of discussions and use only the visible social signals to predict the outcome of a negotiation or a sales pitch, the quality of group decision making, and the roles people assume within the group".[32]

The non-verbal signals that Pentland finds to be highly predictive are largely missing from electronic communications. This could be particularly problematic for lawyers who were inattentive or insensitive to these types of signals in face-to-face interactions before the COVID-19 pandemic and are likely to overlook them entirely in relatively flat electronic interactions. Lawyers' tendency to be unaware of subtle signals and cues is shown in one study of 1,800 lawyers in four law firms. The lawyers' lowest average score was on "Interpersonal Sensitivity", defined as "the degree to which a person is socially sensitive, tactful, and perceptive".[33] The lawyers also scored below a comparison sample of high-level managers and professionals in "Sociability" ("the degree to which a person needs and/or enjoys social interactions"). In an earlier study, the lawyers "had an average Sociability score of only 12.8%, compared to an average of 50% for the general public".[34] (Rainmaker partners, however, "scored nearly three and a half times higher on Sociability than the service partners".)

---

31 Geoff Colvin, *Humans are Underrated*, Portfolio/Penguin, 2015, p130.
32 *Ibid.*
33 Jeff Foster, Larry Richard, Lisa Rohrer and Mark Sirkin, *Understanding Lawyers: The personality traits of successful practitioners*, Hildebrandt Baker Robbins, 2010.
34 Larry Richard, "Herding Cats: The Lawyer Personality Revealed", Report to Legal Management, Altman Weil, 2002.

4.2 Reduced creativity

Another casualty of the COVID-19 pandemic is creativity. Although creativity is a critical element of effective decision making, it tends to decline under two circumstances evident in this pandemic: uncertainty and lack of personal interactions among colleagues.

Jennifer Mueller, a management professor and author of *Creative Change*, has conducted extensive research to determine why "organizations, scientific institutions, and decision makers routinely reject creative ideas even when espousing creativity as an important goal". She finds that, although people express positive views of creativity, they actually harbour deep biases against creativity when they have strong feelings of uncertainty. In high uncertainty conditions, study participants taking an implicit association test relate creativity with words like 'vomit', 'hell', 'agony' and 'poison'. A sense of uncertainty not only provokes a negative reaction to creativity but also interferes with our ability to identify and accurately evaluate creative ideas. As Mueller explains, uncertainty "makes us less able to recognise creativity, perhaps when we need it most".

Creativity also declines as interactive, in-person communication declines. Spontaneous interactions at offices are a major source of creativity, as Walter Isaacson explains in his biography of Apple co-founder Steve Jobs:

> *There's a temptation in our networked age to think that ideas can be developed by e-mail and iChat. That's crazy. Creativity comes from spontaneous meetings, from random discussions. You run into someone, you ask what they're doing, you say 'Wow,' and soon you're cooking up all sorts of ideas.*[35]

Although people who work remotely often report high levels of productivity, research indicates that, in the absence of "serendipitous interactions" at the office, they are less creative.[36] "The ability to walk into somebody's office, meet someone in the hallway or in the elevator or at the coffee machine are all catalysts for creative collaboration," states Jay Neveloff, the chair of Kramer Levin's real estate practice. "Working from home limits that interaction."[37]

---

35   Walter Isaacson, *Steve Jobs: The Exclusive Biography,* Simon & Schuster, 2011, p430.
36   Colvin, *supra* note 31 at 168.
37   Mary Ellen Egan, "Leading Questions: Kramer Levin Real Estate Chair Jay Neveloff", *Bloomberg Law,* 8 January 2021, https://news.bloomberglaw.com/business-and-practice/leading-questions-kramer-levin-real-estate-chair-jay-neveloff.

Attorneys working remotely are particularly prone to declines in creativity because they may not have been very creative before the pandemic. In one study, law firm attorneys scored relatively low on inquisitiveness and imagination; in another study, in-house lawyers also scored low on "idea orientation", measuring their "preference for thinking creatively and generating new ways to solve problems".[38] The risks to creative thinking, after the pandemic dissipates, are extremely high because many lawyers express a preference for remote working and intend to continue near-exclusive remote working, if permitted by their law firms. Remote working could decrease creativity in a profession that already demonstrates a preference for precedence over originality.

5. Changes in conflict resolution forums

In addition to monitoring decision-making quality during the pandemic, lawyers also should consider *where* future decision making will occur. The selection of forums in international contracts has become increasingly important and controversial because traditional venues like London and New York may expose clients and witnesses to above-average health risks. Both the United States and the United Kingdom are perceived to have done a poor job of handling the COVID-19 crisis.[39] In the United States, visa, immigration and security policies and practices under President Donald Trump also heightened the risk that key witnesses would be prevented from entering the country to participate in mediation and testify in court or at arbitration hearings.

The health and travel risks attendant to dispute resolution in the United States are accompanied by perceptions that the rule of law has encountered and continues to encounter significant challenges in that country. In 2020, for the first time, the United States dropped from the Top 20 list of countries ranked by the World Justice Project for their adherence to the rule of law. Lawyers who have assumed that the United States has a superior system of civil and criminal justice, free of corruption and discrimination, should consider the World Justice Project factor rankings in Table 1 in deciding whether

---

38 Foster, *supra* note 29. Markus Hartmann, Bill Mordan, Thomas E Schoenfelder and Patrick Sweeney, "The Perfect Legal Personality", *ACC Docket,* July/August 2011.
39 "All publics surveyed ranked the US Coronavirus response the lowest", Pew Research Center, 15 September 2020, www.pewresearch.org/global/2020/09/15/us-image-plummets-internationally-as-most-say-country-has-handled-coronavirus-badly/.

Table 1. US and UK rankings in rule of law factors

Factor	US (UK) Global rank
Civil justice	36 (17)
Order and security	28 (24)
Fundamental rights	26 (13)
Constraints on government powers	22 (13)
Criminal justice	22 (12)
Regulatory enforcement	20 (13)
Absence of corruption	19 (10)
Open government	13 (11)

Source: Table based on data from World Justice Project, Rule of Law Index 2020, pp155–156

the United States still qualifies as the default dispute resolution forum in their clients' international contracts.

It is puzzling that two countries often seen as reliable, fair enforcers of legal rights and obligations in international disputes do not achieve high World Justice Project scores for administering and enforcing the rule of law in their own countries.

Although forum selection clauses are often regarded as 'boilerplate' and receive scant attention in contract drafting, prudent lawyers might consider the possibility of legal malpractice exposure in routinely designating cities in the United States and the United Kingdom. Both countries are distinguished by poor methods and outcomes in handling the COVID-19 public health crisis, and selecting a forum that is known to pose above-average health risks may constitute a breach of the duty of care. The potential liability exposure is heightened when clients' directors, officers and employees cannot enter a country to testify in person.

Lawyers also might need to advise their clients to obtain separate counsel regarding forum selection clauses. A conflict of interest arguably arises when lawyers routinely designate forums that facilitate their law firms' continued representation of the same client in the event mediation, arbitration or litigation occur. (Disclaimer: This Section 5 is cautionary and does not contain and is not intended to be a substitute for legal advice. Lawyers should conduct independent research and consult with the appropriate professionals before taking any specific action.)

In previous years, popular forums for international dispute resolution have included New York, London, Zurich, Geneva, Paris, Stockholm and Singapore. The changing perceptions and fortunes of the United States and the United Kingdom may result in a shift away from New York and London to the other popular forums and more frequent designations of new competitors like Frankfurt, Toronto, Oslo, Seoul, Taipei and Tokyo.

6. Conclusion

The COVID-19 pandemic has inflicted severe stress on lawyers and law firms. Severe stress often induces a longing for a return to "the way things used to be" and invokes unrealistically fond recollections of previous structures, systems and relationships. The post-crisis "new normal" then becomes functionally similar to the old normal with mild changes in form and nomenclature.

Before returning to previous practices that satisfy lawyers' need for security, affluence and routines, law firm leaders could pause and thoughtfully consider these questions.

- Will the firm's practices and leadership increase lawyers' level of engagement and commitment every year?
- Is the business model of raising rates despite flat or declining demand sustainable?
- Are current practices consistent with lawyers' duties to perform *pro bono* services and improve the nation's legal systems?
- How will continued expense reductions, especially in professional development budgets, affect long-term attorney performance and inculcation and adoption of the firm's culture?
- Do the firm's business practices and compensation systems perpetuate lawyers' contributions to extreme income inequality?
- Will gender, ethnic and racial disparities in attorney income and equity partner selection be corrected within three years or less?
- Are the firm's criteria for selecting, developing, evaluating and promoting attorneys based on empirical evidence demonstrating a robust correlation between the criteria and actual client service and satisfaction?

- Are the firm's goals set primarily to achieve a competitive economic advantage or to effectuate an independent concept of professionalism?

If the COVID-19 pandemic yields any positive results other than the income derived from law firms' surprisingly strong financial results in 2020, it will be firms' candid and socially responsible answers to questions like these.

Law firm real estate: emerging considerations in a post-COVID-19 environment

Matt Brainard
Savills
Tiffany Winne
Stream Realty Partners

The COVID-19 pandemic has accelerated the urgency of several key questions regarding law firm office space. With real estate typically amounting to a firm's second largest cost, law firms have long been contemplating strategies for optimising their spend in this area. COVID-19 and its attendant work-from-home phenomenon has placed this issue even more squarely in the spotlight. In this chapter we examine how COVID-19 has impacted law firm thinking on real estate in the months since its onset and offer perspectives as to what its long-term impact will be on the sector.

1. **Responses in the early days of COVID-19**
It is generally accepted that law firms need office space, and typically this is higher-end office space relative to corporate users and even other professional services firms. Particularly since the Great Recession of 2008, Corporate America has been in a period of great innovation and experimentation in the way that it uses office space. In contrast, law firms have been more restrained in their exploration of new ways of utilising the workspace. While many firms have adopted universal sized offices, reduced the amount of space devoted to physical files and added new amenities, the building blocks of most law firm offices remain the same: private offices for all attorneys.

COVID-19 has occasioned fundamental questions about the role of office space. As firms watched their expensive office space sit empty for months, questions naturally arose as to its usefulness and efficacy in general. Even firms who fared well from a revenue and Paycheck Protection Program (PPP) perspective during this time wondered what this would mean for their priorities going forward.

The following real client quotes typify what we have heard from many of our law firm clients during 2020.
- "Work from home is going better than we ever thought it would. Without the pandemic, we may never have conducted this experiment, but we like it."
- "Our lawyers are enjoying working from home, we may want this to be a permanent fixture in our real estate strategy."
- "Our lawyers want to come back to the office, but not nearly as many days per week as they did prior to COVID. We can use this to shrink way down."

At many law firms, these are just musings. At others, they are the sentiments driving serious strategic planning initiatives. Many law firms without lease expirations looming were able to take their time, digest data from within their firm and across the industry, and plan for what this means for the future. Some firms, however, did not have the luxury of waiting and were confronting major, unavoidable lease expirations. Amongst firms facing these situations, we saw many firms taking a wait-and-see approach, executing short-term renewals, typically one to three years, in order to bide time and gather more insight until a vaccine was introduced and lawyers were able to come back to the office. Others who had recently signed or were mid-negotiation on new leases chose to proceed. Amongst these firms, we noted an interesting trend of adopting a new way of working that departed from the traditional model of one office per attorney. Though there were only a handful of major Am Law 100 firms across the country designing space during COVID, we did note some interesting commonalities across them.
- Several Am Law 100 firms planning new offices across the country drastically reduced the amount of square footage they had planned to take prior to the onset of COVID.
- These square footage reductions ranged from 10–25% reductions *relative to the space plans those firms were working on in late 2019*.
- One common theme amongst the major projects we saw was the implementation of day-officing, a strategy whereby attorneys would occupy non-dedicated offices when they were physically present in the office. This trend is also known as 'hoteling', 'agile working' or 'flexible working'.
- In most of these cases, until the onset of COVID-19 the firms had not planned to implement day-officing to any notable extent as a part of their real estate strategies. After COVID, they

- planned to have a portion of their attorney base ranging from 10–25% actively day-officing. Some firms are contemplating future implementations of 50% or higher.
- Potential benefits of this approach cited have been: cost reduction/increased profits per partner, recruiting advantage and better attorney engagement. Some project that the avoidance of daily commutes will increase the billable hours, though this point remains controversial and the actual outcome remains to be seen.
- The "sharing ratios" of these approaches, defined as the number of seats per active attorney, ranged from .74–.88.
- In most cases, the attorneys who were slated to day-office were more experienced practitioners, versus first or second year associates.
- Adaptation of day-officing also appears to vary depending on practice area, with some practices (eg, tax, corporate, licensing, environment, regulation) thought to be more conducive to flexible working than others (eg, complex litigation and trial practice groups that work on larger cases).
- Interestingly, we saw almost no firms offering special compensation in exchange for an attorney giving up their dedicated offices. Most leaders we talked to shied away from the idea of offering special compensation for this, citing the "Pandora's Box" effect this would have if certain lawyers started requesting compensation if they availed themselves of internal services less than others.
- Lastly, it is important to note that while many of these trends are legitimate, some law firm leaders are voiding concerns over the potential negative ramifications of these new practices, including the lack of partner-to-associate collaboration is having on their business. While productivity may be sustainable, the quality of that productivity has been dampened by the absence of an associate's ability to fully interact with senior attorneys. Long-term effects of these reduced interactions may result in more associate turnover and or limited critical thinking and business development experience. Others have voiced concerns about a long-term work-from-home strategy on recruiting efforts, both at the associate and lateral levels.

Albeit a small sample size, we were struck by the number of them that quickly swung from an approach that included *no* day officing to one with a significant percentage of their lawyers slated to adopt this new way of working. Those of us who advise law firms were quick to note that another major trend in law firm real estate, the universalisation of office sizes, gained fairly widespread adaptation, but it took over 10 years for this trend to really take hold. In contrast, in just a few months' time we saw major global law firms who seek to attract and retain top talent make significant commitments to this new way of working.

2. Quantifying the day-officing phenomenon

In October 2020 we conducted an internal survey of the members of our Legal Tenant Practice Group (LTPG), a cadre of senior brokers who each manage multiple multi-market relationships with major law firms. In addition to the set of projects we describe above we also observed that questions around day-officing had begun to dominate the conversations our clients were having with us, even amongst those without pending lease expirations. We were frequently being asked for benchmarking data to help them make sense of this idea, and to understand how it is playing out in the legal sector more broadly. We asked each professional to characterise the internal strategic planning efforts at their law firm clients relative to the concept of day officing. In an effort to help quantify these conversations, we tapped the LTPG professionals within our firm and asked them to anonymously categorise the strategic planning efforts they witness unfolding in law firms they advise. In total, our advisers' responses cover 200+ law firms, spanning every major market nationwide. Our key findings included the following.

- The largest contingent – nearly half of the firms (48%) – are interested in the concept of day-officing, but remained agnostic and did not yet know whether it will fit their culture. These firms have no active implementations of the concept, but consider it 'under review'.
- 42% of all firms are either already actively day-officing, implementing a day-officing strategy, or planning to implement a day-officing strategy in the future. *(Please note: This is a broad contingent including firms who say today that they plan to employ this approach when leases roll in the coming years, but may have no active commitment to the idea today.)*
- The LTPG reported that only 10% of its law firms were currently rejecting the concept of a day-officing strategy, indicating that it had no place in their current or future strategy and was not a fit for their culture.

This data, combined with the class of major law firms who have already begun implementing day-officing during COVID, suggests to us that there is a place going forward for the idea that attorneys may work in a location not permanently assigned to them. Obviously, this represents an opportunity for law firms to lease less square footage, resulting in a reduced cost structure. We predict that there will be no one-size-fits all prescription for the use of this concept, and that each interested firm will need to figure out how this fits their culture, workforce and priorities. As this concept is developed more fully across the legal sector, we pose the following questions.

- Will this 'mini-trend' of major firms making high-ticket capital commitments involving day-officing become commonplace? Will we see this as a widespread phenomenon, or will this turn out in retrospect to be an isolated number of cases, enacted during the height of the pandemic?
- What will emerge as 'rule-of-thumb' sharing ratios for attorneys?
- Given that law firms lean heavily on personal interaction for training, mentoring and cross-selling, how well will a day-officing strategy support these needs?
- Traditionally, the best work and promotion opportunities in law firms have come from forming relationships in the office. How will day-officing affect those dynamics?
- How will firms with heavy work-from-home contingents compete recruiting-wise against those who maintain robust in-office cultures?
- We perceive potential concerns regarding how day-officing practices could potentially counterpoise firms' efforts at diversity and inclusion. Is there a scenario in some firms where offering dedicated offices to some attorneys and non-dedicated offices to others may create an elevated prejudice and a new caste system?

3. A broader view

As prevalent as discussions regarding work-from-home and day officing have become this year, we want to recommend a step back from this singular topic to a broader framework for thinking about law firm office real estate. We believe that COVID-19 has created levels of disruption so severe that, ironically, it creates the perfect conditions for re-thinking law firm real estate, ie, an atmosphere wherein traditional assumptions are tested and questioned, and a greater openness to new models may prevail. Against this backdrop,

we challenge our law firm clients to ask themselves the following questions.
- What is our office space *for*?
- What purpose does it serve?
- What are we trying to accomplish with this very significant expenditure?

Answers to this question will vary widely but will form the basis of a firm's real estate strategy. For some firms, office space serves the purpose of housing attorneys. For others, the space is very client-facing and an important part of their marketing strategy. For others, it is an important driver of talent attraction. While so many firms these days seek to do more with less and to minimise their expenditures on real estate, we strongly assert that minimising the office footprint is not necessarily the only axis of consideration. Fitting the maximum number of practising attorneys into the smallest possible footprint may be the right answer for some firms, but for many it is not the whole picture.

Consider a recent case study from our practice. A long-time client of ours, a prominent Am Law 200 law firm with ~20 offices across the country, was looking to take advantage of the tenant-friendly market conditions to restructure its headquarters lease. Based on its target attorney ratios, it had too much space with approximately 75,000 sq. ft under lease. Based on industry ratios alone, it could more appropriately house itself in ~50,000 sq. ft. The idea of reducing its footprint by nearly a third was undoubtedly tempting for the partnership base. If the answer to the question, "What is our space *for*?" had been "to house our attorneys and enable their day-to-day work", then ~50,000 sq.ft would have been the right answer for them. This firm, however, is very marketing-oriented and has a strong tradition of hosting frequent high-end client events in its office space and at other offsite event venues in the area. It thinks of its office space as not just a *work*place, but also a *show*place. When faced with the exciting prospect of shedding ~30% of its space and enjoying the resulting cost savings, the firm instead took a more measured approach to its lease restructure. They did indeed shed some of their office space, but simultaneously decided to take advantage of a unique opportunity: leasing a former high-profile bank space consisting of 5,000 sq. ft on the ground floor of their building to create a 'public' amenity space for its clients. This space will act not only as their reception area, but also as a high-end, technology-enabled 'club' and concierge-based, amenity-driven space where their clients can be welcomed, both informally and for events. This space will be unique among law firms in their market and will also give them very prominent exposure to high levels of daily foot traffic in that market's central business district and marquis lobby signage that promotes the firm's branding.

Including this space, the law firm ultimately leased ~61,000 sq. ft. Even with this new commitment, the firm's overall real estate costs still dropped due to the space give-back on their office floors. In asking themselves what purpose their office space investment served, they decided to shift their functional mix slightly away from *production* (ie, attorneys working) in favour of *marketing* (ie, creating a unique client experience). Prompted by COVID, this client asked itself what its real estate was for. The answer involved rebalancing away from attorney workspace in favour of the marketing benefits of this unique client space.

We present this not as an exemplary solution for all firms, but rather an illustration of one firm's strategy irrespective of COVID-driven occupancy decisions. Given the uncertainty created by COVID, many firms are 'hunkering down' and trying to reduce their space as much as they can, there are counterexamples as well of firms thinking more broadly about their real estate as a strategic advantage.

4. **Health as a real estate consideration**

Another aspect of the legal sector's response to COVID-19 is a focus on healthy workplaces. Driven by the impact of COVID-19, the importance of health and wellness in the office is becoming a critical issue in multiple ways.

- Some firms view this as key to recruiting and retention of both laterals and newly minted associates in the long term.
- Others view it as part of their overall branding efforts and want to communicate to clients and the general public that they are serious and committed to this issue.
- For almost all firms, this is an immediate short-term concern for attracting lawyers back to the office once vaccines are widely available and workers migrate back to the office in force.

Health issues now figure so prominently in people's minds since COVID-19 began to permeate our collective consciousness, and we believe that this mindset will persist even after this immediate threat has passed. One key way that firms have begun codifying and demonstrating their commitment to health issues in the workplace is through the pursuit of wellness-related certifications. Even prior to COVID, many forward-thinking office tenants had begun pursuing these for their office space and landlords for office buildings. The most relevant of these certifications are Fitwel[1] and WELL,[2] with Fitwel being more focused, flexible, less expensive and easier to achieve while WELL is more rigorous, more expensive and requires significant advance planning. Fitwel was originally created by the US Centers for Disease Control and Prevention (CDC) and US General Services Administration. The CDC remains the research and evaluation partner for Fitwel.

Based on the model popularised years ago by LEED for certification for environmental considerations, Fitwel certification affords companies a recognised imprimatur for their efforts to provide a healthy and wellness-oriented workplace. Factors on which a company seeking the certification are judged include: employee access to natural daylight, indoor air quality, access to healthy food choices, walkability, access to public transportation and access to fitness facilities.

Fitwel awards its certifications on three levels: 1 Star, 2 Star and 3 Star, with three being the highest level of attainment. Steptoe and Johnson is the only law firm to date to achieve a Fitwel certification. They qualified for a 2-star rating at its Washington DC headquarters. It is notable to recognise that this was accomplished post-occupancy and other law firms can as well, depending on how recently their build-out was completed. Some of the features on which Steptoe's certification was based include natural daylight throughout the majority of the workplace; sit/stand desks; staffed exercise room with showers; a bike storage room; a multi-purpose room for wellness activities; an indoor air quality policy; and one certified first responder per 100 people. The firm reports rave reviews from its employees.

In the summer of 2020, two new certifications were announced in response to COVID: Fitwel's Viral Response Module[3] and IWBI's Well Health Safety Rating.[4] Largely informed by experiences with COVID, these certifications focus on air quality, cleaning/sanitation, hand hygiene, PPP provision, etc and require annual recertification.

---

1 www.fitwel.org/.
2 www.wellcertified.com/.
3 www.fitwel.org/viral-response-module/.
4 www.wellcertified.com/health-safety/.

While WELL and Fitwel were in existence prior to COVID, we expect them to become more broadly adopted once the virus has been brought under control. Many progressive organisations have long recognised that a healthy workplace boosts productivity, reduces healthcare costs and lowers absenteeism. We believe in the wake of COVID-19 that law firms, like many other types of tenants, will find themselves 'marketing' the wellness aspects of their offices to their employee base in an effort to coax them to re-enter the office, and stay there long term. Additionally, wellness is anticipated to play a key role in future recruitment as well.

5. Implementing real estate strategies in a post-COVID-19 environment

As law firms work to identify their evolving business drivers, vision for the firm and decide what, if any, adaptations must be made in the wake of COVID-19, there are a variety of real estate strategies they might implement in order to realise their goals.

5.1 Space disposition

As many firms move towards the goal of consolidating and reducing their overall space footprint in an effort to decrease real estate occupancy costs and increase profit margins, a very common approach often pursued is subleasing a portion or all of their space in a given location. In markets where available law firm space supply is generally low and demand is healthy, subleasing can be an effective strategy. This is especially the case if the space being offered for sublease has newer improvements, an efficient layout, and is even equipped with quality furniture in good condition. Conversely, in markets with an abundance of supply and low demand, subleasing is often difficult or even ineffective. Since the beginning of the global pandemic, North American commercial office space markets have seen available sublease space increase by 52% across all markets, with increases of up to 177% in some markets.[5] This, coupled with the fact that demand from law firms and most other types of businesses to relocate during these times is at an all-time low with leasing activity falling 40% year over year, makes the odds of subletting space extremely challenging.

When considering a sublease disposition strategy, it is critical that a firm's real estate adviser carefully assess the marketability of

---

5   Savills Research.

the subject space, sublease provisions in the lease and the supply vs demand subleasing and leasing activity metrics in the market. Realistic expectations for the time it could take to successfully sublease the space and what potential economic recovery might be achieved are essential. Oftentimes, if reduction of costs is the primary objective, other strategies should be explored in parallel with subleasing. Depending on a law firm's existing lease obligation, building ownership, current condition of space and local market conditions, a restructure of the lease or relocation might be worth exploring.

5.2 Lease restructuring

As the global pandemic has accelerated and many law firms focus on reducing real estate footprints and occupancy costs, the lease restructure has emerged as an increasingly prevalent strategy for a variety of reasons.

A lease restructure is defined as a renegotiation of terms without the triggering event of an imminent lease expiration. The objective is to achieve more favourable economics and flexibility in the lease. Very often, a tenant's contracted lease rate is higher than the new current market rents, and a lease restructure could enable them to adjust their rents to a current market rate. Alternatively, a tenant may be able to shed excess space in exchange for a lease extension. Depending on a variety of variables, including the existing lease term, creditworthiness of the tenant, landlord's financial position, loan structure and lender profile on the building, current market conditions and tenant's overall size, concessions such as rental abatements, tenant improvement allowances, options to expand, options to contract and options to terminate may be achievable.

Why would a landlord entertain an early lease restructure? Generally, landlords are far more motivated to do whatever they realistically can in order to keep a tenant in their building for the long term. A longer-term lease helps landlords stabilise their asset by locking in an income stream. This not only benefits ownership from a cashflow perspective, but also in their ability to sell or refinance the building. Furthermore, the cost to lose and replace a tenant is often far greater than the cost to keep them. This is especially the case during a softer, more tenant favoured market where demand for office space is lower and the amount of time a space might sit vacant is longer than it would have been in a landlord favoured market.

In addition to market conditions, if a tenant has an option to terminate their lease early, this can often be used as leverage to enter a lease restructure dialogue with a landlord. Most of the time, a tenant's option to terminate must be exercised between nine and 15 months from their lease expiration and includes a fee equivalent to the landlord's unamortised transaction costs (eg, tenant improvement allowances, brokerage commissions, etc), plus in some instances several months of rent. Despite this fee, the tenant's economic advantages to exercising the option and obtaining a suitable lower cost lease alternative elsewhere, may outweigh the fee. Furthermore, the landlord's economic downside of losing the tenant may be far greater than any termination fee they receive, compelling them to do whatever they can to convince the tenant to recommit to the building.

Ultimately, in order to rationalise a longer lease term, it is essential the lease restructure achieves a law firm's short- and longer-term objectives. The precise mix of outcomes in lease restructure situations tend to be highly situationally dependent and assessing them requires more sophisticated financial analysis than a typical space acquisition scenario. Whether it be a reduced space footprint, occupancy cost reductions, improvements to reconfigure or upgrade the space or to create more flexibility during its tenancy, it is important a law firm's real estate adviser help define these objectives at the outset and develop a clear strategic plan to achieve these goals.

5.3 Relocation

The volume of space relocations by national law firms has been down significantly during the global pandemic. Relocating a law firm entirely typically requires far more capital outlay than staying in place due to tenant improvement costs, furniture, fixtures and equipment costs, technology infrastructure and general move costs.

This being said, as the number of high-quality direct spaces offered by landlords and new subleases come available to the market triggered by the current economic downcycle, the supply and demand metrics will continue to shift in the tenant's favour, often substantially depending on the market. Furthermore, motivated building owners and sublandlords have become more willing to offer aggressive economics which may have seemed impossible to achieve prior to the pandemic. These negotiated concessions can be a great equaliser when comparing a relocation versus a stay-in-place scenario.

Provided a law firm's real estate adviser correctly runs a strategically sound process during tenant-favoured markets, it is not uncommon to garner enough economic concessions to cover most or all of the required cost to build out and move into a new space.

A relocation space may also provide more efficiencies, enabling a law firm to fit into less space than possible in their current building. The reduced footprint of the relocation space may equate to significant cost savings over the term of the new lease.

Ultimately, the relocation scenario will, in most cases, be a law firm's strongest leverage card when negotiating with its existing landlord to remain in place. Even if a law firm has no interest or intention of moving to a new space, it is important all viable relocation scenarios are sufficiently evaluated, as this will be the best way to understanding what economic and non-financial concessions are achievable in the market at any given time. It is also worth noting that there have been countess instances of law firms at the outset of their real estate process determined to simply remain in their current space and negotiate the most favourable terms with their landlord who ultimately relocated to a new space at the end of their process, as they found the benefits of the relocation scenario far too compelling.

5.4 Do nothing

As referenced earlier on in the chapter, many firms have elected to take a wait-and-see approach to their real estate strategy during the global pandemic. Most often, this means doing nothing with respect to their existing lease obligation, assuming they have ample term remaining, or doing a short-term (1–2 year) extension if necessary. This approach also allows a law firm to limit capital expenditures within the space. The value of this approach is the opportunity to bide time, waiting for the critical mass implementation of the vaccine to take place, and to observe how the world around us will unfold. Waiting can often afford a firm clarity as more data becomes available regarding nascent work-from-home dynamics and fluctuating market conditions.

Each firm needs to balance the value of waiting with the timing of market recovery. Many firms believe that market conditions will continue to move in tenants' favour. This said, there is also data to suggest that as vaccines become prevalent, markets will improve. As landlords grow more confident, fewer tenant concessions and flexibility will be offered in lease negotiations. It is important to take both perspectives under consideration when implementing a do-nothing strategy and working with a qualified real estate adviser to have contingency plans in place that contemplate market volatility.

6. **Conclusion**

While the real estate strategies described above are commonly implemented by law firms during healthy economic cycles, recessionary downturns and everything in between, it is important to point out that these are by no means fully prescriptive. Just as every law firm has their own culture, business drivers and unique set of circumstances, building owners and markets will vary tremendously. The right solution for an individual law firm will only be reached with careful consideration of these myriad factors. As complex a process as formulating a proper law firm real estate strategy was prior to COVID-19, the advent of the virus has magnified the challenges law firms face in crafting the right solution. It is critical as a law firm weighs its options not only to have a qualified adviser, but also to involve firm leadership at the highest level in these very important questions.

Effective financial management post-pandemic

Thomas P Fitzgerald
Winston & Strawn

1. Introduction

The year 2020 will remain in our memories for decades to come. A global pandemic, millions of deaths, with millions more out of work, unable to work, or forced to lock down their businesses and their very economic lifelines. Too many episodes of racial injustice, rioting and looting, a contentious election in the United States, and all culminating with an attack on the US Capitol and an affront to the very rule of law so many in our industry work tirelessly to uphold. Families in disarray, remote learning, colleagues confused over how to interact with one another, and, for those of us fortunate to continue to work, endless days and nights filled with video calls and 'always on' ways of working while dealing with countless issues in our personal lives.

And yet, law firms found a way to survive, and even thrive. For many law firms, crisis created opportunity. Clients need help from the legal profession to navigate unforeseen challenges and opportunities, swiftly changing laws, guidelines, and even government intervention. In addition to helping clients succeed during unprecedented times, law firms had the opportunity to take a hard look at their operations, processes, real estate footprint, technology, staffing models, expense management and just about everything in between. Great firms found appropriate ways to make substantial, significant improvements to their operating models which will sustain them for years to come.[1]

In this chapter, we will review the following key areas that firms addressed during the pandemic, and that will be a hallmark of any great firm going forward.

---

[1] At our firm, professional staff continued to provide outstanding support during the pandemic, and I would specifically like to thank my colleagues David McDonald, Scot Farrell and Howard Kravitz for their significant contributions to this chapter.

- Creating and maintaining a healthy and safe work environment.
- Managing and optimising cash flow.
- Making lateral investments and identifying opportunities for new revenue growth.
- Rigorous focus on expense management, tightening administrative and financial controls and re-imagining staffing, structure and work processes.

2. Creating and maintaining a healthy and safe work environment

On 17 March 2020, days after our Asian and European offices had gone remote, we made the decision to move our entire US workforce to a remote operating model. To put that in perspective, before that date, we had anywhere from 100 to 120 people using our remote technology to work on nights, weekends, or the occasional work from home situation. On 18 March, close to 1,800 people, with more than 2,200 devices, were using our remote servers to get their work done from a location other than our offices. The technology we had put in place over the years would suddenly face its toughest test, and we passed with flying colours!

But we knew that some people still wanted or needed to come to an office. And in some states in the US, law firms were considered 'essential businesses'. There were different restrictions in different parts of the country and the world. We had to make sure that if a person entered our physical space, they would be safe and protected from a virus that was spreading through droplets, surfaces and in unknown ways. We needed staff in our offices to support lawyers who required access to files, services and technology. While people were working, they needed staples such as water, coffee and bathroom accessibility. They wanted to know elevators were safe and clean. Parking would be available and protected, and protocols would be in place to ensure their health and well-being.

We also knew that clients and courts would have similarly stringent requirements regarding in-person visits. Physical events, conferences, sponsorships and entertainment would be dramatically curtailed as safety protocols were being put in place all over the world. We knew the culture of our firm relied heavily on mentorship and interaction among partners, associates and staff, and immediately put in place ways for people to stay connected to each other. Some of the elements of our plan will remain in place as we re-imagine the way we work. Others will be reduced as vaccinations increase and the current pandemic fades from view.

Like many firms, we followed to the letter all guidelines issued by the Centers for Disease Control and Prevention (CDC) and in the state or country governments where we operated.

But we did not stop there. We took additional actions to make certain our people stayed safe while continuing to serve the needs of our clients and maintain the culture of our firm. We also felt it was critical to demonstrate empathic leadership during a crisis and further cement loyalties among partners, associates and staff. We knew this was a critical moment in our 168-year history, and that we must act in the best of interests of all involved. Some of the additional actions we took included the following.

- Provided regular communication regarding positive cases of COVID-19, including the dates, times and floors where people may have come in contact with the individual testing positive. This included building employees or contractors working on our premises.
- Held numerous 'town hall' meetings for partners, associates and staff.
- Initiated procedures to stay in touch with all personnel.
- Conducted daily or weekly department, office or practice group meetings to foster connectivity and camaraderie.
- Began daily 'return to office' surveys to monitor in-office attendance and requirements for support services.
- Increased mental health and well-being workshops, programmes and access to mental health professionals.
- Increased the stipend for computer and internet services.
- Conducted business continuity exercises, evaluating the state of preparedness for offices, technology, client communications and public relations.

Many of these will remain in place post-pandemic, as any great law firm must take appropriate steps to protect the health and safety of its people and its clients. We will monitor our travel needs, enhance our connectivity as remote work is likely here to stay, and continue to invest in mental health and well-being initiatives. We learned the value of regular communications in a remote environment and the importance of leaders checking in with people regularly to simply ask "How are you doing?" and "What can we do to help?".

Perhaps the greatest lesson we learned during this time is the value of information and the impact it can have on morale, client service, securing a strong revenue stream and properly managing the firm. These are lessons we will take with us into the 'new norm'.

3. Managing and optimising cash flow

We thought we were pretty good at this pre-pandemic! In fact, we prided ourselves on our management of our balance sheet, our ability to project revenue and optimise our cash flow. For several years, we had predicted our monthly and annual budgets with uncanny accuracy. Our partners were diligent in managing their time entries, client accounts receivables and collections. We monitored our rate increases and our realisation rates. What we learned during the pandemic – we could do even more during a crisis, and we can incorporate some of those best practices into how we manage our firm going forward.

First, we formed an operational and financial task force comprised of the chairman, vice chairman, department leaders, and our CFO and COO. During the early stages of the pandemic, this group met daily to discuss pipeline, billing and expense management, and to monitor the financial well-being of our clients relative to the impact of COVID-19. We established a new operating budget for the firm, which incorporated new revenue projections, decreased operating expenses and the impact on partner compensation.

We were in unchartered waters and had to make difficult decisions to protect the long-term financial health of the firm and continue to serve the ever-evolving needs of our clients. We looked at everything and enacted a plan with several key components appropriate for the circumstances. We believe they will have substantial and significant impact on the firm for years to come.

We secured short-term borrowing capacity with our lender group. Given the uncertainty of the times, the potential need for capital and the anticipation that clients may delay their payments to us, we immediately turned to our bankers to negotiate amounts and terms that would be available. We were fortunate that with interest rates so low, borrowing short-term money was considered "cheap". As a testament to our great firm, and our partners, we never needed one additional dollar to run the firm, but we were prepared! We reviewed our options, and the potential impact to our balance sheet, and realised this was an exercise we should do regularly with our lender group and will continue to do so going forward. Understanding the cost of borrowing versus the maturity curve of our accounts receivable, client demand and disbursements along with potential contingency awards allows us to better manage our cash flow and understand our collection needs.

We enacted a new policy for daily time entry by all timekeepers. In the absence of a global pandemic, we may not have been able to enact this policy which we now know is key for any great law firm. Did we receive pushback? Sure, we did. Did we have non-compliance issues? You bet we did. But, for the most part, we were able to get most timekeepers to enter their billing daily instead of the prior weekly requirement, further enhancing our forecasting, projections and, ultimately, helping us better understand the status of our accounts receivable and make our collection goals very clear.

We worked with office managing partners, practice group leaders and department heads to help enact this policy, and made daily and weekly calls to timekeepers who were delinquent on their entries. We rolled the information into daily billable hours by department, practice group, offices, partners and associates and used that information in the regular meetings with the operational and financial task force. We have realised this type of discipline will be an essential part of our approach to financial management going forward, giving us deeper insight into our cash flow and potential borrowing needs, while improving our financial projections.

We focused on improving collections and reducing accounts receivable. Take a moment to think about how challenging this was and will continue to be. Traditionally, law firms collect much of their revenue in the fourth quarter of their fiscal year. Smoothing out that cycle is key for managing cash flow, especially in a year where there was concern that clients may delay payment to help manage their own cash flow. We decided to have regular, frank conversations with our clients to discuss their financial management challenges, our bills and the timing of payment. Ultimately, this had the effect of bringing us closer to our clients and resulted in a reduction in our collections cycle and a strengthening of our key relationships.

In addition to discussing client financials, we enhanced our client outreach through a dedicated client outreach programme. We initiated virtual client visits from the CEO and created a targeting programme for all partners to stay in touch with clients. Utilising content created by attorneys throughout the firm and made available to clients in our COVID-19 resource centre, we made certain clients were given regular guidance on how to navigate the pandemic and associated legal issues. These efforts helped us stay top of mind with clients, consistently adding value to them and identifying new opportunities for the firm. The targeted outreach was a contributing factor to meeting the revenue targets established in our updated budget.

We will continue to focus on having in-depth dialogues with clients and work towards reducing our accounts receivables and improving our collections cycle. This has proved to be a very appropriate strategy that will yield substantial and significant benefits to our firm.

Through rigorous fiscal management, increased client outreach and renewed help from our lender group, we were able to sustain a very slight reduction in client demand during one of the great challenges of our collective lifetimes. We learned that our culture is stronger than ever, and that in our moment of need, we could rely on the owners of our great firm to be a very real part of the solution. If actions truly speak louder than words, the actions of our partners demonstrated a commitment to our Firm we all hope will not be needed again anytime soon.

4. **Making lateral investments and identifying new opportunities for revenue growth**

The Chinese symbol for the word 'crisis' is generally thought to be a combination of two words – danger and opportunity. While there are many different interpretations of what this means, there is little doubt that the global pandemic resulted in a crisis that allowed law firms to look for lateral investments and to identify new opportunities for revenue growth. It is a risky business, and only time will tell if the investments a firm made during this period in history will pay off. It's a little like evaluating the draft of a professional sports team in year one. Things can look good on paper, but it often takes years to determine the winners and losers.

Great law firms seize on these moments and create their opportunities. There have been, and will be, 'stranded assets' because of the pandemic. Individuals, groups and firms will realise they might not have the scale to compete in the 'next norm'. Perhaps they found their current firms do not have the technology needed to operate in the future and are unlikely to have the economic scale to make the investments needed. Perhaps they have realised their current firms do not have the geographic footprint required for their practice areas. Maybe their leadership does not have a similar view of the growth potential for them. There are myriad reasons why partners leave one firm to join another. And during 2020, we also had a transition in Congress and the White House which left many in government positions searching for a job.

So, what should a firm do? Economic, legal and internal analysis are fundamental to identifying lateral and revenue growth opportunities. There is an overused cliché in business that hails from Wayne Gretzky's famous quote, "Skate to where the puck is going, not where it's been".[2] This quote appears in countless PowerPoint presentations because it rings so true. Of course, firms tend to move in packs, so if an opportunity is attractive to one firm, it is likely attractive to others. Great law firms have "known for" practices, and often, to be "known for", a firm needs a deep bench of world-renowned attorneys who clients want to turn to for their most important matters.

Key questions to consider include the following.

- Where are businesses moving to? What geographic expansion might be needed?
- What are economic and potential demographic factors that need to be considered?
- What practice areas were hit hardest during the pandemic? Or which practice areas were unable to capitalise on opportunities created during the pandemic?
- What practice areas or industry groups are we 'known for'? Is exponential growth possible if we add to our benches in those areas? Could 1 + 1 = 3?
- What cross-selling opportunities are we missing?
- What changes to the law can we expect to see with a new administration? Do we need to add capabilities in emerging areas of the law?
- What are our competitors in the industry doing? Do we need to add capabilities to keep up with the competition?
- How do our financials stack up against our peers and our aspirational peers? What do our financials need to look like to attract top talent?
- How will our partners help or hurt any potential laterals, acquisitions or the addition of new capabilities?

During the past year, we created a strategic alliance with a top Chinese firm in the People's Republic of China, grew our presence on the West Coast in the US, added capabilities in our 'known for' practices, and made investments in areas where we needed breadth and depth because of shifting economic and regulatory practices stemming from the pandemic. In all, we added more than 20 partners across our geographies while forming and co-sourcing work

---

2   See www.brainyquote.com/quotes/wayne_gretzky_383282.

with the strategic alliance that includes approximately 40 lawyers. We integrated everyone virtually, created or updated our strategic plans for these groups, and implemented business development initiatives to raise awareness and improve our cross-selling efforts.

We also asked our partners and associates to become more familiar with changing laws and regulations resulting from a global pandemic. We created a COVID-19 Task Force, chaired by three partners, and established a searchable intranet repository for memos and client alerts that our attorneys could use to answer client inquiries. Like many firms, we asked our lawyers to 'get smarter' about new issues our clients would be facing so we could increase our opportunities for revenue growth, both now, and in the future.

We also saw how a balanced portfolio of service offerings helped diversify our revenue stream. Yes, our litigation revenue was impacted by court closings and trial delays, but practices relating to transactions and counselling saw an uptick in volume and receivables. This is an important lesson to take going forward. Great law firms are able to withstand ebbs and flows in revenue because they have a diversified portfolio catering to multiple clients' needs. Identifying holes in your capabilities and actively pursuing opportunities to close those gaps as we come out of the pandemic should be an essential part of any law firm strategy.

5. **Focus on expense management, administrative and financial controls, and staffing, structure and work processes**

   Most law firm managing partners or CEOs will tell you they always focus on expense management, while remaining open to new ways of working or staffing the firm. Not until a global pandemic threatened the sustainability of a firm were people willing to really take a hard look at their operating models and their expense management. For example, much has been written about real estate costs, or what the in-office work experience may look like in the future. Many firms have reduced the size of partner offices, standardised layouts and created common work areas for collaboration, teaming and mentorship. Our firm was among those on that path. We had reduced the size of offices in our flagship Park Avenue, NY office to 140 square feet, and followed similar approaches for new office layouts around the globe.

   And then the pandemic hit, and we realised that real estate costs were excessive. Here we were, with sunk real estate costs and fewer people utilising our space. Problem was, we had far fewer people in our offices. And we seemed to be operating well, serving clients, driving demand and holding the line on revenue. So, we turned our eyes to other professional services firms like the Big Four, who broached this challenge years ago. Their real estate and rent costs accounted for a much lower percentage of their total revenue, dramatically lowering their expense base and retaining more earnings for partners or for important investments. Essentially, very few people have permanent offices in those firms, with most operating with hoteling privileges.

Could we do it? Could we move to a virtual or remote model for work? Did we have the technology to provide the highest quality of service to our clients and stay connected with each other? Would partners be willing to work part time from the office? Would they give up their personal space? Which staff functions could be performed virtually? What staff functions would need to be in a physical office to provide the needed support functions for our lawyers? The questions were endless. And the more questions we asked ourselves, the more potential opportunities we identified to re-imagine the way we work, what our staffing models looked like, how we could reduce our operating expenses and potentially pass savings on to clients and partners alike.

In the 'next normal', law firms will operate as more of a hybrid model. Moving away from the traditional, in-office model, firms will provide a host of services through technology while still allowing for critical in-office work, mentorship and camaraderie. It's hard to imagine technology replacing the 'war room' model for trial prep or transaction due diligence, but it's easy to see how document management and processing can be done virtually. Timekeeping, billing, payroll, financial analysis, conflicts, certain business development and marketing activities, programming, hosting virtual events and work product collaboration are just some of the activities that can be done remotely. Over time, firms will reduce their real estate costs, driving them down to a much lower percentage of revenue, moving closer to the metrics of other, larger professional services firms.

Make no mistake, this is going to take time. We are talking years, not months. Many firms have signed long-term leases for space with little to no chance of sub-leasing, particularly in this environment. Many have office space in prime locations which have been traditionally aligned to critical economic hubs. Some are convinced the business of law must be conducted in person. The industry may be slow to adopt new ways of operating. As businesses in general re-imagine the balance between in-office and remote work, many are re-thinking their own real-estate footprint and shifting operations to new, burgeoning economic centres in locations outside of the traditional 'big city' footprint.

And once you realise that fewer people are likely to be in the office, firms will begin to rethink their in-office staffing needs. We implemented an entirely new legal support model that impacted every domestic office and several of our administrative departments. The new model includes a 24/7 Winston Resource Center (WRC), the newly created position of practice coordinator, and the centralisation of additional legal support services. The new model – designed to provide better service and improved staff satisfaction at a lower cost – was conceptualised and implemented in less than six months, a remarkable feat in the slow-to-change legal industry.

This project's success was based on creativity, hard work and effective leadership. The project's core concept was shaped by a small leadership design team that took a wholistic look at the day-to-day operations and found that many processes could be streamlined and improved. In their early stages, the group pursued the answer to one fundamental question: how do we enhance the level of support we provide to attorneys and clients?

In answer to their question, the concept of a 'Yes Center' emerged as a centralised resource that would be available 24/7. This tool would be staffed by tenured and talented Winston professionals, strategically positioned across time zones (a 'follow the sun' approach) and equipped to handle tasks that could be performed remotely with no sacrifice to quality. The Resource Center is a virtual operating model that allowed for improved efficiencies and streamlined workflows, maximising the use of technology. Once partners realised they may not have needed an assistant stationed outside their offices, we were free to find new, improved ways of servicing their needs with a more streamlined approach to workflows. Firms will continue to evaluate outsourcing and third-party options for traditional in-office services, like reception, concierge, food service, cleaning, mail room operations, printing, copying and scanning.

Further efficiencies will likely be gained through technology and centralised functions with increased self-service options. Firms have learned that customised solutions for any partner comes with a cost that may be too great to bear. We expect to see tiering of service levels, highly dependent on production, client ranking and opportunity sizing. Change management will be critical, as not all will be ready to adopt new ways of working. As firms consider a host of expense management initiatives and re-imagine their staffing, structure and workflows, change management teams consisting of partners, lawyers, staff department leaders and human resources professionals should be included in all decision making and implementation efforts.

6. **Key takeaways**

The pandemic of 2020 provided an unforeseen opportunity for law firms to hit the pause button on their strategies, operations, culture and future. It's not hard to imagine rampant consolidation in the industry, with many smaller boutique firms being consumed by larger firms with a greater diversity of practices, the economic scale to make critical infrastructure investments and to implement 'best in class' expense management protocols.

But we also learned there is no reason to wait. Great firms used 2020 to implement changes that will have long-lasting effects on their balance sheet, their profits per partner and the efficiencies they can deliver to their clients. As we head into this next decade, we should all be prepared for significant changes in our operating models as the industry works to catch up to our clients, competitors and potential new entrants into our world.

Well-being of partners and the workforce

Eric Ho
Health for Success

In a very real sense, we are all aliens on a strange planet. We spend most of our lives reaching out and trying to communicate. If during our whole lifetime, we could reach out and really communicate with just two people, we are indeed very fortunate. Star Trek creator, Gene Roddenberry

1. A wicked problem and a social mess

The nature of the COVID-19 pandemic lends itself to being described as a "wicked problem" – a problem that is difficult or impossible to solve because of incomplete, contradictory and changing requirements that are often difficult to recognise. It refers to an idea or problem that cannot be fixed, where there is no single solution to the problem, and "wicked" denotes resistance to resolution, rather than evil.

The Harvard political scientist, Robert Horn, extended the concept of a wicked problem to define what he called a "social mess".[1] It is characterised by:

- *no unique 'correct' view of the problem;*
- *different views of the problem and contradictory solutions;*
- *most problems are connected to other problems;*
- *data is often uncertain or missing;*
- *multiple value conflicts;*
- *ideological and cultural constraints;*
- *political constraints;*
- *economic constraints;*
- *often a-logical or illogical or multi-valued thinking;*
- *numerous possible intervention points;*
- *consequences difficult to imagine;*
- *considerable uncertainty, ambiguity;*

---

1 Robert E Horn and Robert P Weber, *New Tools For Resolving Wicked Problems: Mess Mapping and Resolution Mapping Processes*, 2007.

- *great resistance to change; and*
- *problem solver(s) out of contact with the problems and potential solution.*

Human beings do not do well – collectively, or individually – with wicked problems and social mess.

They trigger our fight-flight-freeze, or survival, response, but we get stuck in the 'freeze' setting. We can neither fight nor flee. This is the worst type of stress for humans to endure. The danger for our health and well-being is when this stress become chronic.

As lawyers, our judgement is one of the skills that our clients rely on us for. The ability to sift through what the law says, how it is interpreted and how it applies in practice to your client's particular commercial circumstances is a large part of your success.

However, when your judgement turns towards solving problems that have contradictory solutions, value conflicts and change that faces great resistance – or even that you are out of contact with the problems and the potential solution – how are you able to rely on that finely honed skill?

As we will see later, perhaps the most challenging exercise of judgement that managing partners and law firms face is resolving the tension of opposites between, on the one hand, the cost and efficiency benefits of remote working and, on the other, the human and social disconnection that has emerged with it, including the negative consequences on the health and well-being of partners and staff alike.

1.1 It is no surprise the pandemic has had a transformative impact on how we lead our lives at work and at home

As the pandemic unfolds, organisations and leaders are being forced to re-think the way work is done. Leaders are scrutinising traditional models of working – from office allocation of workspaces to remote working policies. Plans that might recently have been strategic now seem obsolete.

Aside from the question of profitability within law firms and legal teams, the pandemic is forcing firms and their leadership to peer behind the curtain of the lives of their staff much more so than was needed in the past.

The pandemic has fused together our work and personal lives; the boundaries that separated the two – however loosely they were held – have blurred.

Whether they remain hidden or come into public view, we are experiencing more intense emotions in our daily lives, and these emotions, often viewed or experienced as negative, are entering into workplace dynamics: fear, pessimism, exasperation, loneliness, overwhelm, insecurity, withdrawal, weariness and anxiety.

This coincides with many more universal humans needs not being met, and so we are experiencing a lack of security, stability, justice, autonomy, balance, inclusion, fellowship, belonging and structure.

As a leader in a law firm, your ability to be aware of these emotions and human needs in yourself and in others is a critical skill to cultivate. Awareness leads to empathy, and that helps restore the human and social connections that have fractured as a result of forced remote working. Awareness is also critical in solving wicked problems and social messes: it creates perspective and allows us to rely not only on our finely tuned skill of judgement, but also on the creative solutions having that awareness opens up.

As we will see, creativity and stress are not compatible bedfellows, and so exercising judgement without that creativity might not be delivering the most appropriate solutions to your firm's challenges.

1.2 **Our capacity to adapt has taken on a new dimension as the pandemic has upended professional, social and personal norms.**

The pandemic has brutally laid bare the entire spectrum of how humans deal with challenging situations.

(a) *Judgement is a lawyer's superpower, but how is it best deployed in solving wicked problems and social messes?*

Experiencing stress is a common occurrence for any successful lawyer. Closing deals on time to meet a client's commercial objectives and ensuring your team and the work product is 'right' are some of the potential sources of stress that come from striving for excellence in service and technical capability.

When we have trained our brains to apply logic to solving abstract problems and deliver real-life solutions, most lawyers might feel they are in their sweet spot.

But as law firms are peering behind the curtain of the lives of their staff, emotions and human needs are showing up more often, and demanding the capacity for leaders to handle these too.

How do partners deal with social isolation in the workplace, the feelings of loss, and worry about families and careers, let alone exercise their judgement about resolving this wicked problem and social mess as it affects their law firm?

Resolving these 'problems' are not found in our brains and logic alone, but in our hearts and our gut.

The solution lies in building awareness and, with it, empathy.

(b) **Reacting has become our norm**

There is another challenge, though. When we are stressed or anxious, our bodies switch to readying us for survival and that impairs how we make decisions.

In normal times we can find ourselves reacting without thinking. Often this happens with those with whom we are in close quarters or who challenge views we hold strongly: colleagues who are annoying us, family members who press our buttons effortlessly, trolls on social media.

Imagine a day in which you start noticing what you are grateful for. You drive to work, you see someone walk into the road in front of you as you're pulling away from the traffic lights. You stop, concerned if the pedestrian is harmed. There's traffic, but you don't fight it; you listen to your favourite music and don't let the other drivers bother you. Today, you feel accomplished because you've been working recently to create connection and psychological safety in your team. On the way home, your partner calls you and asks you to stop for some groceries they have forgotten to buy. It'll delay your arrival at home, but you remind yourself that it is only another 15 minutes. You wind down in the evening, read a bit in bed before sleeping, and finish a day that you took in your stride. It was busy, but everything just clicked and it felt effortless.

Now imagine starting the same day. This time you wake up, check your inbox and see there's another 200 emails overnight. On the drive into work, you see someone walk into the road in front of you at a set of traffic lights and curse their stupidity. You are frustrated by how slowly every driver in front of you is driving, wondering how any of them passed their driving test. Your partner phones you to pick up some groceries. You just want to get home and rest, and this detour will add another 15 minutes to your day. You're in bed trying to get to sleep, but feeling resentful about having had to go to the supermarket to compensate for your partner's forgetfulness.

In these two imaginary days, the same things happened. All that was different was how your brain dealt with them.

When you feel safe, satisfied and contented, your body is in its rest-digest-relax state. You feel calm. It might be a busy and challenging day, but you're not buffeted negatively by the events of the day. This state is also when you feel connected, you have a sense of belonging, compassion and kindness.

When you are threatened, experience loss or rejection, your body shifts to survival mode. Our negativity bias kicks in to protect us from more of this kind of danger. Instead of a day that feels busy, but effortless, you feel pulled in different directions and apprehensive. You apply assumptions and judgements to what people say or do and give them an interpretation that may never have been present.

In mindfulness, we name the manner in which our brain responds in the example of the effortless day as a response. We are responding, rather than – the alternative – reacting.

Now imagine having to exercise your finely honed skill of judgement when you are in reactive mode, rather than responsive. How might that affect you, and the people around you?

Responding requires us to be self-aware, take in the situation, and decide the best course of action. But the benefits on our health are profound. I'll come back to this below.

(c) ***Our self-imposed high standards as lawyers increase our stress and anxiety levels***

As lawyers, we are known for striving not just for excellence, but perfection; the consequences of seemingly minor mistakes can have outsized repercussions. Falling short of our self-imposed expectations is one of the root causes of the deterioration in our health and well-being resulting from the pandemic. So it will also not be a surprise that the partners I have spoken to talk of stress and anxiety arising more frequently within their organisations as a result of the pandemic.

Why is this happening during the pandemic in particular?

First, the usual challenges and uncertainties at work have increased, and have been equalled, if not surpassed, by the increase in personal challenges and uncertainties at home.

Members of your teams are burdened with a barrage of questions that even the most resilient of them will find challenging.

- Am I now expected to answer emails when I would have been commuting to work?
- What does work–life balance mean when my child starts crying in the middle of a conference call with a client when my childcare arrangements have fallen through?

- How will my job be affected? What are my prospects of promotion when I don't have face-time with the decision makers and don't feel part of my team?
- I haven't heard from my boss for a few days. I wonder if I've done something wrong?

Partners are themselves not only dealing with their own uncertainties at home, but are under intense pressure from the individuals in their teams to show empathy and to lead through these challenging times. On the one hand, that could involve agreeing to pay for a home printer, on the other, dealing with a colleague's social isolation, mental health issues and even suicide.

Second, our capacity to respond to wicked problems and social mess, and our ability to hold the tension of opposites has been tested to the extreme.

The pandemic is depleting our individual reserves of, and capacity for, resilience, hope, maintaining optimism, and our self-efficacy to "keep going" as the months of pandemic restrictions continue. These are the classic traits (referred to as 'HERO')[2] that positive psychology research shows us are helpful for overcoming challenging times and circumstances.

Expectations of clients do not seem to have changed either. On the contrary, partners are keen to demonstrate remote working policies and practice do not impact client service delivery. Lawyers are responding to more emails at times that they previously would not have done.

For senior management, one of the key challenges is the ability to hold the tension of opposites, as we will explore later.

Our individual capacity to respond differs from person to person. Some, for example, are able to adapt to remote working effortlessly, some are not – particularly those who are socially isolated or juggling the immediate demands of a loved one who needs looking after. However, when the challenging situations and decisions we are grappling with involve wicked problems and a social mess, our capacity to respond to them is challenged even more.

Third, the increase in remote working has disrupted social connections and the glue that binds humans together – whether

---

[2] Fred Luthans, Kyle W Luthans and Brett C Luthans, "Positive Psychological Capital: Beyond Human and Social Capital", *Business Horizons*, Elsevier, 2004, 47(1), pp45–50.

that is among family units, teams or organisations. This is, perhaps, the most pervasive aspect of the pandemic, and is a major contributor for not just poor health and well-being outcomes, but lower happiness and productivity.

1.3 The pandemic has removed a key aspect of what it is to be a happy and healthy human being: social connection

(a) *The consequences*

As the boundaries between work and home have blurred, as our routines and habits have been disrupted, and as our capacities to be resilient, hopeful and optimistic have been tested relentlessly, the following is what emerges.

We've lost so many of the ways we connect socially as human beings. Touch and close contact are to be avoided. We are more connected than ever before through our devices and video communication tools, and yet we feel more isolated and alone.

Human beings communicate in a rich and sophisticated way that sets us apart from all other species on our planet. No other animals can communicate like we can. We communicate with incredible detail using language, but we are also probably more detailed visual communicators than other animals.

The communication channels we use – sound, vision, touch and smell – are all being impacted by the absence of physical proximity and the quality of electronic communications. This results in a loss of the richness of information that we have been designed to use to assess another person's emotions and needs. In other words, to be aware and be empathetic.

There are also more practical issues. The opportunities, for example, to spot a junior lawyer in the corridor and invite them to join an impromptu meeting are more difficult to cultivate in a digitally connected workforce. The knowledge sharing and skills acquisition from these interactive moments of connection disappear with ease.

(b) *Our innate and fundamental need for human connection is not being met and is a threat to our health and well-being*

When our hunter-gatherer ancestors became separated from their tribes, they were more likely to fare poorly and, for example, be eaten by prey. There was comfort and safety being in the group.

That is why we have been designed with physiological and emotional systems to help us survive in those situations. We trigger our fight-flight-freeze response that has evolved to help us when facing threats to our life.

Being in this survival mode triggers a cascade of hormonal responses to afford us the best chance of survival: our heart rate and respiration increases, nutrients are mobilised, stress hormones like cortisol are released, our immune system is activated, our awareness heightened, and resources are diverted from non-survival activities, such as digestion and reproduction. All of this allows us to survive in a dangerous natural environment.

In our modern world the threats that trigger the same survival response happen when a client calls the relationship partner, threatening to use another law firm. Or when a junior lawyer receives an email from their boss asking them to "call me".

The threat may be perceived or real; whether in ancestral times or in the modern day they all trigger the same survival response.

However, unless we do something to manage our stress response, our modern environment can lead us into a state of chronic stress. It is this that has had the most negative impact on our physical and emotional health and well-being during the pandemic.

In the following sections, we'll explore some specific areas where the impact of the pandemic is being felt most acutely by organisations and the partners leading the organisation and teams.

I'll also offer some thoughts about how to weather the storm by creating a foundation where well-being and work become equals so that leadership becomes effortless.

2. Health and well-being issues related to remote working

2.1 Forced remote working has ripped apart the fabric of an organisation's human connections

Many organisations, including those in the legal profession, have recognised a need to enable staff to work from home. Policies and benefits have been designed to afford staff a better work–life balance in recognition of evolving working patterns pre-pandemic.

However, none could have anticipated many teams working from home in some parts of the world every day with limited or no interaction in a workplace office environment.

Continual remote working has brought into sharp relief the social connection, knowledge sharing and learning that individuals (particularly those in more junior positions or who are new to the organisation or team) lose by not being together physically, and with it, the threads that connect humans together.

There have without doubt been successes in remote working.

Standards of service clients receive do not seem to have suffered. Indeed, one of the key questions when organisations implemented remote working policies in the past was whether clients would be affected by where their staff worked. But what is the cost to the health and well-being of individual staff?

2.2 The pandemic has eliminated for many staff key drivers for well-being and productivity at work

One of the key drivers for employee well-being in the workplace is one's social relationships at work, especially with supervisors. Making jobs more interesting and improving work–life balance are two other interventions.[3]

These insights are important as they point to the challenge that continual remote working poses to employee well-being. For managing partners, this is important because employee well-being is linked to productivity.

According to the Global Happiness and Wellbeing Policy Report 2019:[4]

> *it is estimated that there is a "positive correlation between employee wellbeing and productivity, and [… a] growing evidence base documenting this being a causal effect. Recent experimental evidence suggests that a meaningful increase in wellbeing yields, on average, an increase in productivity of about 10%".*

(a) Being connected but feeling isolated contributes to deterioration in social relationships

Our remote working allows us to continue to work together in teams, but we are not socialising in teams in the same way.

We have lost many of the human signals and micro expressions when we are physically present with someone that colour our conversations with nuance and specificity.

A slight nod or a lighting up of one's eyes denoting approval and appreciation might be lost entirely during a video-conferencing

---

3   C Krekel, G Ward and J-E De Neve, "Work and Wellbeing: A Global Perspective", in Sachs, J (ed), *Global Happiness Policy Report*, Global Happiness Council, 2018.
4   Global Happiness Council, Global Happiness and Wellbeing Policy Report 2019, www.happinesscouncil.org/report/2019/global-happiness-and-well-being-policy-report.

facility with a poor connection, or a screen filled with multiple participants.

We are much less able to 'read the room'.

There are also the lost fleeting moments when someone asks you a question in the corridor, or invites you to join a meeting as you're filling your water glass in the office kitchen.

Being connected but feeling isolated is amplifying the stress response, reducing happiness, well-being and productivity. The reality is that our work families are fragmenting through widespread, long-term remote working.

(b) *Being connected but feeling isolated can lead to poor health*

As we saw above, when we human beings feel socially isolated, our brains consider this a potential threat to our life, triggering our stress response.

There are multitudes of other sources of stress that have been highlighted earlier.

But what is the consequence of stress that is chronic and is not managed?

(c) *Chronic stress leads to poor, long-term health outcomes*

While some stress (eustress) can be good for us, like adapting to weight-bearing activity or exercising, prolonged, chronic stress increases our risks for:
- heart disease;
- diabetes;
- hypothyroidism; and
- autoimmunity.

Stress also affects:
- blood sugar control;
- weight gain by promoting it;
- increases inflammatory markers such as C-reactive protein (CRP);
- the onset and severity of asthma and allergies;
- impairs cognitive function and mental health; and
- triggers or worsens autoimmune diseases such as MS, Crohn's, psoriasis and rheumatoid arthritis.

You may experience stress in the following ways:
- fatigue;
- headaches;

- decreased immunity;
- sleep problems;
- mood swings;
- sugar and caffeine cravings;
- irritability or light-headedness between meals;
- eating to relieve fatigue;
- dizziness when moving from sitting or lying to standing; and
- digestive distress.

Chronic stress upsets the balance between our fight-flight-freeze response and our rest-relax-digest response because our sympathetic nervous system, which triggers that fight-flight-freeze response, stays switched on, if that stress is not moderated.

(d) ***The pandemic has upended routines that can manage stress effectively***

The insidious problem when individuals experience chronic stress as a result of the pandemic is that the ways to manage that stress, to turn on our rest-relax-digest systems, and to lead effortlessly, are much more difficult to activate.

Why? They all involve maintaining or changing behaviours. Behaviour change is hard enough in normal times, let alone when juggling the competing priorities during a pandemic and making judgements about how to resolve the wicked problem or social mess that affects the future of your firm and your staff.

About 85% of the risk for disease is environmental, not genetic.[5] So changing our diet, lifestyle and behaviours is the key to good health and preventing disease.

These lifestyle and behaviours, drawn from a functional medicine and ancestral health perspective, serve to reduce inflammation sources, reduce stressors and improve mood, sleep, weight, skin and much more, and include:
- eating real food;
- managing stress and incorporating play;
- moving frequently and engaging in weight-bearing activity, preferably outdoors;
- getting sufficient, good-quality sleep; and

---

5 Stephen M Rappaport, "Genetic Factors Are Not the Major Causes of Chronic Diseases", *PLOS ONE*, 22 April 2016, https://journals.plos.org/plosone/article?id=10.1371/journal.pone.0154387.

- managing our exposure to environmental toxins, like pesticides, heavy metals, hormone disruptors (contained in many personal care and household cleaning products) and mould.

It is no wonder then that if these behaviours are not already part of our daily routines, adding them to our lives during a pandemic will prove challenging, if not unrealistic.

Instead, our default might be that we are:
- sitting more;
- looking at our digital screens more;
- eating for convenience rather than health;
- moving and exercising less;
- spending less time outdoors;
- sleeping more poorly;
- incorporating less play;
- a cause of our staff's anxiety; and
- anxious or concerned about the welfare of our staff and challenged to find truly effective ways to support their health and well-being at work.

At the end of this chapter, we'll explore what can be done about it.

3. We're all in the same storm, but we're not all in the same boat

3.1 While our external circumstances can create an 'us and them' divide ...

One of the things we do as humans is to compare and contrast our own experience with those around us. We see this, for example, in sibling rivalry when children are figuring out what is unique and special about themselves, a developmental process known as differentiation.

The pandemic is shining a light on the personal lives and circumstances in which we find ourselves and our colleagues. Some of these may have never been revealed or known to the outside world before video conferencing brought colleagues into your home.

Partners who have children are having to manage home schooling, or child-care. Others are looking after vulnerable or infirm family members. That in itself places a big dividing line between those who have time for work and play, and self-care practices to manage stress, and those whose time must be divided with other competing priorities.

When we look at these external circumstances from the perspective of human connection, perhaps the biggest impact on law firms is on staff who are new or learning the ropes.

Members who are new to an organisation have not been able to invest in the relationships and connections in the ways that long-standing members of an organisation have been. That latter group has already stored up their human capital and are now able to draw down on those reserves to continue exploiting the culture and unwritten rules and norms of an organisation. Or not.

For the others, everything is done via screen. They are at a stage of infancy in establishing their professional and social relationships. They are not meeting colleagues for coffee breaks or lunches, or the spontaneous transfer of legal and/or business expertise and skills.

Newer and junior members are also finding learning challenging, hampered by the lack of opportunities to learn by observing someone else's doing (sitting in on conference calls or observing a masterful mentor in action).

For partners, remote working has also enabled those who do not want to lead to avoid leadership – at least the leadership that is demonstrated by being present and available to staff in an office in what has historically been described as an "open door policy". Those benefits have silently evaporated.

Some may have a boss that is naturally empathetic or who has developed this capacity, and can create the social and human connection that is possible even in a remote working environment.

But it is those junior members of staff and those who haven't adapted their coping strategies, in particular, who will need support to deal with loss of human connection that builds an organisation's human capital.

3.2 ... it is our internal capacities that can help us focus on the opportunities that unite us rather than the problems that divide us

As mentioned above, our individual capacity to face a challenging situation and respond, rather than react, differs from person to person.

Despite the comparisons we might make with the situations we find ourselves in compared to our colleagues, we can boost our capacity to deal with challenging situations by building our psychological capital, our HERO traits.

What are these traits?
- **Hope** is a feeling of expectation and desire for a certain thing to happen, and reflects the belief that one can find pathways to desired goals and become motivated to use those pathways.
- **Self-efficacy** is how confident we are that we will succeed in what we set out to do.
- **Resilience** is our capacity to bounce back from adversity and grow stronger from overcoming negative events.
- **Optimism** is a skill of both balance and perspective and is a belief that good things will happen to us in the future, no matter what. Even pessimists can develop optimism as a skill.

There is good reason why might we want to start cultivating these capacities now. Higher levels of psychological capital have been shown to relate positively to employee and job satisfaction.[6]

4. **The workforce that leaves to work remotely is not the same workforce that returns post-pandemic**

Although senior leaders in law firms have demonstrated that they can deploy technology to deliver the same (or superior) level of service to their clients, the pandemic is introducing a new dimension when it comes to the workforce that returns post-pandemic.

I shared earlier that the pandemic is forcing firms and their leadership to peer behind the curtain of the lives of their staff much more so than was needed in the past.

This dynamic has the possibility of creating opportunities for staff members to take advantage of some of the benefits experienced from full-time remote working as firms and teams pivot from working remotely full-time to a post-pandemic "business as usual".

While the pandemic has forced all of us to react to our changing work and home circumstances, a common refrain is that it is given

---

[6] M Abbas, U Raja, WA Darr, and D Bouckenooghe, "Combined Effects of Perceived Politics and Psychological Capital on Job Satisfaction, Turnover Intentions and Performance", *Journal of Management*, 40(7), 1813–183 (2012); F Luthans, BJ Avolio, JB Avey and SM Norman, "Positive Psychological Capital: Measurement and Relationship with Performance and Satisfaction", *Personnel Psychology*, 60, 541–572 (2007); F Luthans and CM Youssef, "Emerging Positive Organizational Behavior", *Journal of Management*, 6, 321–349 (2007); and CM Youssef and F Luthans, "Positive Organizational Behaviour in the Workplace: The Impact of Hope, Optimism and Resilience", *Journal of Management*, 33, 774–800 (2007).

the opportunity for individuals to re-evaluate what is important to them in life, not just at work or at home.

There are a number of benefits that partners and associates I speak to have identified about working during the pandemic. Organisations have the opportunity to embrace these changes, and incorporate them into revised remote working policies suitable for post-pandemic circumstances and reflect the value in fostering human connection in workplace dynamics.

- Space and privacy at work – those who have a lack of privacy or space at home may welcome spending more time in the office, while those who have the luxury of a study and/or office facilities at home may wish to spend more of their week working from home.
- Office facilities that promote efficiency – depending on the firm, security protocols can mean that staff cannot print at home. Offices can continue to offer ways to make work easier.
- Social connection – being physically proximate to your colleagues in the office and enabling fleeting conversations will reaffirm the bonds that bind organisations and their employees together. Whilst it is entirely possible to set and foster an organisation's culture virtually, leaders may breathe a sigh of relief in returning to more traditional ways of connecting people together.
- Enjoying family relationships and reduction in business travel – staff members who live with their families and who travelled frequently before the pandemic report enjoying spending time with their families and anticipate maintaining significant time investing in those relationships and travelling to meet clients and suppliers less frequently.

As for how individuals will approach returning to the office, to a large extent it depends on an individual's personal circumstances, but also how each individual sees these options as opportunities or threats.

Humans are wired to see threats. This negativity bias helped us evolve and survive. Given that many of us who have endured the emotional ups and downs of the pandemic will still be experiencing chronic stress, the possibility of envisaging returning to work as an opportunity may be a distant one for many staff.

5. How do law firms and their partners steer a path out of the pandemic when every decision involves resolving a paradox that relates to the health of every employee?

One of the biggest challenges and burdens on managing partners has been the need to make workplace decisions that directly affect the health outcomes of every employee, and are likely to give rise to conflicts with the values that individual staff members hold.

Some of these decisions have been taken out of an organisation's hands because governments and authorities have imposed overriding rules.

But in the absence of those rules, or where some discretion has been left to firms to interpret them, those decisions have given rise to the need for leaders to grapple with holding the tension of opposites. It is a concept that people who can hold the discomfort of paradox are truly the most transformative leaders among us.

Lawyers, perhaps, are most challenged by the discipline of holding the tension of opposites because we are trained to exercise our finely honed skill of judgement and to "win arguments". But how does one do that when the challenge we are facing is a wicked problem and a social mess and where there is no winning argument, the solutions are contradictory, and the problems invite a solution that derives from the heart and gut (feelings and needs) rather than solely from the brain (abstract reasoning and logic)?

Holding the tension of opposites is a rare skill set among leaders because it demands comfort with ambiguity. Those individuals who have the discipline to hold this discomfort of paradox grow bigger and become less rigid, more flexible, less judgemental and more tolerant. It results in leaders who are fearless and able to hold affection for the teams they lead.

So what happens when an individual's needs that are rooted in their values, beliefs and behaviours do not align with the decision an organisation wishes to make or has made?

For the individual, whether a partner or a member of staff, this misalignment, or cognitive dissonance, can lead to anxiety and depression.

For managing partners and chairs of law firms, however, the paradoxes come from many angles.

- "Firm: We can hire any lawyer from anywhere in the world" vs "Firm: We want to create a community of staff that represents the values and culture of the firm."

- "Firm: We're paying rent on our office space and it remains empty" vs "Firm: Our staff should return to the office as soon as possible."
- "Firm: Please return to the office" vs "Individual: I don't feel safe as I haven't had the vaccine and I don't intend to."
- "Firm: To maintain our cultural identity and social connection, we require our staff to be in the office at least three days a week" vs "Individual: I work more effectively at home, and do not want to expose myself to the risk of working in the office, because I'm looking after a vulnerable family member."

Perhaps the most important tension to resolve, given the topic of this chapter, is the balance that organisations, leaders and teams will need to strike between balancing the benefits and efficiencies to the organisation of staff working remotely against the benefits for health, well-being and productivity that come when workplace environments foster social connection.

When it comes to this discomfort of paradox, the goal is to develop a higher tolerance for being present with uncertainty. There are a number of ways leaders can cultivate this.

- We can learn to switch from thinking in 'either/or' terms to 'both/and' thinking.
- When individuals hold opposite views to us, we often identify without much effort their negative traits. By bringing forth and focusing on their positive qualities, like their strengths and values, we are more able to hold the tension of opposites.
- Within law firms, we can help individuals align their personal beliefs, values and visions with what the firm's vision and values are. It is often the case that when an organisation carries out an exercise to articulate its vision and values, the work stops at defining what those vision and values are for the organisation itself. However, when organisations take a further step and support staff members in identifying how their own vision and values can align with those of the organisation, it can help drive staff engagement in the work they do.

We all must struggle over the moral and ethical issues the pandemic presents us with, and then handle the emotions of those who are in our care. Many individuals will have a tendency to avoid this struggle and deny its existence. But this approach results in further suffering. Instead, and particularly for partners, we need to embrace the choices when they feel diametrically opposed to one another in some way, and hold that tension until our way becomes clear. We do not move away from it, rather we move towards it. It requires trust in the process of holding these paradoxes.

6. **Beyond the pandemic**

The transformative impact of the pandemic on our lives – both work and personal – will continue beyond the pandemic.

It is those partners who have the skills and traits to adapt, in a way that is aligned with how we have been designed as human beings to thrive, that will bounce back, perhaps even stronger than before. These skills and traits are disciplines that can be learned and practised. In my experience of working with leaders, it results in leadership that feels effortless, and where your success feels fun and authentic: where work and well-being (including social connection) become equals.

In the world of conventional medicine we look to our medical professionals to diagnose what is wrong with us, and we often have the expectation that taking a pill can solve our ailments.

However, when we look at our health and well-being through a functional medicine and ancestral health lens, a pill is not usually the first port of call. Rather than a pill treating the symptoms, functional medicine looks to the root cause and where the problem in the systems in our bodies lie.

That approach acknowledges the importance of establishing a foundation – a bottom-up, rather than top-down approach.

There are numerous functional medicine interventions that are effective in moderating the impact of COVID-19 on an individual's health and well-being, particularly in connection with long-COVID. These are beyond the scope of this chapter.

However, functional medicine and ancestral health can offer us a foundation that supports our health and well-being to put us in the best position to deal with this wicked problem and social mess.

Here are some ideas and suggestions to enable you to create your own optimal health and well-being and to be able to adapt to challenges in life, whether they flow from the pandemic or not. They overlap with some of the key drivers of employee well-being and productivity mentioned above (social relationships at work, especially with supervisors, making jobs more interesting and improving work–life balance).

6.1 Practices for individuals

(a) ***Build your foundations for overall health and well-being***
Given about 85% of the risk for disease is environmental, not genetic, focusing on our diet, lifestyle and behaviours is the key to good health and preventing disease.[7]

Here are the most common steps that partners can experiment with to build their own foundations for overall health and well-being that results in effortless leadership.

- **Eat real, whole food:** if it comes in a bag or a box, avoid it. These are likely to be food-like substances, rather than real food. Eat what would have existed in your great-grandmother's time. Avoid the key, modern day sources of inflammation: industrial seed oils, refined flours and refined sugars.

  What you eat, or not, impacts your mood, your energy levels through the link between your gut and the parts and systems in your body: the gut–brain axis, the gut–skin axis, the gut–heart axis, and so on.

- **Manage stress and incorporate play:** chronic stress raises cortisol levels with dire health consequences. Set aside time to practise mindfulness so you can be aware of your current thoughts, feelings, sensations, and surrounding environment, instead of worrying about the past or future. Even just 10 minutes of a day can reduce stress and dampen inflammation[8] and protect against cognitive decline.[9]

  Adopt mind–body practices, like meditation, mindfulness, yoga. Be playful. Working during the hours when you might previously have been commuting is an easy routine to fall into. Use that time for bringing play into your life.

- **Moving frequently and engage in weight-bearing activity:** our sedentary lifestyles impair our metabolic function by decreasing the activity of an enzyme (lipoprotein lipase, LPL) which is associated with higher triglycerides,

---

7   Stephen M Rappaport, "Genetic Factors Are Not the Major Causes of Chronic Diseases", *PLOS ONE*, 22 April 2016, https://journals.plos.org/plosone/article?id=10.1371/journal.pone.0154387.
8   Ruby Nadler, Julie J Carswell and John Paul Minda, "Online Mindfulness Training Increases Well-being, Trait Emotional Intelligence and Workplace Competency Ratings: A Randomised Waitlist-controlled Trial", *Frontiers in Psychology*, 21 February 2020, www.ncbi.nlm.nih.gov/pmc/articles/PMC7048000/.
9   Ted Kheng Siang Ng *et al*, "Mindfulness Improves Inflammatory Biomarker Levels in Older Adults with Mild Cognitive Impairment: A Randomized Controlled Trial", *Translational Psychiatry*, 21 January 2020, https://pubmed.ncbi.nlm.nih.gov/32066726/.

lower levels of HDL, increased risk of cardiovascular disease. Aim to stand and move around every 30–40 minutes if you are sitting for long periods.

We start losing muscle mass once we turn 30, and it begins to accelerate as we get older. Sarcopenia is detrimental to health, and it is a predictor of mortality. Incorporate strength-based training into your routine.

- **Get sufficient, good quality sleep:** Although science cannot yet fully explain the functions of sleep, we know it is essential for good health. Not getting enough sleep increases inflammation and negatively affects cognitive function,[10,11,12]

Chronic sleep deprivation is linked to learning deficits, depression and Alzheimer's disease.[13]

There are many solutions for busy partners to get better sleep that are beyond the scope of this chapter. There is no one magic solution but a good start is going outside first thing to kick-start your circadian rhythm, and focusing on the other foundations shared here, particularly eating real food, whole food.

- **Manage your exposure to environmental toxins:** environmental toxins can be inhaled, applied to our skin, ingested with our food or injected. Commonly they are found in pesticides and herbicides, heavy metals, hormone disruptors (contained in plastics and many personal care and household cleaning products) and mould. Low doses of these toxins can be harmful and they can often accumulate in our bodies over many years before symptoms emerge. Avoid them as much as you are able.

(b) *Seek support for change*

Most of the activities that will build your foundations for health and well-being are not new.

---

10 Giuseppe Curcio, Michele Ferrara and Luigi De Gennaroa, "Sleep Loss, Learning Capacity and Academic Performance", *Sleep Medicine Reviews*, 10(5), 2006, pp323–337, https://doi.org/10.1016/j.smrv.2005.11.001.
11 TA Bedrosian and RJ Nelson, "Timing of Light Exposure Affects Mood and Brain Circuits", *Translational Psychiatry*, 31 January 2017, 7(1): e1017, doi: 10.1038/tp.2016.262. PMID: 28140399; PMCID: PMC5299389.
12 G Medic, M Wille and ME Hemels, "Short- and Long-term Health Consequences of Sleep Disruption", *Nat Sci Sleep*, 9:151–161 (2017).
13 MR Irwin, MR Opp, "Sleep Health: Reciprocal Regulation of Sleep and Innate Immunity", *Neuropsychopharmacology*, 42(1), 129–155 (2017); OM Bubu, M Brannick, J Mortimer, O Umasabor-Bubu, YV Sebastião, Y Wen, S Schwartz, AR Borenstein, Y Wu, D Morgan, WM Anderson, "Sleep, Cognitive impairment, and Alzheimer's disease: A Systematic Review and Meta-Analysis", *Sleep*, Jan 1;40(1) (2017).

You may have read the suggestions above, and like the leaders who start working with me, think in terms of "buts".

"I know this, but ...
- I don't have time;
- I am too busy;
- I am too tired."

Fundamentally, we know what we need to do in this regard, but the changes to our routines and the stress the pandemic has brought about has challenged our ability to achieve what we know is good for us.

Health coaches are experts in change when it comes to health and well-being and can support the shift from someone knowing what is good for them to achieving it. Masterful coaches do not help clients solve their problems by planning with them what action needs to be taken. Rather they help clients uncover the insights about themselves they do not see yet. These insights and awareness of them is the foundation for change.

(c) ***Start with the key foundation for your change: awareness***
Lawyers who strive not just for excellence, but perfection, are setting up a perfect storm for themselves when it comes to deal with the challenges of the pandemic in our work and home lives.

How to be compassionate to oneself is beyond the scope of this chapter.

However, the starting point for any behaviour change is awareness. Take the time – perhaps during your mindfulness practice, or when you have a couple of minutes in bed in the morning and at night – to observe your emotions and feelings. Notice the patterns that emerge when thinking about those moments when perfect seems necessary.

(d) ***Create boundaries for your self-care***
One of the consequences of the blurring of boundaries between work and home has been the disruption to self-care routines.

When creating a foundation for your own health and well-being, what is important to you? Identify your top self-care practice and schedule it as if it were an important meeting.

These do not have to be big and bold actions. Here are some ideas.
- Make yourself less available and pace your day differently.
- Cut down your screen time by 30 minutes each day.

- Set aside 15 minutes two mornings a week to practise mindfulness.
- Reduce the number of calls you have via video conference and use the telephone instead.

(e) *Take one, almost-impossibly-small, next step*

Generally speaking, partners are masterful at solving problems. What accompanies that capacity is often the belief that anything they turn their hand to is achievable.

With the disruption the pandemic is causing, if you are looking to change your behaviours, aim to take (only) one, almost-impossibly-small, next step. Your next step should be so small that failure is impossible. If you think your goal is too small, that is a good sign that it is just right to incorporate in the middle of a pandemic, or any other challenging situation. A good indicator is when you share your almost-impossibly-small next step with someone else, and you laugh out loud at how ridiculously small that step feels. That's the right amount to begin with.

Aim small, not large. You'll eventually reach your larger goal, but if you set that larger goal straight away, you're less likely to benefit from the sense of achievement from having had many small wins along the way.

So rather than an hour of exercise every day of the week, aim for 10 minutes one day a week to begin with.

6.2 Practices for organisations and leaders

(a) *As a leader, be vulnerable!*

Time and time again, partners and senior management hear the call for empathetic leadership. Empathetic leadership connects us as human beings. Expressing one's human vulnerability is part of that. "Rumbling with vulnerability" is what Brené Brown identifies as a hallmark of a powerful leadership.[14] Expressing vulnerability is to be human.

Leaders can effectively re-establish some of the glue that binds us together in a workplace team or community by being courageous and expressing publicly the challenges they are facing.

This is more than just having regular meetings with your staff. Checking in with your team members is important: one should

---

14   Brené Brown, *Dare to Lead: Brave Work. Tough Conversations*, Whole Hearts, 2018.

not be emulating the experience I discovered of one junior lawyer whose boss had not spoken to them in three months.

Leaders need to take the first step, rather than waiting for their staff to express their own vulnerability. Your vulnerability unlocks everyone else's.

This is not a call to run a therapy session in your meetings. It may be as simple as acknowledging to your team that you are extremely tired because you are worried about the health of a loved one.

Or that you are anxious and scared because of the stress that your team is enduring.

If you find identifying emotions and feelings difficult, you might share what your "personal weather forecast" is at the beginning of a team meeting: "I feel cloudy with sunny spells."

Those who look up to leaders are looking for guidance and permission that what could be seen as an admission of "failure" is a normal part of the human experience in a work environment.

(b) Affirm the individuals in your team

Being vulnerable usually means offering something to others that is challenging you. But it is important to focus on the positive experiences too.

One of the lessons Motivational Interviewing offers us is the power of giving affirmations. Research shows that giving affirmations to an individual increases their "change talk". This is the language we hear when an individual is on the path of achieving the change they want.[15]

Affirmations are a statement about an individual's strengths, achievements, values or effort.

- "You persevered with grace with that client, even though they were impatient."
- "You lifted the team's spirits with your joke."
- "You went above and beyond to cover for your colleague when she was looking after her relative."
- "You are a dignified person."

Affirmations when given and received create powerful connections between human beings. Keep them short and succinct.

---

15   Timothy R Apodaca *et al*, "Which Individual Therapist Behaviors Elicit Client Change Talk and Sustain Talk in Motivational Interviewing?", *Journal of Substance Abuse Treatment*, 20 September 2015, www.journalofsubstanceabusetreatment.com/article/S0740-5472(15)00243-3/fulltext.

Aim to give them orally, rather than in writing. Offering them in a team/public setting will help encourage others to do the same.

(c) ***Express your gratitude***
Be intentional and vocal about your gratitude for what your team are doing. It sounds obvious but thinking about the good job someone has done is different to picking up the phone or jumping onto a video conference to do so.

7. Closing thoughts

The pandemic is but one example of a challenging situation that organisations and individuals will face. There will be more, and perhaps they will also be in the nature of a wicked problem or a social mess.

What this pandemic has demonstrated is that each of us can choose how to respond to the situations we experience, and a key part of ensuring our health, well-being and productivity is connecting to our fellow colleagues, family members and friends in order to experience our fullest lives as human beings.

Effortless leadership is within the reach of all leaders in law firms. What could effortless leadership offer you that you don't already experience? Where will you choose to focus your attention? As William James wrote in *The Principles of Psychology* in 1890: "My experience is what I agree to attend to."

About the authors

Sara Andrews
Assistant director, New Perimeter,
Senior international *pro bono* counsel,
DLA Piper
sara.k.andrews@us.dlapiper.com

Sara Andrews helps lead the strategic direction of New Perimeter, DLA Piper's non-profit affiliate that provides long-term *pro bono* legal assistance in underserved regions around the world. She initiates, develops and contributes to New Perimeter projects and manages global teams of DLA Piper lawyers. Sara develops long-term partnerships with international NGOs, government agencies and other joint venture partners. She has led projects focused on legal education, law reform, access to justice, women's rights and economic development throughout Africa, Asia, the Balkans and Latin America. Before joining New Perimeter full-time, Sara practised in DLA Piper's litigation group. Sara received her BA, *magna cum laude*, from Amherst College and her JD from Northwestern Pritzker School of Law.

Naomi Beard Nelson
Founder and CEO, Naomi Beard & Associates
naomi@naomibeardinc.com

Naomi Beard Nelson is the founder and CEO of Naomi Beard & Associates, Inc., a full-service law firm consultancy that has, for over 15 years, partnered with leading law firms across all markets to enable them to attract, develop and retain top talent. She regularly advises firms on leadership development, performance management, talent development framework design, compensation systems, mentoring programmes and engagement initiatives. Through bespoke executive coaching and career transition services, Naomi and her team help firms and their people optimise success. She and her team also perform a range of organisation-wide assessments, including 360° reviews, upward reviews and performance evaluations.

Before founding NB&A, Naomi practised law for 10 years in the US offices of two global law firms. She is a formally trained and credentialled executive coach, a frequent presenter at law firm and professional association events, and a contributor to a variety of industry publications.

Jennifer Bluestein
Chief talent officer, Perkins Coie LLP
Jbluestein@perkinscoie.com

A strategic talent development leader, Jennifer Bluestein, chief talent officer, is responsible for all talent strategy and human resources functions at

Perkins Coie, including lawyer and staff recruitment, development, compensation and benefits.

Prior to joining Perkins Coie, Jennifer, a former employment lawyer, spent more than 15 years in professional development at Greenberg Traurig and Baker & McKenzie and has a law degree from Pritzker Northwestern University School of Law.

Jennifer has authored two books for PLI on attorney development, *An Associate's First Year: A Guide to Thriving at a Law Firm* in 2018 and *Stepping It Up: A Guide for Mid-Level Associates* in 2020.

Matt Brainard
Senior managing director, Savills
mbrainard@savills.us

For two decades, Matt Brainard has specialised in representing law firms and corporate tenants on a local, national and global basis. He works closely with his clients helping them define what their future workspace and lease structure looks like and how this will enable their business to thrive.

As a member of the Legal Tenant Practice Group and Technology Practice Group, Matt has negotiated large and complex commercial real estate transactions allotting more than five million square feet on behalf of legal, tech, media and professional services companies. Matt and his team deliver a full scope of integrated services including site search and selection, occupancy cost reductions, capital containment, lease and sale negotiations, transaction management, financial modelling, workplace strategy, project management, critical technology facilities, lease administration, operating expense audits and multi-location portfolio advisory.

David Cunningham
Chief innovation officer,
Reed Smith
dcunningham@reedsmith.com

David Cunningham is the chief innovation officer of global firm Reed Smith. He guides the firm in thoughtful review of modern legal service delivery models, working to create a firm that is driven by the value it can measure and provide to its clients and employees. David is also the founder Legal Metrics, a data-driven 'legal ops' and diversity metrics initiative. He has engaged over a hundred legal departments and law firms to improve how legal ops metrics are calculated and benchmarked. He was also deeply involved with the Corporate Legal Operations Consortium (CLOC) in its earliest days and has spoken on the topic of legal ops metrics at all the CLOC US Institute events.

David was previously the chief information officer of Winston & Strawn, where he was responsible for creating and sustaining a competitive edge with technology, data and improved processes. His role included leadership for IT, risk management, information governance, innovation, data analytics, research, project management and one of the industry's largest e-discovery/managed services teams. David was previously a managing director of Hildebrandt Baker Robbins (now HBR Consulting) for the technology strategy and risk practices. Over 20 years, he worked with 200 US and UK/European firms.

Lisa Dewey
Pro bono partner and director, New Perimeter, DLA Piper
elizabeth.dewey@us.dlapiper.com

As DLA Piper's full-time *pro bono* partner, Lisa Dewey cultivates DLA Piper's strategic thinking on *pro bono*, including the vision for DLA Piper's US *pro bono* programme. Lisa leads the firm's US *pro bono* practice, including working with firm corporate clients to develop and deliver collaborative *pro bono* projects. Additionally, Lisa serves as the director for New Perimeter, DLA Piper's global *pro bono* initiative dedicated to providing long-term *pro bono* legal assistance in underserved regions around the world to support access to justice, social and economic development, sound legal institutions, and women's advancement.

Lisa teaches and frequently lectures on access to justice and *pro bono*. Her experience includes representing clients in death penalty, family law and asylum matters, as well as corporations and individuals in criminal investigations and federal jury trials. Lisa received her JD, *summa cum laude*, from American University's Washington College of Law.

Alex Dimitrief
Partner, Zeughauser Group
dimitrief@consultzg.com

Alex Dimitrief is a partner at Zeughauser Group. He is also a lecturer on law at Harvard Law School, where he teaches a new class on "The Corporation as a Citizen", and a distinguished adjunct professor at New York Law School, where he teaches on corporations. Alex was the president and CEO of General Electric's Global Growth Organization in 2018–2019 and previously served as the general counsel of GE Energy, GE Capital and then GE. Before joining GE in 2007, he was a trial lawyer at Kirkland & Ellis LLP for 20 years.

Thomas P Fitzgerald
Chairman, Winston & Strawn
tfitzgerald@winston.com

Thomas P Fitzgerald currently serves as the firm's chairman and leads its Executive Committee. He has led the firm since 2006, and during his tenure the firm opened 10 additional offices on three continents and significantly expanded its practice offerings. Tom coordinates the firm's acquisition of new talent, leads client development and feedback initiatives, and manages the firm's operations across the world.

Anne Geraghty Helms
Director & counsel, US *pro bono* programmes, DLA Piper
anne.helms@us.dlapiper.com

Anne Geraghty Helms is responsible for helping to develop, lead and manage DLA Piper's *pro bono* programme in the United States. Working collaboratively with the legal aid community, her role is to engage every DLA Piper lawyer in the United States, often in partnership with firm clients, in meaningful opportunities to give back through legal *pro bono*. Anne concentrates her own practice on juvenile and criminal justice issues but also has worked on a range of initiatives that touch on *pro bono* and access to justice – helping to establish legal clinics in domestic violence and landlord–tenant court, presenting at law schools in Mexico City on *pro bono* and juvenile justice as part of the firm's New Perimeter project focused on helping to strengthen *pro bono* culture in Mexico, and co-drafting a report for the Legal Services Corporation's Pro bono Task Force. Anne received her JD, *magna cum laude*, from Georgetown University Law Center.

Eric Ho
Founder and director, Health for Success
eric.ho@healthforsuccess.com

Eric Ho has been a lawyer for over 20 years. He trained as an M&A lawyer and was group head of legal for Anglo American plc's commodity trading business. He is also a leadership health coach, one of a small handful of US National Board-certified Health and Wellness Coaches based in the UK (NBC-HWC), an ADAPT-Certified Functional Health Coach (A-CFHC), and an ambassador of the UK Health Coaches Association.

Eric founded Health for Success to help high-performing individuals and teams rediscover authentic success: success without the overwhelm, burnout, and poor physical and mental health. His work focuses on leadership and the ways in which health, happiness and productivity overlap.

He collaborates with licensed health practitioners globally, focusing on cognitive decline, to support patients achieve their health goals in a lasting and sustainable way. Eric loves using his multi-lingual, multi-cultural background to help professionals use health as a foundation to be their best.

Michelle Holford
Director of business development, Slaughter and May
michelle.holford@slaughterandmay.com

Michelle Holford is currently the director of business development at Slaughter and May, leading a multi-discipline team to help grow, develop and support the firm's client relationships. An experienced marketing and business development leader, she has over 20 years' experience across a range of professional services sectors including legal, corporate finance and private equity. Prior to joining Slaughter and May in 2018, Michelle was head of client solutions at Freshfields Bruckhaus Deringer, where she was responsible for the marketing the firm's services on a global basis. Before Freshfields she was a deal originator at corporate finance firm Livingstone Partners (now Arrowpoint Advisory, part of Rothschild), responsible for generating new clients and opportunities for the firm.

Randall Kiser
Principal analyst, DecisionSet®
rkiser@decisionset.com

Randall Kiser is a principal analyst at DecisionSet®, a professional development and decision services firm. He is recognised as "the pre-eminent scholar of the US legal profession" and is also regarded as "a brilliant scholar and legal consultant", "the leading scholar in attorney decision processes" and "an internationally acclaimed researcher and consultant on legal decision making and trial risk assessments". Randall is the author of four books on law firm and attorney performance. He has taught law school courses at major universities and served as a scholar-in-residence at the Indiana University Maurer School of Law. His work has been featured in media ranging from *The New York Times* to the *Harvard Negotiation Law Review*. Randall received his law degree in 1978 from the University of California at Berkeley and was awarded his undergraduate degree with highest honours in 1975 from the University of California at Davis.

Tiffani G Lee
Partner, Holland & Knight LLP
tiffani.lee@hklaw.com

Tiffani G Lee is a partner in the South Florida Litigation Group of Holland & Knight in Miami. Since 2008, Tiffani has served as the firm's diversity partner. As diversity partner, she leads the firmwide Diversity Council, serves on the Practice and Operations Committee (the firm's highest governance body), and serves on the firm's Partner Compensation Committee.

Tiffani is recognised nationally for her DEI work and frequently speaks and writes on these issues. After the killing of George Floyd, Tiffani authored a *Law360* article titled "Lawyers Must Address Racial Injustice with Radical Candor". In the article, Tiffani wrote about the necessity of lawyers and law firms addressing racial injustice and how, as guardians of justice, lawyers have an obligation to work for the greater good.

Tiffany Winne
Executive managing director and partner, Stream Realty Partners
tiffany.winne@streamrealty.com

Tiffany Winne is an executive managing director and partner at Stream Realty Partners, where she leads the strategic direction and operations of the Arizona office. Tiffany's primary responsibilities include leading Stream's acquisition, development, leasing and property management services. Throughout her two-decade real estate career Tiffany has been devoted to representing commercial tenants with a particular focus on the legal sector, creating solutions to enhance opportunity and mitigate risk for law firms.

Tiffany was declared one of the top 50 most influential women in commercial real estate nationwide on the 2017 Women of Influence list by the *Real Estate Forum*. She has been quoted in diverse publications including *Business Week*, *Phoenix Business Journal*, *Chicago Tribune*, *Crain's Chicago Business*, *Commercial Property News*, *Illinois Real Estate Journal* and *Real Estate Forum*. Additionally, Tiffany serves as a community board member of the Translational Genomics Research Institute.

Peter Zeughauser
Chair, Zeughauser Group
zeughauser@consultzg.com

Peter Zeughauser is the chair of Zeughauser Group, a leading international law firm consultancy. He is a trusted adviser to the leadership of market leading global, international,

national, regional and boutique law firms on the challenges and opportunities they face as a result of increasing competition for sought-after high-performing talent, consolidation, segmentation and globalisation of the market for legal services. He has served as an adviser on the industry's most consequential and precedent setting mergers and acquisitions and regularly advises firms on leadership enhancement, improved financial performance, governance, succession planning, partnership structure and compensation systems. Peter is the author of *Lawyers are from Mercury, Clients are From Pluto* (ClientFocus Press, 1998). He served as a contributing editor to *The American Lawyer Magazine* for 20 years. Before consulting, Peter served as senior vice president and general counsel of the Irvine Company for over a decade until 1996. He served as chair of the Corporate Counsel Association in 1991 and as an adjunct professor of law at University of California – Irvine School of Law in 2021.